Ferdinand Christian Baur

A Philological Introduction to Greek and Latin for Students

Ferdinand Christian Baur

A Philological Introduction to Greek and Latin for Students

ISBN/EAN: 9783743407817

Manufactured in Europe, USA, Canada, Australia, Japa

Cover: Foto ©Suzi / pixelio.de

Manufactured and distributed by brebook publishing software (www.brebook.com)

Ferdinand Christian Baur

A Philological Introduction to Greek and Latin for Students

A PHILOLOGICAL INTRODUCTION

TO

GREEK AND LATIN.

AN OUTLINE OF ENGLISH SPEECHCRAFT. By WILLIAM BARNES. Crown 8vo. Cloth, price 4s.

THE LIFE AND GROWTH OF LANGUAGE. By WILLIAM DWIGHT WHITNEY, Professor of Sanskrit and Comparative Philology in Yale College, New Haven. Third Edition. Crown 8vo. Cloth, price 5s. *Copyright Edition.* Volume XVI. of the International Scientific Series.

ESSENTIALS OF ENGLISH GRAMMAR. By WILLIAM DWIGHT WHITNEY, Author of "Life and Growth of Language." Crown 8vo. Cloth, price 3s. 6d.

ENGLISH GRAMMAR FOR BEGINNERS. By. H. C. BOWEN, Author of "Studies in English," etc. Fcap. 8vo. Cloth, price 1s.

LONDON: KEGAN PAUL, TRENCH, & CO.

A PHILOLOGICAL INTRODUCTION TO GREEK AND LATIN FOR STUDENTS.

Translated from the German of

FERDINAND BAUR, Dr. Ph.,

Professor in Maulbronn.

BY

C. KEGAN PAUL, M.A., Oxon,

And E. D. STONE, M.A.,

Late Fellow of King's College, Cambridge, and Assistant-Master at Eton

THIRD EDITION REVISED.

LONDON:
KEGAN PAUL, TRENCH, & CO., 1 PATERNOSTER SQUARE
1883.

LONDON AND AYLESBURY

HAZELL, WATSON, AND VINEY, PRINTERS.

(The rights of Translation and Reproduction are reserved.)

PREFACE.

THE translators of the following little treatise have simply endeavoured to put Professor Baur's ideas before English students. The only liberty they have taken is that of breaking up the German sentences, and thus in some degree making the work less difficult than the original, although it has not even now the doubtful merit of easiness. English equivalents are given for Greek and Latin words wherever Professor Baur has given German renderings.

The translators' best thanks are due to the Rev. A. H. SAYCE and the Rev. G. W. COX for many valuable suggestions while the work was passing through the press.

CONTENTS.

Section		Page
I.—The Nature and Origin of Language		1
II.—The Elements of Language		4
III.—The Divisions of Philology		6
IV.—Classes and Stages of Language		7
V.—The Indo Germanic, or Aryan Family of Languages		8
VI.—The Græco-Latin Language		9

PART I.
THE SCIENCE OF SOUND.—GLOTTOLOGY.

I. VOWELS.

VII.—Analysis of Sounds in Greek and Latin	11
VIII.—Changes of Vowels	12
IX.—Change of Vowels under Consonantal Influence	14

II. CONSONANTS.

X.— The Greek Consonantal System	17
XI.—Spirants and Aspirates	18
XII.—Significance of Consonants to Philology	20

Section	Page
XIII.—Etymology	21
XIV.—Consonantal Change in the Indo-Germanic Languages	23
XV.—Consonantal Relation between Greek and Latin	25

THE CONSONANTS AS ROOT CONSONANTS.

A. MUTES.

1. TENUES. K. T. Π.

XVI.—The Guttural Tenuis K, corresponding to the Latin *c, q*, also to Gothic *g*, and H. G. and E. *h*	27
XVII.—The Dental Tenuis T, Latin *t*, Gothic *th*, H. G. *d*, and E. *t, th, d*	30
XVIII.—The Labial Tenuis Π, Latin *p*; for this H. G. and E. have *f* in the beginning of a word	31
XIX.—Change of the Guttural, Labial, and Dental Tenuis, K, Π, T, in Greek and Latin	34

2. MEDIALS. Γ. Δ. B.

XX.—The Guttural Medial Γ, corresponding to the Latin *g*, Gothic *k*, English *k*	37
XXI.—The Dental Medial Δ, corresponding to the Latin *d*, Gothic and Lower German *t*, German *z*, English *t*	38
XXII.—The Labial Medial B.	41

3. ASPIRATES X. Θ. Φ.

XXIII.—The Guttural Aspirate X, corresponding to the Latin *h, f, g,* in the beginning of a word *g,* Gothic *g*	43

Contents.

SECTION	PAGE
XXIV.—The Dental Aspirate Θ. On account of the want of a dental aspirate the Latin equivalent for this is often *f* in the beginning of a word, *d* and *b* in the body of it; Gothic *d*, German *t*, English *d*	45
XXV.—The Labial Aspirate Φ, corresponding to the Latin *f* = *bh*, at the beginning of a word *b*, in German and English *b*	46

B. SEMI-VOWELS. PERSISTENT SOUND OF CONSONANTS.

1. LIQUIDS.

XXVI.—The Nasal and Dental Liquid N	49
XXVII.—The Nasal and Labial Liquid M	50
XXVIII.—The Lingual Liquid Λ. *l*	51
XXIX.—The Lingual Liquid P. *r*	53

2. ORIGINAL SPIRANTS. Σ (SPIRITUS ASPER). ϝ. JOD.

XXX.—The Sibilant Σ and its Substitute the Rough Breathing	56
XXXI.—The Labial, Semi-Vowel Spirant ϝ, corresponding to the Latin *v*, sporadically represented by the rough breathing in Greek, at the beginning of a word	60
XXXII.—The Palatal, Semi-Vowel Spirant Jod has disappeared in Greek, and is retained as the Latin *j*, English *y*, *g*	61
XXXIII.—Greek Pure Vowel Roots	63
XXXIV.—Consonantal Laws of Sound	63
XXXV.—The Laws of the Ending	68

PART II.

FORMATION OF ROOTS AND STEMS.

Section	Page
XXXVI.—Conception of Roots and their Formation—Reduplication—Primary and Secondary Roots	70
XXXVII.—Marks and Peculiarities of the Root	74
XXXVIII.—Stems of Words	76
XXXIX.—(1) Verbal Stems	78
XL.—(2) Nominal Stems, including Participle and Infinitive	81
XLI.—Comparative and Superlative Stems	83
XLII.—Stems of the Numerals	85

PART III.

WORD-FORMATION OR INFLEXION.

XLIII.—The Word	87

I. THE NOMINAL INFLEXION. DECLENSION.

XLIV.—Elements	88
XLV.—Signs of Gender	89
XLVI.—Declensions	90
XLVII.—Case-endings	91
XLVIII.—Pronouns and Pronominal Declension	97
XLIX.—Adverbs and Prepositions	99

II. THE INFLEXION OF VERBS. CONJUGATIONS.

L.—Elements	101

1. PERSONAL ENDINGS.

LI.—Primary and Secondary Personal Endings. Augment. Imperative 103
LII.—Personal Endings of the Active . . . 105
LIII.—Greek Middle-Passive 111
LIV.—Latin Middle-Passive 112

2. MODAL ELEMENTS.

LV.—Greek Conjunctive and Optative 113
LVI.—Latin Conjunctive-Optative 115

3. TENSE-STEMS.

LVII.—Idea and Classes of Tense 117

(1) SIMPLE TENSE-STEMS.

LVIII.—The Greek Simple Perfect and Pluperfect . . 119
LIX.—Latin Simple or Strong Perfect 122
LX.—Greek Simple or Strong, so-called Second, Aorist 125
LXI.—Greek and Latin Present Stems 127
LXII.—Greek Imperfect 134

(2) COMPOUND TENSE-STEMS.

A. GREEK COMPOUND TENSES.

LXIII.—Compound Aorist. Weak or Sigmatic (so-called 'First') Aorist 135
LXIV.—The Greek Future 137
LXV.—The Compound or Weak Greek Perfect and Pluperfect, together with the Futurum Exactum . 140
LXVI.—The Greek Aorist and Future Passive . . . 141

B. LATIN COMPOUND TENSES.

SECTION	PAGE
LXVII.—Summary	143
LXVIII.—Weak Latin Perfect	144
LXIX.—Tenses and Moods formed from the Perfect	146
LXX.—Future in *bo*	148
LXXI.—Imperfect Indicative	149
LXXII.—Imperfect Conjunctive	150

The following abbreviations are used :—

E.	English.	O. H. G.	Old High German.
H. G.	High German.	O. L.	Old Latin.
O. E.	Old English.	O. L. G.	Old Low German.
O. G.	Old German.	Skr.	Sanskrit.

A PHILOLOGICAL INTRODUCTION

TO

GREEK AND LATIN.

I.—THE NATURE AND ORIGIN OF LANGUAGE.

1. LANGUAGE is the phonetic representation of thought: thought vocalized.

It is no work of human art, arbitrarily invented for the purpose of communicating thought; but a product which has grown naturally out of the essential development of human reason: it has originated φύσει, not θέσει.

There are two current theories on the origin of language—(α) the so-called onomatopœic, which refers language to the mere imitation of sounds, as *cuckoo*, *rataplan*, *tomtom;* (β) the interjectional, which refers it to the sounds arising from sensation, mere animal cries—*ah*, *ache*, ἄχος.

Neither of these can independently and alone explain the origin of language.

Reason and language are inseparable. Without language, there is no reason; without reason, there is no

I

language. Or, to put this in other words, there are no definite and clear thoughts, except such as can find expression in articulate sound; there are no articulate sounds except such as are intimately connected with definite conceptions and ideas. Thought which can be grasped is impossible without language. Words and conceptions exist only for each other,—words being the phonetic embodiments and the only exponents of conceptions.

2. All phonetic expressions are originally the reflex of impressions on the senses, and this is true whether we consider them under the form of an imitation of sounds, or of interjections, *i.e.* sounds arising from a sensation.

The phonetic expressions which, primarily, are either imitations of sounds, or interjections, are, secondarily, tokens of the object which produces the sound, or causes the sensation.

A number of phonetic expressions for identical impressions on the senses are fused into one collective expression, and this becomes a sign of a general conception which includes them all.

From an unlimited number of such possible conceptions, together with their phonetic expressions, a limited selection is made by language; each of these selected expressions, or phonetic types, becomes the sign of some one conception or object essential to human life.

The process by which these are selected is instinctive and rational, not arbitrary or conventional.

These phonetic types are the fundamental elements

of language; and to discover them is the goal and result of philology. They form, for us, the irreducible residuum of linguistic analysis, or, in other words, that which cannot be further explained.

3. These elementary phonetic types or roots represent originally impressions on the senses, and convey concrete material meanings.

They then become signs of ideas, which, though concrete, are extremely wide and general, and may therefore be called abstract.

The same idea being connected with a variety of objects—some concrete, others abstract—all such objects may be ranged under a general category.

Thus, for example, *equus*, ἵππος, anciently ἴκκος, Sanskrit *açvas*, from the root *ac*, *sharp* or *quick*, may be compared with *acus*, a *needle*.

All abstract words, which express immaterial conceptions, had originally material concrete meanings, and are borrowed by metaphor from phenomena of the world of sense.

Thus compare ἄνεμος, *animus;* *spiritus, spirare;* θυμός, θύω, *I boil;* αἰών, *aevum, time,* which last originally came from the root *i, to go*.

Metaphor is the transference of a name from the object to which it properly belongs to other objects which appear in some measure to participate in the peculiarities of the first.

This is done by means of the imagination, which is especially vigorous in the early periods of language.

Metaphor is an essential implement of language, a powerful means of linguistic development.

II.—THE ELEMENTS OF LANGUAGE.

1. Single letters, vowels, and consonants, are not the elements of language. Letters in themselves have no meaning; they contain no intelligible principle. Lingual sound only can be analysed in them, not language itself.

The elements of language are those sounds which are full of significance, or complex sounds, the so-called roots, or "exponents of conceptions." Through the union of these, whether in one word, or in a number of words, thought can find expression.

2. Complete lingual sound, however, as exhibited in any one language, expresses two things—
   - (α) Meaning, that is to say, perceptions, ideas, and conceptions.
   - (β) Relation to something else which lies beyond, and is not contained in the sound.

Complete lingual sound then contains a material, or radical, and a formal element, a predicative and a demonstrative root; and to discover these is the work of a complete grammatical analysis.

Complex sounds, which express meaning only, and which remain when all principle of relation is abstracted from a given word-form, are roots, in the narrow sense of the word. Roots are the indivisible atoms of language, the primitive and ultimate elements of words, which cannot further be analysed.

But the word, the complete form of language, is composed of meaning and relation, predicative and demonstrative elements united in a phonetic whole. The root and the word are the two poles between which the analysis of language moves.

The root is the expression of a general idea. If on the one side we consider this analytically, and from the stand-point of complete language, it is a pure abstraction of diffused and indistinct meaning. It is, therefore, not used by itself in more developed language.

On the other side, however, if considered synthetically, and followed from its origin through all its phases and changes, it is an original word. It existed for itself in the creative period of language; it is a real living germ, growing, and ever thrusting forth new shoots.

But when words are formed, whatever is added to the root as an affix, was itself, originally, an independent, self-existent word. It has coalesced with the root as its suffix, in virtue of the innate power of growth possessed by the root, and in the process of amalgamation has been worn down to mere syllables and letters.

3. The word is the single phonetic expression of a complete and independent perception. It allows this perception to appear either as an existing entity or as an incident of time, as a noun or as a verb.

The noun and the verb are both, for us, equally original forms of lingual expression. In itself, however, the distinction between the parts of speech must be considered as a product of the development of language.

The root, considered abstractedly, is not concerned with this distinction. It necessarily takes to itself further elements of language, and thus out of the universality of its meanings it gradually assumes nominal and verbal expression; differentiates itself into noun and verb.

All the relational elements of the noun and of the verb—that is to say all nominal and verbal suffixes, all inflexions, whether of cases or persons—are themselves originally roots, demonstrative or pronominal.

4. Between the root and the word lies the stem, that which remains after grammatical analysis has taken away the inflexional endings. It is not a mere root, therefore it is not unconcerned with the difference between noun and verb; it has in itself, over and above the root, a general nominal or verbal formative element. This is far more relative than the root, and is negative only to the more definite conceptions. Thus there are nominal and verbal stems.

The word then may be defined as the complete combination of sounds which express meaning and relation. It contains, so far as root and stem are not coincident, Sec. 38, 2, three elements—the Root, the Stem, the Inflexion.

III.—THE DIVISIONS OF PHILOLOGY.

The material basis of sound, which is originally physiological, underlies the complete linguistic form as well as its elements.

Divisions of Philology. 7

It is conditioned by the constitution of the human organs of speech, and is again, in each language, individually modified by usage. The sounds which are its separate constituents, enter into union with each other in part, only according to the definite laws of each language and the laws of sound.

The science of sound treats these laws as its elementary part, and thus results the division of Philology into the science of sound—Glottology, and the science of form—Grammar.

The latter, considered generally, in the widest sense of the science of lingual form, is in part the science of root and stem formation, in part the science of word formation or inflexion.

IV.—CLASSES AND STAGES OF LANGUAGE.

1. Isolating or radical languages. These consist of sounds of unalterable meaning, susceptible of no modification—mere roots. There is in them no difference between root and word, or between noun and verb; every word is a root; there are no inflexions. Such is Old Chinese.

2. Agglutinative languages. In these, two or more roots grow together in a single word. One of these maintains its radical independence, and remains unaltered by phonetic decay. The others constitute a dependent affix, as prefix, suffix, or infix, that is to say the addition of a sound of relation at the beginning, at the end, or in

the middle of a word. The word is thus a conglomerate without strict unity. Such is the Turanian family of languages.

3. Inflexional languages, of which the following are the steps. The root and the modifications made in it by the sounds of relation are blended together, Sec. 2, 2, β. The root is capable of a regular alteration with a view to the expression of relation, and of the addition to the root of the sound expressing relation. These are the Semitic and Indo-Germanic branches of language. The two branches are thoroughly different in grammatical construction, but this does not exclude the possibility of an original identity of their material elements, that is to say of the roots.

The characteristic tokens of these languages are—

(α) A regular change of the root vowel, strictly limited to a definite order of vowels.

(β) The addition of the expression of relation exclusively at the end of the root in the form of suffixes. To this the only exceptions are the verbal augments and the reduplications, of which more hereafter.

(γ) That all their roots are monosyllables.

V.—THE INDO-GERMANIC, OR ARYAN FAMILY OF LANGUAGES.

[The word Aryan is here used in its widest sense.]

The original Indo-Germanic language—the existence of which is inferred from a consideration of known allied languages—divides into,

1. The Asiatic or Aryan group. [The word Aryan is here used in its narrower sense.]
   (a) The old Indian language of the Vedas, which was afterwards the written language Sanskrit. This was the elder sister and not the parent of the other languages of the family.
   (β) The Iranian languages. The word Iran or Eran is derived from Arya. These are the old Bactrian or Zend (East Iranic), and old Persian (West Iranic, the language of the Achæmenid cuneiform inscriptions).

2. The south-western European group: Greek, Italian including Latin, Umbrian and Oscan, and Keltic.

3. The northern European group: Slavo-Lithuanian and German, this last including Gothic, Low German and English, High German and Scandinavian.

VI.—THE GRÆCO-LATIN LANGUAGE.

1. The Græco-Italian group of languages is a link in the chain of language which extends from India to Western Europe. It is further removed from the original Indo-Germanic language than is the old Indian, but is nearer to it than is the Slavonic-German group.

Sanskrit, Greek, and Latin are sisters, belonging to the same order and class of languages, but the first has a character of greater originality. Greek, however, exhibits high antiquity, especially in the preservation of the old tense and mood forms.

2. In the Greek language the Doric and Æolic dialects are older than the Ionic-Attic.

The Greek forms, as we find them in classical authors, have arisen through phonetic decay, through degradation and mutilation of an older and fuller form. They have gone through a series of processes of paring and decomposition, by which the meaning of the language is refined in the same proportion as are its forms. Its historical development, at the same time, lies under the physical law of *vis inertiæ*. The original simple and fundamental vowels become changed and modified.

3. The sounds of Latin and the Italian languages are —so far as the consonants are concerned—in much closer relation with the original sounds than those of the Greek.

Compare, for instance, *ves* in *vestis* with ἕ in ἕννυμι = Ϝεσνυμι, Sanskrit *vas ;* ἥμι, *semi*, originally *semis ;* ἑπτά, *septem*, Skr. *saptán ;* τέσσαρες, *quattuor*, Skr. *katvaras ;* τί, *quid*, originally *ki ;* ἧπαρ, *jecur*, Skr. *jakrt ;* νέος, *novus*, Skr. *navas ;* ἕπομαι, *sequor*, Skr. root *sak ;* ἵππος, nearly the original ἴκκος = ἰκϜος, *equus*, Skr. *aɤvas ;* οὖλε, *salve,* ἰός, *virus*, etc.

On the other hand, in the case of the vowels, Latin is monotonous and weak, in comparison with the manifold development and subtle divisions of the Greek vowel system. It is poor in diphthongs, and original old Latin diphthongs become modified into single sounds.

PART I.
THE SCIENCE OF SOUND.—GLOTTOLOGY.
I. VOWELS.

VII.—Analysis of Sounds in Greek and Latin

1. The Indo-Germanic fundamental vowels are *a, i, u*. The first of these, made by opening the lips as widely as possible, is clear and hard, and incapable of any transition into consonants. The last two, made by contracting more and more the opening of the lips, are weak and fluid, nearly related to the semi-vowels *j*, or jod, and *f*, or vau. [N.B. The letter *j* is retained throughout the following pages because of necessity so printed in Latin words. It answers, however, to the sound of the English *y*.]

These fundamental vowels are originally short, and therefore short in all roots: they have been gradually extended and lengthened by the reception of formal elements. The diphthongs *ai* and *au* are made by the combination of the hard *a* with the weak *i* and *u*.

2. *A* was first modified into *e* and *o*, or rather was differentiated into *a, e, o*. Then arose further diphthongs, ει and οι, connected with αι; ευ and ου connected with αυ.

From the gradual change of α, ε, ο, to ᾱ, η, ω, there arose other spurious diphthongs from the combination of these hard vowels with ι. These had a *j* sound, which is now wholly lost, and hence the iota subscript ᾳ, ῃ, ῳ. Others arose through the combination with υ—ᾱυ, ηυ, ωυ; ᾱυ Attic-Doric, ηυ Attic-Ionic, ωυ Ionic.

3. The old Latin diphthongs were *au, ou, eu; ai, oi, ei;* which were modified into the single sounds ō, ū; *ae, oe, ē, ī.* Compare *Claudius—Clodius; jous—jus; Lucius* = Λεύκιος; *aquai—aquae; ploirume—plurimi;* ποινή— *poena—punio; oenus—unus; populei—populi; foidos— foedus; hoi—hi;* οἶνος—*vinum;* οἶκος—*vicus; amem* = *amaim,* an archaic form.

VIII.—Changes of Vowels.

1. A-Series. The original *a* vanishes altogether, as in πίπτω = πιπετω from πετ = *pat;* in the same way, γίγνομαι from γεν = *gan.*

It is weakened or thinned into *i,* generally before two consonants: ἴσθι, connected with ἔστω = *asdhi* from the root ες = *as;* ἱστίη Ion. connected with ἑστία, *Vesta* from *vas* = *us* in *uro* = *uso;* ἵππος, Sec. 6, 3; κίρνημι— κεράννυμι; πίτνημι—πετάννυμι; πίλναμαι, πιλνάω—πελάζω; σκίδναμαι—σκεδάννυμι; χράω—χρίμπτω, ἐγχρίμπτω; σκήπτω (σκαπ)—σκίμπτω, ἐνσκίμπτω, Il. XVII. 437; πίτνω, πιτνέω —πεσεῖν—*pet, pat;* τίκτω—τεκ, *tak.* This takes place regularly in the present reduplication, Sec. 61, 3; and in Latin compounds: *facio, conficio,* compare *Juppiter.*

Changes of Vowels.

It is modified into *e:* ἕδω = *admi,* ἕζομαι from ἑδ = *sed* = *sad;* ἐστι = *asti;* into *o:* ποδός from *pad;* εἴκοσι = Ϝίκατι Æol.; ἄκρις—ὄκρις; ὕρχαμος—ἄρχω; ἀγκών—ὄγκος; ἅμ —ὁμοῦ.

The original *a* is retained in ἀκωκή (*ac*): ἄγω (*ag*); λαμβάνω—λαβ; πατήρ, stem πατερ, *patar*.

a and ε are interchanged : in ἅτερος Dor.—ἕτερος; ἕταμον ἕτεμον; τρέφω ἕτραφον; κτείνω (κτενϳω) ἕκτανον, κτανῶ.

Gradual changes. First stage: ε to ο, especially in the formation of noun stems: φόρος from φέρω *bhar;* τόκος from τεκ; λόγος from λεγ; ἕκτονα from κτεν; *a* to ā, η (ᾱ the older and Doric; η Ion.-Att. form gradually descended from a); λέληθα, λήθη from λαθ; ἕαγα, ἕηγα from Ϝαγ; εἴληχα from λαχ; εἴληφα from λαβ. Compare *plango, plāga; ăgo, ambāges, ēgi; tango, contāgio.* Second stage: ā, η to ω: ἔρρωγα, ῥήγνυμι, Ϝραγ; πτώξ, πτώσσω, πτωσκάζω Il. IV. 372—πτήσσω—πτακ; ἀρωγός, ἀρήγω; τρώγω, ἕτραγον; ἀκωκή, ὠκύς from ἀκ in ἀκή, ἄκρος. Compare *ăcies, ăcus, ăcuo, ācer, ōcior; lăbare, lăbi, lābes* = *fall* and *stain,* λώβη *shame.*

2. I-Series. The fundamental vowel is ῐ in ἴμεν = *imasi,* ἴθι from the root ι *to go;* ἕλιπον from λιπ, ἕπιθον from πιθ. The first stage is into ει, ῑ: εἶμι, πείθω, στείχω, στιχ in στίχος. The second stage is into οι: οἶμος from εἶμι, ι; λέλοιπα, πέποιθα, στοῖχος; οἶδα—εἰδῶ; εἰδέω connected with ἰδέω, Il. XIV. 235, as ἰδυῖα is connected with εἰδυῖα—ἴσμεν = ἴδμεν, Ϝιδ; ἀμοιβή—ἀμείβω. Compare *fĭdes, fĭd, perfĭdus, fīdo* = *feido, infĭdus, foedus, foidos;* λίς, λιτός, *smooth,* λεῖος, *lēvis, leivis; vīcus,* οἶκος = Ϝοικος; *vīnum,* οἶνος = Ϝοινος.

3. U-Series. The fundamental vowel v, *u* in σύ, *tu*, originally *tŭ;* ἔφυγον, φυγή, φυγ, *fug;* ζυγόν, *jug* in *jŭgum, jungo*. The first stage is into ευ: φεύγω, ζεύγνυμι, ῥεῦμα, from the root ῥυ, πνεῦμα—πνυ. The second stage is into ου, *ū:* ἐλυθ—ἐλεύσομαι—εἰλήλουθα; σπουδή—σπεύδω; σοῦμαι connected with σεύομαι, root συ; or into ω: ζώννυμι, ζωστήρ, from the root ζυ == ζυγ in ζεύγνυμι; χώννυμι from χέω = χεϝω = χεύω, root χυ. Compare *jūs, right = yoke, bond = jous*, from *ju = jug =* ζυ, ζυγ, *to bind*, in *jungo; jūs, soup = jous*, from *ju =* ζυ, *to mix*, in ζύμη, ζωμός; *ūro = ouso*, from *us*, compare εὔω, εὔω, *I singe.*

IX. CHANGE OF VOWELS UNDER CONSONANTAL INFLUENCE.

1. The vowels were affected by the original Indo-Germanic spirants *j, v, s*, Sec. 11. The Greek language resisted their influence, and hence,

(a) They were changed into vowels: *j* into ι: nominal-suffix *ja* in πάτριος, ἅγιος; comparative-suffix ιον, originally *jans*, in ἡδίων, stem ἥδιον; genit. sing. of the O-stems into οιο from *ojo*, originally *osjo*, Sec. 47, 2; optative-element ιη from *ja:* εἴην == ἐσίην = ἐσίημ = *asjam;* Doric future into σιω from *sjw*, πραξίω == πραγσίω. *v* spirant ϝ to υ vowel: δύο, *duo* = δϝω, Sanskrit *dva, bis = dvis;* χεύω, πνεύω Æol., from χεϝω, πνεϝω, χυ, πνυ; compare αὐίαχος Il. XIII. 41 = ἀϝιϝαχ; ἰαύω from ἀϝ; ταναύποδα Od. IX. 464 = ταναϝπο; ταλαύρινος. *j* to ε: πλευσοῦμαι == — εομαι == — σjομαι; so also φευξοῦμαι; compare κενεός = κενjος, στερεός, ἠνορέη.

(b) *j, v* were transposed as the vowels ι, υ before consonants: ι in κτείνω=κτενjω; so φαίνω, φθείρω, ὀφείλω; μέλαινα = ανja; so again μάκαιρα, λέαινα, δέσποινα = δεσποτνja, νείαιρα, *the abdomen*, δότειρα, τέρεινα; χείρων=χερjων, μείζων = μεγjων, κρείσσων = κρετjων from the stem κρατ in κρατύς (ζ = γj, σσ = τj), strictly speaking therefore ι is epenthetic, or is a doubled power of j; it affects the consonant, which becomes a mixed sound, Sec. 34, 3, and at the same time passes over as ι into the preceding syllable; compare φοίνιος from φόνος, connected with φοινός Il. XVI. 159. v = ϝ: γουνός = γονϝος from γόνυ, γοῦνα, compare *genua*, δοῦρα; οὖλος, Ion. = ὄλϝος, ὅλος, *salvus*, old Latin *sollus;* ἐλαύνω = ἐλανϝω; compare *nervus*, νεῦρον.

(c) *j*, *v*, *s* disappear, whence it follows that vowels are massed together and contracted. s, φέρῃ = φερεσαι; μένους from μενεσος; εἴην from ἐσjην; εἰπόμην from ἐσεπομην from ἐπ = σεπ, compare *sequor;* εἶρπον = ἐσερπον from ἕρπω = σερπω. v = ϝ, νέος = νεϝος, *novus;* εἰργασάμην = ἐϝεργ; εἶπον, ἔειπον = ἐϝεϝεπον, redupl. aor. from the root ϝεπ. *j*, in so-called contracted verbs in αω—εω—οω, from αjω, εjω, οjω.

2. A syllable was lengthened in compensation for the loss of consonants: of ϝ; the Ion.-Ep. genit. βασιλῆος, τοκῆος, νηός = βασιλεϝος, ναϝος, and thence with a change in quantity came the Attic form εως; of *j* in Homeric πόληος = πολεjος, Attic πόλεως; of ν in Ionic ξεῖνος, from Æolic ξέννος = Doric ξένϝος, Attic ξένος; of ν before σ: φέρουσι = φερονσι = φεροντι; τούς = τονς; πᾶς = πανς; τιθείς = τιθενς = τιθεντς; χαρίεις=χαριϝεντς, τιμήεις —contracted τιμῆς, not τιμῆς, Il. IX. 605, since the ι is not organic, = τιμηεντς; of σ; εἰμί from ἐσμι, connected

with the Æolic ἔμμι, εἶμαι=ἔσμαι; in the compound aor. when σ disappears after λ, μ, ν, ρ: ἔνειμα = ἔνεμσα; ἔφηνα = ἔφανσα from the root φαν; ἔστειλα = ἐστελσα, στελ in στέλλω = στελjω, connected with the Æolic ἔστελλα with assimilation of the σ; ἐκάθᾱρα; in the nomin. singul. when s disappears: ποιμήν = ποιμενς; πατήρ = πατερς; εὐμενής = εὐμενεσς; φέρων = φεροντς; δαίμων = δαιμονς. Compare pĕs = pĕds connected with pĕdis; cāsum = cadtum; abiēs, abiĕtis; exāmen, exăgmen; flāmen, flagmen, compare flagrcre, φλεγ; contāmen = contagmen; ājo = agio; mājor = măgior; jūmentum from jŭg; on the other hand, stĭmulus, stĭlus, connected with instīgare, from stig; pōno from posno, posino.

3. The sound of ι was introduced into the preceding syllable when the word ended in σι: in the dat. plur. ταῖς, τοῖς from ταῖσι, τοῖσι, Ion.-Ep. τῇσι, = tasi, tosi, pronoun-stem ta, suff. σι; in 2 pers. sing. φέρεις = φερεσι, φέρῃς = φερησι.

4. A vowel was inserted after ρ and λ: ὀρέγω connected with ὀργ in ὀργυιά; ἀρήγω from ἀρκ—ἀρακ in ἀρκέω; ταράσσω from the root τραχ, τέτρηχα τραχύς; ἤλυθον or ἦλθον; ἀλέξω, ἀλ in ἀλαλκεῖν; compare μόλυβος plumbum.

5. A vowel was prefixed occasionally before one, oftener before more than one, consonant: ἄσταχυς—στάχυς, ἀστήρ—stella, root στορ, ster, Sec. 17, ἀστράπτω—στράπτω; ἀφλοισμός Il. XV. 607, φλοῖσβος; ἀβληχρός, βληχρός, soft, weak; ἰγνύη, poples, Il. XIII. 212, γόνυ; ὀφρύς, H. G. braue; E. brow; ἐχθές, χθές; before simple liquid, and nasal letters: ἀμύνω—μύνη, ἀμαλός—μαλακός, μαλθακός; ἐννέα, ἐννεϝα, novem, ν being doubled after ε

prefixed; ὄνυξ, *unguis*, H. G. *nagel*, E. *nail;* ὄνομα, originally ὀγνομα, *nomen;* ἐρείπω, ῥίπτω; ἐρυθρός, *ruber;* ἐρεύγεσθαι, *ructare;* ἀράσσω, ῥήσσω; ἐρωή, ῥώομαι; ὀρέγω, *rego;* before ϝ: ἔρση, ϝερση, ἔερση = ἐϝερση, Il. XXIII. 598; ἔεργω, Sec. 20; ἐείκοσι, ἐϝεικοσι, or εἴκοσι, ϝίκατι; ἔεδνον, connected with ἔδνον, ϝεδνον; before gutturals : ὀδούς, *dens;* ὀδάξ, δάκνω; ὀδύρομαι, δύρομαι; before labials : *opimus*, πίων.

II.

CONSONANTS.

X. THE GREEK CONSONANTAL SYSTEM.

The consonants fall naturally into classes regulated by the nature and duration of their sound; that is to say, according as they are audible or inaudible without a vowel, and according as their sound is momentary or lasting. These classes are,

(1) *Mutes*, or soundless, momentary consonants. These are divided (a) according to the organs which produce hem, into Gutturals, κ, γ, χ; Dentals, τ, δ, θ; Labials, π, β, φ. (b) According to their harder or weaker pronunciation or degree of sound, into Tenues, ψιλά="without a breathing," κ, τ, π; Medials, or weak, γ, δ, β; Aspirates, or mutes with a breathing added, χ, θ, φ. These last do not exist in Latin, and are designated as foreign sounds by *ch, th, ph* (on φ = *f*, Sec. 11, 4).

2

(2) *Semivowels,* or lasting sounds. These are (a) Liquids, and are partly nasal, γ (before gutturals), ν also a dental, μ also a labial ; and partly lingual, λ, ρ. (b) Spirants and Sibilants, breathing and hissing sounds, ‘ (*h*), ϝ (*v*), σ ς. To these must also be added Double Consonants, double sibilants or mixed sounds, σσ (*ss*), ξ (*x* = *ks*), ψ = πσ, *ps*, ζ = δσ.

XI.—Spirants and Aspirates.

1. *J*, one of the three original spirants of the Indo-Germanic languages, *J, V, S,* has disappeared in Greek, and is now only to be recognized by its effects. It is sometimes turned into a vowel, Sec. 9, 1 ; sometimes assimilated, Sec. 34, 1 ; sometimes fused down with other consonants into a mixed sound, Sec. 34, 3 ; sometimes changed at the beginning of a word into the rough breathing; sometimes it disappears altogether in the beginning, Sec. 32, and in the middle of a word, Sec. 9, 1, c.

2. *V* is retained as ϝ, the digamma, the old vau, in the older language—that is to say, in the Doric and Æolic dialects. In the later language, as we find it in the Homeric text, the digamma becomes an aspirate at the beginning of a word, or is altogether absorbed, αἷμα, ἄγνυμι. In the body of a word it is sometimes absorbed, ὄϊς = *ovis,* νέος = *novus,* νηός = νηϝος ; sometimes weakened into the vowel υ [*y*], ·as in ναῦς, εὔαδεν, βοῦς, Ζεύς, compare *Jov,* Sec. 9, 1 ; sometimes

Spirants and Aspirates. 19

assimilated in contracted syllables, Sec. 34, 1, b ; or it is thrust aside by the strengthening of the preceding vowel, οὖλος = ὄλϝος, γοῦνα; compare Sec. 9, 1, b.

This spirant, however, ϝ = v, survives in its effects, partly in the syllabic augment before a vowel, ἐάγη, ἐῳνοχόει, even in the Attic dialect, ἑάλων, ἑώρων, ἐωνούμην, partly in the dialect of the Homeric poems. In these its influence is felt both in the quantity of the preceding syllable, and in the elision. In this latter case, however, some wavering may be noticed between the older and more recent Ionic dialects—for example, in ἄναξ and ϝάναξ. Digammated words originally made the preceding syllable long by position—Il. I. 108; IV. 18, 214; V. 7, 836; XIII. 495; XVI. 502; Od. IX. 196; XIV. 479; long vowels at the end of a word remained long before it—Il. III. 392; VI. 91; VIII. 513; XVIII. 473; Od. X. 510; XI. 108; XVIII. 56; XXI. 405; short vowels were not cut off—Il. I. 462; V. 161, 757; IX. 40; XV. 288; XVI. 178, 424; XXI. 309, and there was instead only an apparent elision.

3. The original *s* remains predominant in Greek at the end of words only, compare Sec. 35, and before mutes. At the beginning of a word it is usually changed into *h*, and between vowels it is wholly thrust out, Sec. 9, 1, c, Sec. 30.

The elision and excision of the original spirants—their alteration, assimilation, and fusion with other consonants —cause remarkable changes in the character of the original sounds, and are a very noteworthy peculiarity of the Greek language. All the dentals disappear before σ s. So also does ν, with a compensatory lengthening of the preceding vowel, Secs. 9, 2 ; 34, 7.

In Latin, *s*, between vowels and at the end of a word, is simply changed into *r*: *Lares — Lases, eram* from *esam, erit—esit, quaero — quaeso, arbor — arbos;* it disappears in the middle of a word before *m, n, l, d,* compare *cano, Camena (Casmena),* connected with *carmen, idem,* and between vowels, *diei, spei,* Sec. 47 ; at the end of a word, *parricida(s), familiai(s),* Sec. 47, and after *l, n, r, sol, vigil, puer, leo = leons.*

4. Greek is averse to the accumulation of aspirates, Sec. 34, 5 ; 9.

Latin has no aspirates; their place is taken by the corresponding breath-sounds. Instead of the dental aspirate θ, we have in Latin at the beginning of a word simply *f*, Sec. 25. This *f* is not an aspirated tenuis, *ph*, but a labial breath-sound = *bh*,* and often used for *dh* and *gh*. Only in later periods of the language *f* = φ, Secs. 22—25. For the difference of sound between φ and *f*, see Quintilian xii. 10, 29.

XII.—SIGNIFICANCE OF CONSONANTS TO PHILOLOGY.

1. Consonants are the stable element, the skeleton, as it were, of language, which remains generally the same through all the changes of a root. This is true

* Therefore the reduplicated perfect is *fefelli,* not *pefelli.*

not only within each single language, but also in the languages which are akin to each other.

Consonants not only form, phonetically, the fixed bodies of words, but they are also the exponents of thought, the significant elements, which have naturally become interwoven with the conception of a word. They make, therefore, stronger resistance to phonetic changes than do the vowel elements of words. Vowels are exposed to far greater changes; they are fluctuating, tend to melt into each other, and are therefore less easy to grasp.

2. But the consonants of the same root are also subject to numerous changes. These occur in the transition from one Indo-Germanic language, group of languages, or stage of linguistic development, to another, as well as within the same language, during the process of word formation. These changes can be reduced to laws.

3. These laws relate to the consonantal change of sound in a root or a stem, partly in the passage from one Indo-Germanic language to another, according to their grades, partly within each separate language.

The first is the law of sound-shifting; the last is the consonantal law of sound in Greek and Latin.

These laws are the foundation of scientific etymology.

XIII.—ETYMOLOGY.

1. Etymology is the science of what is true and genuine in language, of what is ἔτυμον; it is the knowledge of the

true and original signification of a word in conformity with its derivation, and the tracing it down from its stem-word and root-word.

It does not merely show by analysis that a word is generally derived from one which is more original and simple, that is to say from a root; but, starting from the root, follows the word synthetically and genetically, tracing it through all its wanderings, both within the several languages, and from one to another of those which are related. It explains how one word has been gently and gradually altered into another by the regular law of phonetic change. It discloses especially the laws or analogies which regulate and direct the consonantal changes of sound in the history of language.

2. Therefore the identity or resemblance of the sound, as well as of the meaning of two words, are only of subordinate importance for methodical etymology. Words of quite different sounds, which have not a single letter in common, may be shown by scientific analysis to be words of the same origin; compare, for example, χέω—*fundo*, Sec. 23, ἀήρ—*ventus*, εἷμα—*vestis*, Sec. 31; and others, again, of wholly different meaning, as, for example, πέτομαι—πίπτω—*peto*, Sec. 18, 37, φηγός, *the esculent oak—fagus, the beech*. The last is an example of the way in which a word may alter its meaning by change of language, time, and country.

In the development of language the successive changes of meaning go hand in hand with **phonetic change.**

3. But through all changes of form and meaning the original condition of a language, or family of languages, remains unaltered in its essential elements. These constantly produce new forms with modified meaning, and enrich the language with words and conceptions, but nothing whatever can be arbitrarily added to them.

The observation of these changes of form and meaning is a peculiarly delightful study, and opens a glimpse into the wondrous household of human language which is able to subsist on such simple means.

XIV.—CONSONANTAL CHANGE IN THE INDO-GERMANIC LANGUAGES.

Almost the entire consonantal structure of the Indo-Germanic languages is conditioned by the phonetic law discovered by Jacob Grimm.

This law of *sound-shifting* concerns the common roots or words of this family of languages, and explains the changes of sound gradually made in the mutes from tenues to aspirates, from aspirates to medials. It also explains the changes of sound in the guttural, dental, and labial groups of consonants in the various stages of language.

1. Sanskrit, Greek, Latin, Slavonic, Keltic.
2. Gothic, with Low German and English.
3. Old High German.

These rules are especially valid for consonants at the beginning of words, and in a far less degree for those in the middle and at the end of words: they are thus expressed:—

1. Where there is a tenuis, *k*, *t*, *p*, in the first stage of development in language, its place is taken in the second stage by the corresponding aspirate or spirant, and in the third stage by the corresponding medial. The medial is however retained only in the dental class; compare Sec. 17, τερσ-; in O. H. G. *h* and *f* were used instead of *g* and *b*.

2. Where aspirates, χ, θ, φ, occur in the first stage, their place is taken in the second stage by medials, *g*, *d*, *b*, and in the third by tenues, *k*, *t*, *p*. Compare Sec. 24, θήρ, θυγάτηρ; Sec. 20, ῥαγ—*frag*. But instead of the *k* and *p*, which might be expected, *g* and *b* often remain in H. G.; compare Sec. 25, root φυ; Sec. 23, χυ; the dental *d*, on the contrary, becomes changeable into *t*.

3. When medials, *g*, *d*, *b*, occur in the first stage, the corresponding tenues appear in the second stage, and aspirates in the third; compare δάκρυ, Sec. 21; *duco*, Gothic *tiuhan*, O. H. G. *ziohan*, H. G. *ziehen*; $z = ts$, the dental spirant for the dental aspirate.

This law undergoes modification through the want of strict aspirates in Latin, Sec. 11, 4, and Sec. 15, as well as to some extent also in Gothic and Old High German. The aspirates thus lacking are generally replaced by the corresponding breath-sounds or spirants.

XV.—CONSONANTAL RELATION BETWEEN GREEK AND LATIN.

The consonantal differences between identical roots or words of these two languages, which are related, and stand on the same linguistic stage of development, are, in regard to their relation with each other, mainly conditioned by the following characteristic peculiarities:—

1. By the fact of the exchange of the guttural, labial, and dental tenues k, p, t, both in the transition from one language to the other, and within the boundaries of each of the two languages, Sec. 19.

With this is closely connected the development of the guttural tenuis k in Latin into the guttural tenuis with a labial secondary sound; that is to say into $qu = kv$, which often arises within the bounds of Latin from the fact that $c = k$. This qu is a transitional sound from the guttural to the labial tenuis, that is, from k to p, and explains the frequent interchange of k and p in Latin and Greek.

2. By the want of a proper aspirate in Latin, Sec. 11, 4. In the place of the Greek aspirates, χ, θ, ϕ, the corresponding breath-sounds are used in the beginning of a word, often f, or even the medial, for χ and θ. In the middle of a word d and b are found in the place of θ. For examples, Secs. 23—25.

3. By the tendency of the Greek language to dispense with spirants, and the entire absence of the spirant j,

which has only a latent effect, Sec. 11, 1. *J* is, on the contrary, very prevalent in Latin, both in the beginning and in the body of a word, as in the root *jug*, and in *ajo*, *major*. It often however becomes a vowel, and disappears both between vowels and after consonants, *cuncti* = *cojuncti ; deicit* = *dejicit; obex, obicis* = *objex, objicis ; minor* = *minjor*.

4. By the frequent transition of *s* in Greek into the rough breathing at the beginning of a word, though it may also pass into the smooth breathing, Secs. 11, 3 ; 30. On the other hand, *s* is changed into *r* between vowels, and at the end of a word in Latin, Sec. 11, 3. Compare H. G. *war, waren* = *was, wasen;* E. *was, were;* H. G. *küren* = *kiusen;* E. *choose*.

5. By the continuance of the old vau. This was a half-vowel, and as such was frequently weakened into vowels in the body of a word, as in the diphthongs *au* and *ou*, and disappeared altogether between vowels.

But it remained at the beginnings of words in Latin, Sec. 31, while it completely disappeared in the written language of Greece, or passed into the rough breathing, Secs. 11, 2 ; 31.

6. By the sporadic weakening of *d* in Latin to *l:* δάκρυ —*lacrima ; lingua* = *dingua*, Gothic *tuggo*, H. G. *zunge*, E. *tongue ;* 'Οδυσσεύς— *Ulysses;* δαήρ —*levir ; olor*—*odor*, ὅδωδα ; *silva* = ἴδη ; compare conversely *adeps*—ἀλείφω ; for the change of β and *g*, β and *v*, β and *f*, see Sec. 22.

7. By the different law in regard to the endings of words in the two languages. Compare for example *lac* = *lact* and γάλα = γαλακτ, Sec. 35.

In the following chapters the consonants are arranged as the elements of Greek and Latin roots and words, which partly remain unchanged, and partly change in the passage from one realm of language to another, according to known laws. A survey is made of the roots and stems common to two or more Indo-Germanic languages, according to the classes of consonants arranged on the basis of Greek. This is the etymological part of linguistic analysis.

THE CONSONANTS AS ROOT CONSONANTS.

A. MUTES.

1. TENUES. K. T. Π.

XVI. THE GUTTURAL TENUIS K, corresponding to Latin *c, q, g,* Gothic, H. G. and E. *h.*

ἀ κ—ἀκή, ἀκαχμένος, προήκης, εὐήκης, νεηκής, Doric νεακής, τανυήκης, πυριήκης, ἀκωκή, ἀκμή, ἀκόνη, ἄκρος, ἄκρις and ὄκρις, ὀξύς, ὠκύς; *acus, acuo, acies, acer, ocior.*

ἀ ρ κ—ἀλκ—ἀρκέω, ἄρκιος, ἀρήγω, Sec. 9, 4; ἀλκή, ἀλαλκεῖν, ἀλέξω; *arceo, arx, arca, Herculus,* originally god of *hurdles* or *sheep-folds.*

εἴκοσι = ϝικοσι = δϝικοσι, Æolic ϝίκατι; *viginti,* Sec. 2.

ἑκατόν, *centum;* Gothic *huna;* E. *hundred.*

Ϝεκ—ἑκών, ἀέκων—ἄκων, ἕκητι, ἀέκητι, ἕκηλος, εὔκηλος, *invītus* = *invic(i)tus*?

ἑκυρός, *socer*; Gothic *svaihra*, Greek rough breathing for σϝ, as ἕ, ϝέ = σϝε, *sve*, thence *se*.

ἰκ—ϝικ—ἔοικα, ἔϊκτην, ἤϊκτο, εἶκε (from a present εἴκω?) Il. XVIII. 520, εἴσκω causative, εἰκάζω; ἴκελος, εἴκελος, ἐπιείκελος, ἀϊκῶς Il. XXII. 336, ἀεικής, μενοεικής, ἀεικέλιος. εἰκών.

Ϝικ—ἴκω, ἰκάνω, ἰκνέομαι, ἱκέτης, ἰκτήρ, ἱκετήσιος, προίκτης, προΐσσομαι (on the other hand see below προῖξ), ἱκανός, ἴκμενος.

καθαρός, καθαίρω; *castus* = *cadtus*.

καί with locative ι, *que* see below τε. Sec. 19, 3.

καλ—καλέω, κλῆσις etc.; *calare, kalendae, nomenclator, classis, clamare.*

καπ—κώπη; *capio, capulum;* H. G. and E. *haft, heft.*

καπ—καπύω, κεκαφηώς, καπνός.

κάπηλος, *caupo;* H. G. *kaufen*, without any shifting of sound at the commencement, which proves that the word is strange to the language.

κάρα, κάρη etc., κρήνη; *cerebrum;* H. G. *hirn.*

καρδ—κῆρ, κέαρ, καρδία, κραδίη; *cor (cord), cordatus, vecors;* Gothic *hairto;* H. G. *herz;* E. *heart.*

καυ—καϝ—ἔκηα, καήμεναι, ἔκαυσα, καίω, καῦμα, κῆλον = κᾶλον, κήλεος, κήλειος Il. XV. 744, κηώδης, κάγκανος, reduplicated and with a nasal sound, Il. XXI. 364.

κελ—κέλης, κελητίζω Il. XV. 679; *celer, Celeres;* κέλλω Sec. 19.

κεφαλή; *caput, capillus;* Gothic *haubith;* H. G. *haupt,* E. *head.*

Root Consonants. 29

κ ι—κει—κεῖμαι, κέαται, κέατο, κοίτη, κοιμάω, κῶμος, κώμη; *quies, quiesco, civis;* H. G. *heim ;* E. *home.*

κ ι—κίω, κιών, μετεκίαθον, κινέω ; *cio, cieo, citus.*

κ λ α—κλάω, κλάδος, κλῆρος.

κ λ ι—κλίνω, κλίμα, κλῖμαξ, κλιτύς ; *inclino,* etc., *clivus.*

κ λ υ—κλύω, κλυτός, κλέος = κλεϝος, κλέομαι, ἔκλεο Il. XXIV. 202 ; *cluo, inclutus, cliens, gloria = closia* (?); H. G. *hlut, laut ;* E. *loud.*

κ λ υ—κλύζω, κλύδων ; *clueo, cluo, cloaca, fossa Cluilia ;* H. G. *hlutar, lauter.*

κ ο λ—κολούω, κόλος ; *incolumis.*

κ ο π—κόπτω, κόπος ; *fatigue = striking down,* κωφός ; Gothic *haunjan ;* H. G. praeterite *hieb,* E. *hew.*

κ ο σ—κόσμος, κοσμέω ; *como = cosmo, comptus.*

κ ρ ι—κρίνω ; *cerno, certus, crimen.*

κ υ π—κύπτω, κύπη, κύπελλον, κύμβαχος = *head-foremost,* and *the crown of a helmet ; cupa,—cumbo, cubare ;* H. G. *kufe ;* E. *coif.*

κ υ ρ—κῦρος, κύριος, κυρόω, κουρίδιος, κουριδίη ἄλοχος = *housewife,* not from κούρη, κόρη.

κ υ ρ τ ο ς, *curvus.*

κ ύ ω ν, *canis ;* Gothic *hunds ;* E. *hound.*

λ α κ—ἔλακον, λάσκω ; *loquor, Locutius.*

λ α κ—λάκος, λακερός ; *lacer, lacero, lacuna.*

οἶκ ο ς, ϝοικ, ϝικ, see above ; *vicus ;* E. *wick = a village.*

σ κ ε π—σκέπτομαι, σκοπή, σκοπός ; *spec—specio—spicio, specula, species, suspicio*—from *suspēcio,* as *subtilis* from *tela, convicium = convōcium,* not = *suspicitio.* In Greek there is a metathesis between *p* and *c;* the Latin root-form is the original.

κ is weakened into γ; ἐφράγην from φράσσω = φρακjω, ἐπλάγην from πλήσσω = πληκjω.

XVII. The Dental Tenuis T, Latin *t*, Gothic *th*, H. G. *d*, and E. *t, th, d*.

σ τ α—στυ—ἔστην, ἴστημι = σιστημι, εἱστήκειν = ἐσεστ., στάσις, ἱστός; ἐπίσταμαι = ἐπι-σταμαι without reduplication, for the meaning compare the H. G. *ver-stân, verstehen;* στεῦται; formations from the extended stem σταθ—σταθμός, στάθμη, etc.; *sto, sisto, status, statio, stamen, stabulum, stabilis, vestibulum = the outstanding place, forecourt; s* disappears in *tabula*, *st* in *locus*, anciently *stlocus* from the extended root *stal, stla* Sec. 37 = *stlocus ;* compare *līs*, originally *stlis = stlits*, O. H. G. *strīt*, Sec. 29, 3; H. G. *stân, stelle, stuhl;* E. *stool, stand.*

σ τ ε π—στέφω, στέμμα, στέφανος; *stipare, stipator, stipulari.*

σ τ ι γ—στίζω = στιγjω, στίγμα, στιγμή; *distinguo, instigare, stimulus, stilus:* H. G. *stich;* E. *stick, stitch.*

σ τ ο ρ — *stra*, *ster*, στόρνυμι, στορέννυμι, στρώννυμι, στρῶμα, στρατός; ἀστήρ, Sec. 9, 5; *sterno, stratus, stramen, stella* = *sterula*, H. G. *stern; strages, struo, strues;* H. G. *strô;* E. *star, strew, straw.*

τ α —ταν—τεν—τῆ, τάσις, τάνυμαι, τανύω, τιταίνω, τείνω, τόνος; τανaός, ταναύποδες Sec. 9, 1, a, τανηλεγής; ἐπίτηδες, ἐπιτήδειος, *tendo, teneo, tenus, protinus, tonare, tonitru;* H. G. *donar, donner;* E. *thunder.*

τ α γ—τεταγών Homeric; *tango, contāgio, contāmen, contāminare.*

τ α κ—τήκω; tā-bes, tabesco.

τ α λ — τλα — tol — τλῆναι, τάλας, ἐτάλασα, τάλαντον, ταλαύρινος, τολμάω; tuli, anciently tetuli, lātus, from tlatus = τλητός, tollo, tolero.

τ α φ—ἔταφον, τάφος; variation of the root in θαπ—τέθηπα, nasalized into θάμβος, θαμβέω.

τ έ γ γ ω, tingo, tinguo.

τ ε κ—ἔτεκον, τέκνον, τόκος, τέχνη; τυκ—τυχ—τετυκεῖν, τετύκοντο, ἔτυχον, τύχη, τυγχάνω, τεύχω; tignum, tēlum = teclum, texo, tēla = texla (compare āla—axilla, mala—maxilla, vēlum—vexillum), subtēmen, subtilis = subtelis, Sec. 16.

τ ε μ—ταμ—τμα—τέμνω, ἔταμον, τμήγω; simple form of the present without consonantal suffix, τέμει, Il. XIII. 707; to this also certainly belongs τετμεῖν = τετεμειν, ἔτετμε, to hit, in spite of the difference of meaning: τομή, τμῆμα, ταμίας.

τ ε ρ—τέρην, τείρω, τέρετρον, τιτραίνω, τρανής; tero, teres, terebra; E. drill, thrill.

τ ε ρ σ—τέρσομαι, τερσαίνω, ταρσός; τάριχος, ταριχεύω; torreo; Gothic thaurstei = durst; O. H. G. darru, H. G. dörre; E. thirst.

totus, Gothic thiuda, people, thiudisko; H. G. diot, diutisk, popular, thence deutsch; E. diet, a public assembly.

XVIII. THE LABIAL TENUIS Π, Latin p; for this H. G. and E. have f in the beginning of a word.

ἐλπ—ϝελπ—ἔλπομαι, ἔολπα = ϝεϝολπα, ἐλπίς; allied to

this, ελδ, Fελδ in ἔλδομαι, ἐέλδωρ, ἔλδωρ, δ for π; *volupis* archaic, *voluptas*.

ἕρπω, *serpo*; *rēpo* from *srepo* by metathesis

λιπ—λίπα, λίπος, λιπαρός, λιπαρής, λιπαρέω, ἀλείφω, ἄλειφαρ, ἄλειφα; *adeps*, an unusual transition, λ into *d*, and on the contrary δ is weakened into *l* in δάκρυ, *lacruma*, Sec. 15, 6, Sec. 21.

πα—πατ *to nourish*—ποτ—πατέομαι, ἐπασάμην, ἄπαστος, πάομαι *to acquire*, πέπαμαι, ἐπασάμην, πατήρ; πόσις = ποτις, *the lord of the house, the husband*, δεσπότης, πότνια, πότνα; *pater, Juppiter, pasco, pascor* inceptive, *pastor, panis, penus, penates; compos, potis, potens, possum, potior*; Gothic *fadar*; O. H. G. *fatar*; E. *father*.

παγ—πακ—ἐπάγην, πήγνυμι, πάγος, πάχνη, πηγυλίς, Od. XIV. 476, πάσσαλος = πακjαλος, πακτόω; *paciscor, pango, pax, pignus, pinguis*, παχύς; E. *fat*.

παθ—πα—παθεῖν, πάσχω = παθσκω, or = πασκω? παθ a further extension of the root πα, compare πῆμα; *patior*.

πεδ—πέδον, πεδίον, ποῦς st. ποδ, *pes* st. *ped*, ἔμπεδον = *oppido, oppidum*; H. G. *fuoz, fuss*; E. *foot*.

πεν—πένομαι, πένης, πενιχρός, πενία, πενέσται, πόνος, πεῖνα, πεινάω; *pēnuria*; compare σπαν—in σπάνις, σπανίζω, Sec. 30.

περ—περάω, to press through, πόρος, πεῖρα, πειράω, διαπρύσιος; *porta, portus, experior, peritus, periculum*; Gothic *faran*; H. G. *erfahrung, gefahr, wohlfahrt*, compare εὐπορία; περ in περάω, *to bring over*, is certainly identical; πέρνημι, πιπράσκω (πρα), πρίαμαι = πιπραμαι (?) *to bring to oneself, to buy*.

πετ—πτα—πέτομαι, ἐπτόμην, ἔπτατο, ἔπτην, etc., εὐπετής,

Root Consonants. 33

ὠκυπέτης, ἰθυπτίων Il. XXI. 169, a later and kindred form ἴπταμαι = πιπτ.; πεσεῖν, Dor. ἔπετον, διιπετής, πίπτω = πιπέτω, πιτνέω, πτῶμα, πτῶσις, πότμος; πεπτηώς see πτακ, *peto, impetus, penna = petna, praepes—pets*, on the other hand *bipennis = bipinnis* from *pinna = pitna, a pinnacle*, compare πίτυς, Sec. 19, 3; H. G. *fedara, feder, fittig;* E. *feather.*

πετάννυμι, πίτνημι, Sec. 8, 1, πέτασος, πέταλον; *pateo, patulus, patina.*

πεύκη, *pinus;* H. G. *fiuhta, fichte*, Sec. 19, 3, πικ—πιτ.

π ι — πο — πίνω, πέπωκα, πόσις, πότος, πῶμα; *pōtus, pōtare, pōtio, pōculum; bibo* weakened and reduplicated.

πιθ—πεπιθεῖν, πείθω, πέποιθα; πίστις = πιθτις, πιθανός, πίσυνος, πειθώ; *fides, Fidius, foedus*, Sec. 8, 2.

πῖλος, *pilus, pileus;* H. G. *filz*, E. *felt.*

πίων, πιαρός, πίειρα, πῖαρ, πιμέλη, πιαίνω; *opīmus.*

πλα—πλέος, πλεῖος, πλέως, πίμπλημι, πλήθω; πλῆθος, πληθύς, πλήρης; *pleo, plenus, plerusque, locuples, plebes, pŏpulus, publicus, Publicola, plus, plurimus.*

πλακ—weakened πλαγ, reduced to πλα —; πλήσσω = πληκjω, ἐπλάγην, πληγή, πλάζω = πλαγjω *I strike off from the path*, τειχεσιπλήτης, δασπλῆτις *torch-swinging*, Od. XV. 234; πελ is interchanged with this in πέλας, connected with πλησίον, πελάζω; πέλαγος *the sea laid flat* (?); *plango, plaga, plecto;* E. *flat.*

πλυ—πλέω = πλεϝω, πλεύω Æolic Sec. 9, 1, πλεύσομαι, πλόος, πλοῦς, πλοῖον; πλώω = πλοϝω, ἔπλων, ἐπιπλώς; πλύνω; *pluit, pluvia;* O. H. G. *fliozan, fluot;* E. *float.*

πνυ—πνέω = πνεϝω, πνεύσομαι, πέπνυμαι, ἄμπνυτο, pres. form, ἄμπνυε Il. XXII. 222, πνεῦμα, πινυτός, πινύσσω

3

to make prudent, Il. XIV. 249, ποιπνύω, with diphthongal, reduplication.

προῖξ, προῖκα, προίκτης, προίσσομαι, see Sec. 16, ṛik; *prex, precor, proco, procus, procax.*

πτακ—πτα—ἔπτακον, πτήσσω = πτηκjω, καταπτήτην Il. VIII. 136, πεπτηώς, ποτιπεπτηυῖαι Od. XIII. 98, παπταίνω, πτώξ, πτώσσω, πτωσκάζω.

πτέρνα, Gothic *fairzna*; H. G. *ferse.*

πτύω—*spuo, pituita, s* has disappeared at the beginning of the word as in Greek; H. G. *spihan, speien;* E *spew, spit.*

πυ—πύθω, πύον = *pus; puteo, putidus;* H. G. *faul;* E. *foul.*

πυκ—πύξ, πύκτης, πυγμή; *pugnus, pugil, pungo, pugno. pugio;* O. H. G. *fûst;* E. *fist.*

XIX. Change of the Guttural, Labial, and Dental Tenuis, Κ, Π, Τ, in Greek and Latin.

1. Greek κ in the middle of a word = Latin *p:*

σκεπ—*spec* by metathesis, see Sec. 16.

σκῦλον, σκυλάω, σκυλεύω—*spolium, spoliare,* on the other hand σκῦτος—*scutum.*

σακ—*sap*—σηκός, Doric σακός; *saepes, saepio, praesēpe, sĕpelio.*

λύκος, *lupus;* Gothic *vulfs;* E. *wolf.*

ὀκ—ὄσσε = ὀκjε, ὄσσομαι = ὀκjομαι, προτιόσσετο Od. XIV. 219; *opinor, inopinus, opinio,* see below ὀπ.

Greek κ at the beginning of a word = Latin *p:*

κέλλω, ὀκέλλω; *pello, appello,* connected with *procella.*

Root Consonants. 35

2. The Greek π is still more common for the original k, Latin c, q :

ἐπ—Ϝεπ—ἔπος, εἶπον, ἔειπον = ἐϜεϜεπον, ὄψ stem ὀπ, ἐνοπή, εὐρύοπα, *far-sounding;* vec in *vox* stem vōc, voco, *invīto* = *invicito* from vec = Ϝεπ, *convīcium* by assimilation of vowels from *convocium ;* so too the Greek κ in ὄσσα = ὀκja; ἴσκεν, *he spake,* Homeric, Od. XXII. 31, = σισεκεν from σεκ = σεπ = Ϝεπ, compare ἔννεπε = ἐνσεπε, ἴσπετε = σεσπετε, ἐνίσπες, ἐνίσπε, ἐνισπήσω, ἐνισπεῖν, θέσπις, θεσπέσιος ; ἐχ—σεχ in ἔχω, ἴσχω, ἔσχον, σχές, is analogous to this variation of roots ἐπ—σεπ.

ἐπ—σεπ—ἕπω, ἕπομαι = σεπομαι, ἕσπον, ἑσπόμην = σεσεπόμην, ἑάφθη (?) Il. XIII. 543 ; XIV. 419,—with syllabic augm. on account of the original σ at the beginning of a word, α instead of ε as ἐτάρφθην from τέρπομαι, ὅπλον ; *sequor, secus, secundus, socius;* so too the Greek κ in Homeric ἀοσσητήρ = ἀσοκjητηρ, compare *as-sec-la.*

ἧπαρ, *jecur,* see Sec. 6, 3.

ἰπ—ἴπτομαι, ἐνίπτω, ἠνίπαπε, ἐνῑπή, ἐνέπιπτε Il. XV. 552 ; *ico ;* so too the Greek κ in ἐνίσσω = ἐνικjω ; ἰάπτω, *jacio,* see Sec. 32, 4.

ἵππος, ἴκκος ; *equus,* Sec. 6, 3, connected with *Epŏna* Juven. VIII. 157.

λιπ—*lic*—λιπεῖν, λείπω, λοιπός; *linquo, reliquus (lic), licet.*

ὀπ—ὤψ, ὄπωπα, ὀπωπή, ὄπις, ὄμμα = ὄπμα, ὀπτήρ, ὄψομαι, ὀψείω, desiderative, Il. XIV. 37, ὀφθαλμός, ἐνωπή, ἐνῶπα Il. XV. 320, εἰσωπός Il. XV. 653, ὑπώπια, ὀπιπεύω reduplicated, παρθενοπῖπα Il. XI. 385 ; *oculus ;* so too the Greek κ in ὄσσε, ὄσσομαι ; Latin *p* in *opinor.*

πέντε, Æolic πέμπε, πεμπτός, πεμπάζω ; the Oscan adverb of time *pomptis*, compare the Sabine *Pompilius*, *quinque;* Gothic *fimf;* E. *five*.

πεπ—πέπτω, πέψω, πέπων; ὀπτάω, ὀπτός = ποπτος, ὄψον; connected with πεκ in πέσσω = πεκjω; *coquo, cocus, coquina;* connected with doubled *p* in *popa, popina, popanum,* πόπανον, *pastry*.

πο—relative and interrogative pronominal-stem whence που, ποθι, πως, πω, ποτε, ποθεν; Ionic κου, κως, κοτε, κόσος, κότερος; Latin stem *quo—cu—*; *quod, quid* Oscan *pid, ubi = quobi,* enclitic—*cubi* in *alicubi, sicubi, necubi; necunde, quantus, uter = quoter, neuter = ne-cuter, alicunde;* Oscan stem *po —*.

τρεπ—τρέπω; *torqueo* by metathesis; so too the Greek κ is retained in ἀτρεκέως, ἀτρεκές, perhaps also in τρώκτης a sharper, not *greedy*, as if from τρώγω; Od. XIV. 289; *tricae, trico, intricare, extricare*.

3. τ = π and stands for the original *k*:

ἀταλός = ἁπαλός; πέντε, *quinque;* πόκα, ὄκα, Doric = πότε, ὄτε; τε = *que*, see above καί Sec. 16, compare ἥττων, ἥκιστα, ἥσσων = ἠκj.

πιτ—πικ—πίτυς, πεύκη, πίσσα = πιτja or πικja, πικρός, πευκάλιμος, πευκεδανός, ἐχεπευκής; *pinus, pix* stem *pic;* H. G. *fiuhta, fichte; pech* without shifting of sound, a foreign word.

4. The change of *k* to π, *p*, and from π, *p* to τ takes place in:

quattuor, Skr. *chatur*—πίσυρες Homeric, πέσσυρες Æolic, πέτταρες Bœotian, Attic τέτταρες, τέσσαρες = τεσϝ. = τετϝ.

quinque—πέμπε Æolic, πέντε, see above.

quis stem *ki,—pis,* Neuter *pid,* Oscan and Umbrian,—τις.

Root Consonants.

2. MEDIALS. Γ. Δ. B.

XX. THE GUTTURAL MEDIAL Γ, corresponding to the Latin *g*, Gothic *k*, English *k*.

ἀγ—ἄγω, ἀγαγεῖν, ἀγός, ἀγινέω, ἡγεῖσθαι; *ago, cōgo, coago, cōgito, coagito, agmen, exāmen* Sec. 9, 2, *exiguus*.

ἀγ—ἀγ—ἅγος, Ion. ἄγος, ἅγιος, ἅζομαι = ἁγίομαι, ἐναγής; ἄγαμαι see below.

Ϝαγ—ἄγνυμι, ἀγή, ἔᾱγα = ϜεϜαγα, Ion. ἔηγα, ἐάγην, ἀκτή, ἰωγή Od. XIV. 533 = ϜιϜωγή with reduplication, compare ἰωή = ἰωϜη from ἀϜ, Sec. 31, κυματωγή.

ἀργ—ἀργός, ἀργής, ἀργεννός, ἄργυρος, ἄργῐλος; *arguo, argutus, argentum, argilla*.

γα—γαϜ—γαυ—γαίω, βουγάϊε vocative Il. XIII. 824, γάνυμαι, γανάω, γάνος, γηθέω, γέγηθα; *gaudeo, gavisus*. Related to this is the stem ἀγα in ἄγαμαι, ἀγάομαι, ἀγαίομαι, ἀγητός, ἄγη, ἄγαν, ἀγανός, ἀγαυός, ἀγαυρός.

γαρ—γῆρυς, γηρύω; *garrio, garrulus*.

γεν — γνα — γα — γένος, γίγ(ε)νομαι, γνήσιος, γεγαώς, νηγάτεος, γυνή; *genus, gig(e)no, gnascor, natura;* Gothic *kuni;* O. H. G. *chunni, chunning,* H. G. *könig;* E. *king,* originally = *father,* O. H. G. *chind,* H. G. *kind* = γόνος; E. *kin*.

γένυς, γένειον, γνάθος; *gena;* Gothic *kinnus;* H. G. *kinn;* E. *chin*.

γευ—γεύομαι; *gusto, gustus;* Gothic *kiusan, kustus;* O. H. G. *chiusu, chust;* H. G. *kiese, küse, koste.*

γνο—originally *gna*—ἔγνων, γιγνώσκω, ὄνομα = ὄγνομα, γνῶσις, γνώμη, γνώμων; *gnosco, gnarus, ignoro,* archaic *gnarigare, narrare, nobilis; agnitus, cognitus* with weakening of the vowel, *nŏtus, ignōtus, gnārus* with strengthening of the vowel; Gothic *kannjan, kunths, kunthi*; E. *ken.*

γ ό ν υ, γνύξ, πρόχνυ, γουνάζομαι, γουνός, ἰγνύη, Sec. 9, 5; *genu;* Gothic *kniu;* E. *knee.*

ἐ ρ γ—Ϝεργ—Ϝρεγ—ἔργον, ἔοργα = ϜεϜοργα, ἐώργει Od. XIV. 289 = εἰοργει from ἐϜεϜ.; ἔρδω = Ϝεργjω, for ἐρζω, ῥέζω = Ϝρεγjω, ἀργός from ἀεργός; Gothic *vaurkjan;* H. G. *werk;* E. *work.*

Ϝ ε ρ γ—εἴργω, ἐέργω, ἔρχαται, ἐέρχαται, ἐρχατόωντο Od. XIV. 15; *urgeo.*

ζ υ γ—*jug* see Sec. 32, 1.

λ υ γ—λ υ γ ρ ό ς, λευγαλέος, λοιγός; *lūgeo, luctus.*

ῥ α γ—Ϝραγ—ῥήγνυμι, ῥηγμίν, ῥωγαλέος; ῥακ—in ῥήσσω, ἐπιρρήσσω; *frag—frango, fragilis;* Gothic *brikan;* O. H. G. *prichan;* E. *break.*

ῥ ε γ—ὀρέγω, ὀργυιά; *rego, rex, rectus, erga, ex rega, in the direction;* H. G. *recken, richten.*

σ τ ε γ—τεγ—στέγω, τέγος; *tego;* O. H. G. *dak* —, H. G. *dach, decke;* E. *deck, thatch.*

XXI. THE DENTAL MEDIAL Δ, corresponding to the Latin *d*, Gothic and Low German *t*, German *z*, English *t*.

ἰ δ—Ϝαδ—*svad*—ἔαδον = ϜεϜαδον, εὔαδον = ἔϜαδον, ἔαδα, ἀνδάνω, ἔεδνον—σϜεδνον, ἐδανός Il. XIV. 172, ἦδος—from which the rough breathing has disappeared, compare below ἴδος—ἄσμενος, a participle become an adjective, like ἴκμενος, ἡδονή, ἥδομαι, ἡδύς, ἥδυμος = νήδυμος (?); *suavis = svadvis, suadeo.*

ἀ ρ δ—ῥαδ—ἄρδω, Homeric ἐρράδαται with the radical δ,

Root Consonants.

compare ἐρηρέδαται, νεαρδής, ῥαίνω = ῥαδνjω. Instead of the medial the aspirate appears in ῥαθάμιγξ, ῥαθαίνω, ῥαθάσσω.

δα—δέδαε, δαῆναι, δαήμων, ἀδαήμων, δαίδαλος, δαιδάλλω, with diphthongal reduplication, δαίφρων *prudent*, Odyss.; root δακ in διδάσκω = διδαχ-σκω, διδαχή, compare *dic* in *disco* = *dicsco*, *doceo*, see below δικ.

δα—δαίω, *I divide*, ἐδασάμην, δαίς, δαίζω, δατέομαι, δασμός, δαιτρός.

δαϝ—δαιω, *I kindle*, δάηται Il. XX. 316, δέδηα, θεσπιδαής, δασπλῆτις see above πλακ—πλα Sec. 18, δαΐς, apocop. dat. δαΐ, δαλός, δανός Od. XV. 322, δαίφρων Il. *warlike*; δήιος, δηιόω, δηιότης, δηλέομαι; *deleo*.

δάκρυ, *lacruma* see Sec. 15, 6; Gothic *tagr*; O. H. G. *zahar*; E. *tear*.

δαμ—δαμῆναι, δαμάω, δαμάζω, δάμνημι, δάμαρ, ἀδμής, δμώς; *domare*, *dominus*, *dominari*; H. G. *zahm*; E. *tame*.

δέκα, *decem*; Gothic *taihun*; O. H. G. *zehan*; E. *ten*.

δεμ—δέμω, δέμας, δόμος, δῶμα; *domus*; Gothic *timrjan*; H. G. *zimmer*; E. *timber*.

δή = *jam* = *dja-m*, compare *Janus*, *Diana*.

δι—stem διε in δίεμαι Il. XXIII. 475, ἐνδίεσαν XVIII. 584, δίωνται XVII. 110, δίοιτο Od. XVII. 317; perf. δέδια, δείδια; pres. δείδω = δειδιω, thence δέδοικα, δειδίσσομαι.

διϝ — *div*, *dju* — = light, God, heaven, day: δῖος, ἔνδιος, εὔδιος, διιπετής; Ζεύς = Δjευς, Διός, Διώνη, kindred form with nasal suffix Ζήν, Ζηνός, acc. Ζῆν Il. XIV. 265, from the stem *dja*, as in *Janus*; δῆλος, δέελος, δέατο Od.

VI. 242, δοάσσατο, stem *dev*; *deus, divus, divinus, Dius fidius, Dialis, Juppiter* = *Djuppiter*, the vowel being weakened in consequence of the deeper sound of the second word in composition, *Jovis* = *Djovis*, *Diana* = *divana*, the heavenly one; *Janus, Janus-pater; dies, diu*, by day in *noctu diuque*, a day long, long time, *interdiu, diutius, diutinus*, stem *diuto, dum* = *dium*; O. H. G. *Zio, Dienstag* = *Ziestag*; E. *Tuesday*.

δικ—δίκη, δείκνυμι; *dicio, condicio, dicis* in *dicis causa, indĭco, dīco, causidĭcus, maledĭcus, judex* = *jusdecs; disco* = *dicsco, doceo* see above δα; Gothic *ga-teihan*; H. G. *zihan, zeihen, zeigen*.

δο—δίδωμι, originally *da, dadāmi;* δοτήρ, δόσις, δῶρον; stem *da* in *do, dos, donum; duim, duam;* see below under Moods; for the relation between δο and θε = *dha*, see Sec. 15, 2 A.; Sec. 24, θε; *cĕdo, give here*, compounded of the demonstrative *ce* and *do* = *da; cette* = *ce-dite* = *date*.

δύο, δίς = δϝις; *duo, bis* as *bellum* from *duellum* = *dvis, dis* —; Gothic *tvai;* H. G. *zwei, zer*—; E. *twain, two*.

ἐδ—ἔδω, ἔδμεναι, without tach-vowel, compare below *est*, ἐδωδή, ἐδητύς, ἔσθω, ἐσθίω; νῆστις, ὠμηστής; *edo, est* = *edt, esurio* = *edsurio, esca* = *edsca*.

ἐδ—σεδ—ἔδυς, εἷσα = ἐσεδσα, ἔσσαι, ἔσαι, ἕσσατο = ἐσεδσ., ἕζομαι (ἐδj.), ἑδοῦμαι, ἵζω with present reduplication = ἱέδjω, ἕδρα; *sed—sedeo, sīdo* = *sisedo, sedes, sella* (*sedla*); Gothic *sitan, sitls;* O. H. G. *sizan, sezal;* E. *sit, settle*.

ἰδ—ϝιδ—ἰδεῖν, εἶδον = ἐϝιδον = ἔϝιδον, οἶδα, ἴδμεν, Ion. ἴσμεν, ἴστωρ, ἴδρις, ἰδρείη, ἰνδάλλομαι, ἄϊστος, ἀϊστόω, Ἀΐδης, ἄδης, νῆις Il. VII. 198, Od. VIII. 179; *video, visus, viso, vitrum*.

Root Consonants.

ἰδ—ἰδ—ϝιδ—σϝιδ—ἴδος, ἰδίω, ἴδιον Od. XX. 204, ἰδρώς, ἰδρόω; *sudo, sudor;* O. G. *sveiz;* E. *sweat.*

καδ—κέκαδον, nothing to do with χάζω, κήδω, κῆδος, κεδνός, active = *careful,* passive = *of value, dear.*

ὀδ—ὄδωδα, ὄζω = ὀδjω, ὀδμή; *odor, oleo, d* being weakened into *l,* see Sec. 15, 6.

ὀδούς, stem ὀδοντ with vowel prefixed, Sec. 9, 5; *dens;* Gothic *tunthus;* H. G. *zand, zahn;* E. *tooth.*

σκεδ—σκεδάννυμι, σκίδνημι, σκίδναμαι for the weak vowel see Sec. 8, 1; *scandula.*

σκιδ—σχιζ—σχίζω, σχίζα; *scindo, scidi,* anciently *scidi* see below simple Latin perfect, *scida;* root *cid—caedo, caementum, caespes;* O. H. G. *sceidan, sceit,* H. G. *scheit;* E. *skid.*

ὑδ—*ud—vad*—ὕδωρ; *unda,* Gothic *vato;* O. H. G. *wazar;* E. *water.*

XXII. The Labial Medial B.

In Greek β is seldom original, and then = Latin *b;* more often = an original *g.*

βα—βαίνω = βανjω, βῆναι, βιβάς with pres.-reduplication, βάσκε, βιβάζω, βιβάσθων, βῆμα, βάδην, βέβαιος, βέβηλος; *betere, arbiter;* instead of *b, v* in *venio;* Gothic *qiman;* O. H. G. *koman, kommen,* points back to the original *g* in Sanskrit, root *gâ,* to go.

βοῦς, Doric βῶς, βουγάϊε, Sec. 20, γα; *bōs* stem *bov;* O. H. G. *chuo,* which points back to the original *g* in Sanskrit, *gaus;* E. *cow.*

β = *b* in βληχή, *balare;* βραχύς, *brĕvis* = *bregvis,*

compare ἐλαχύς, lēvis = legvis Sec. 23; βάρβαρος, balbus.

β = Latin g in βάλανος, glans; βαρύς, gravis.

β ι in βίος, βιόω = γϝι, the γ disappears and the ϝ is hardened into β; Epic future without the characteristic tense-letter βέομαι, βείομαι, vivam, βέῃ Il. XVI. 852; vivo reduplicated verb = gvigvo, vixi, vig-si, with the guttural retained, vīvus, vīta, victus; H. G. queck, quick in erquicken, quecksilber; E. the quick and dead, quickset-hedge; Sanskrit root jiv.

β = original and Latin v:

β ο λ, βόλομαι Il. XI. 319, Od. I. 234, XVI. 387, βούλομαι, βουλή etc.; volo, nolo = ne-volo, malo = magi-volo, voluntas; voluptas, see Sec. 18, ἐλπ—; O. H. G. wellan, willo; E. will.

ἀ μ ε ί β ω, Doric ἀμεύω, ἀμοιβή; original root miv in moveo, mōtus, mōmentum, mūto.

β = φ = f: βασκαίνω, βάσκανος; fascinare, fascinum, from the root φα, fa, Sec. 25 = fascination.

3. Aspirates Χ. Θ. Φ.

XXIII. The Guttural Aspirate Χ, corresponding to the Latin *h, f, g*, in the beginning of a word *g*, Gothic *g*.

ἀ κ—ἀγχ—ἄχος, ἄχομαι, ἀχέω, ἀχεύω, ἤκαχον, ἀκαχοίμην, ἀκάχησε, ἀκάχημαι, ἀκαχήμενος, ἀκηχέδαται, with change of quantity, ἀκαχείατο, ἀκαχήδατο, ἀκαχίζω, ἄχνυμαι, ἄχθομαι, ἄχθος, ἄγχι, ἆσσον = ἀγχjον, ἐπασσύτερος; ango, angor, angustus, anxius; H. G. angst.

Root Consonants. 43

ἐλαχύς, ἐλάσσων, —χjων; *lēvis* = *legvis*.

ἐχ—Fεχ—ὄχος, ὀχέομαι, ὄχημα; *veho, via* (*vea*), *vexo, vēlum* = *veglum, vexillum, vectis;* H. G. *wagen, weg;* E. *way*.

ἐχ—σεχ—ἔχω, ἔσχον = σεσεχον, σχεῖν, εἶχον = ἐσεχον, ἴσχω present reduplication = σισεχω; further formation in σχέθω = σεχθω, ἰσχανάω, ἀσχαλάω; ὄχα compare ὄχωκα = ὄκωχα, ἐχυρός, ὀχυρός, σχῆμα, σχεδόν, ἐπισχερώ, ἐξείης.

λιχ—λείχω, λιχμάω, λίχνος; *lingo, ligurio;* Gothic *bi-claigon—;* H. G. *lecken;* E. *lick*.

στιχ—στίχος, στείχω, στοῖχος; *vestigium, vestibulum* see στα—Sec. 17, *fa-stigium;* Gothic and H. G. *steig —, steg;* E. *step*.

χα—χαν—χαίνω, χάσκω, χάσμα; καχάζω reduplicated, καγχάζω, καγχαλάω reduplicated with nasal sound = *achinno; hio, hisco, hiatus, hiulcus; fatisco* (?); O. H. G. *kin—gin*—H G. *gähnen;* E. *yawn*.

χαδ—ἔχαδον, χανδάνω, κεχανδότα Il. XXIII. 268, κε- χάνδει XXIV. 192; *prehendo* = *prae-hendo, praeda* = *prae hida, praedium* = *praehendium*, compare *praebere* = *prae- hibere, debere* = *de-hibere*.

χαδ—χάζω, κεκάδοντο Il. XV. 574 = ἐχάσαντο; *cēdo, necesse, successus* from *ne-ced-tis, suc-ced-tus*.

χαμαί, feminine locative, χαμάδις, χαμᾶζε, χθαμαλός, χθών; *humus, humi, humilis; homo*, anciently *hemo, nēmo* = *ne-hemo;* Gothic *guma;* O. H. G. *komo*, H. G. *gam* in *bräutigam;* E. *groom*.

χαρ—ἐχάρη, χήρατο Il. XIV. 270, χαίρω, χαρά, χάρις χαρίεις; *gratus, gratia;* O. H. G. *ger, giri, gerôn*.

χελιδών, *hirundo;* compare χάλαζα, *grando*.

χ ε ρ—χείρ, χέρης, according to the meaning = ὑποχείριος, compare *mancipium*, χερείων, χείρων, εὐχερής, χράω *to attack*, ἐγχρίμπτω; *herus, heres, herctum, hercisco.*

χ ή ν; *anser* for *hanser;* O. H. G. *kans,* H. G. *gans;* Bohemian *hus;* E. *goose.*

χ ῆ ρ ο ς, χήρα, χηρεύω, χωρίς, χατίς, χατέω, χατίζω, χῆτος; *ad fatim, adequate, according to desire, fames, fatigo, fessus; fatisco* (?), see above χα.

χ θ έ ς, ἐχθές; *heri* for *hesi,* compare *eram = esam,* Sec. 15, 4, *hesternus;* Gothic *gistra;* O. H. G. *kestre,* H. G. *gestern;* E. *yester.*

χ ι—χιών, χεῖμα, χειμών, χειμάζω; *hiems, hibernus.*

χ ο λ ή; *fel = hel;* O. H. G. *kalla,* H. G. *galle;* E. *gall.*

χ ο ρ δ ή, *chorda,* a foreign word in Latin; stem *haru, the gut,* in *haruspex, hariolus* connected with *fariolus.*

χ ό ρ τ ο ς; *hortus, cohors, a close army corps;* Gothic *gards;* O. H. G. *karto,* H. G. *garten;* E. *garden.*

h o s t i s, also *fostis, hospes = hostipes;* Gothic *gasts;* O. H. G. *kast,* H. G. *gast;* E. *guest.*

χ ρ ι—χρίω, χρῖμα, χρῖσμα; *frio, frico, fricae, frivolus.*

χ ρ υ σ ό ς; Gothic *gulth;* O. H. G. *kold,* H. G. and E. *gold.*

χ υ—χέω = χεϜω, Æolic χεύω, ἔχευα, ἔχεα = ἐχεϜα, ἐχύθην, χεύσω, χύμα, χεῦμα, χοή, ἰοχέαιρα, χώομαι, compare ἰπλέω, πλώω = *confundor, to be troubled;* Latin stem *fud* in *fundo, fons, fūtis, fūtilis, confūto, refūto, effūtio;* Gothic *giutan;* O. H. G. *kiuzu,* H. G. *giesse, guss;* E. *gush.*

XXIV. THE DENTAL ASPIRATE Θ. On account of the want of a dental aspirate the Latin equivalent for this is often *f* in the beginning of a word, *d* and *b* in the body of it; Gothic *d*, German *t*, English *d*.

α ι θ, originally ιθ—αἴθω, αἴθων, αἰθήρ, αἶθοψ, Αἰθίοψ; *aedes*, originally meaning a *fireplace*, *aestus* = *aedtus*, *aestas*.

ἐ ρ υ θ ρ ό ς, with ε prefixed, Sec. 9, 5; *ruber, rufus, robigo, ru-tilus;* O. H. G. *rôt;* E. *red, ruddy*.

θ α—θῆσθαι Homeric = *to suckle,* θήσατο Il. XXIV. 58, θηλή, θῆλυς, γαλαθηνός, τιθήνη, τιθασός, τιθαιβώσσω Od. XIII. 106, ἀτιτάλλω; *fēmina, fīlius, fētus, fēnus, fēcundus* (?) see below φυ.

θ α ν—θνα—θανεῖν, θάνατος, θνήσκω, θνητός, τέθνηκα; Gothic *dauthus ;* O. G. *tôd ;* E. *dead*.

θ ε — Skr. *dha* — τίθημι, θέω in ̓ προθέουσιν Il. I. 291, θέσις, θέμις etc. compare δο, Sec. 21; in the Latin root *da, to give*, and *dha* = θε, *to set*, have coalesced; this last meaning is retained in *condo, abdo, trado*, etc.; θ = *f* in *fămulus, fămilia*, certainly also *facio*, with the root extended by the addition of *c*, compare *jacio*, root ἐ; O. H. G. *tuom, a judge's sentence, tât ;* E. *doom*.

θ ε ν—θείνω ; *fendo* in *offendo, defendo*.

θ ε ρ—θέρω, θέρος, θερμός; O. L. *formus, formucapes*, thence *forceps, fornus, furnus, fornax ;* Gothic *varmjan ,* O. H. G. *waram*, H. G. and E. *warm*.

θ ή ρ, φήρ, Æolic; *ferus, fera, ferox;* Gothic *dius ;* O. H. G. *tior*, H. G. *tier ;* E. *deer*.

θ ι γ—θιγγάνω ; *fingo, figulus, figura, fictile*.

46 An Introduction to Greek and Latin.

θρα—θαρ—θρασύς, θάρσος, θαῤῥεῖν; E. *dare; fretus, fortis.*

θυ—θύω, θύελλα, θυμός, θῦμα, θύος, θυήεις, θυόεις; *suffire, fumus, funus, burning incense for the dead;* Gothic *dauns;* O. H. G. *toum,* H. G. *dunst.* Compare Sec. 37.

θυγάτηρ; Gothic *dauhtar;* O. H. G. *tohtar,* H. G. *tochter;* E. *daughter.*

θύρα; *fores, foris, foras,* French *hors;* Gothic *dauro;* O. H. G. *turi,* H. G. *thor, thüre;* E. *door.*

οὖθαρ; *uber;* O. H. G. *ûtar;* E. *udder.*

πυθμήν; *fundus;* O. H. G. *bodam,* H. G. *Bodensee;* E. *bottom.*

XXV. THE LABIAL ASPIRATE Φ, corresponding to the Latin *f* = *bh*, in the middle of a word *b*, in German and English *b*.

ἀλφ—ἤλφον, ἀλφάνω, ἀλφηστής, ἀλφεσίβοιαι Il. XVIII. 593; *labor (labos), laboro;* O. H. G. *arabeit,* H. G. *arbeit.*

ἄμφω; *ambo;* H. G. *beide;* E. *both.* ἀμφί, *amb—am—an—*in composition, *ambio, ambages, amplector, anquiro.*

ἄφενος, ἀφνειός; stem *op* in *ops,* φ in the middle of a word = *p, opulentus, vol-up-tas* (?)—see Sec. 22 βολ—*vol,* Sec. 18 ἐλπ,—*cōpia* = *coopia;* stem *ap* in *apiscor, aptus, coepi* = *coĕpi* from the original *coapio.*

νέφος, νεφέλη; *nĕbula, nĕbulo, nūbes, nūbo,* but on the other hand, *pronŭba, nubilus, nubila, nimbus;* O. H. G. *nebal,* H. G. *nebel.*

ὀμφαλός; *umbilicus;* O. H. G. *nabulo,* H. G. *nabel;* E. *navel.*

Root Consonants. 47

ὀρφανός; orbus, orbare; O. H. G. arbja, H. G. erbe.
ὀφρύς; O. H. G. prâwa, H. G. braue; E. brow.

φα—φαϝ—φαν—φημί, φατός, φάσκω, φάτις, φήμη, ἀμφασίη, παράφασις, πάρφασις, παραίφασις, παλαίφατος, φωνή; φάε Od. XIV. 502, φάος, φῶς, φάεννος, φαεινός, φαέθω, φαεσίμβροτος, πιφαύσκω, παιφάσσω, *I flash*, Il. II. 450, φαίδιμος, φαιδρός; ἐφάνην, φανερός, φαίνω, πεφήσεται Il. XVII. 155, παμφαίνω with nasal reduplication, φάσμα; from φαϝ by hardening the digamma, giving a nasal sound, and changing the a into ε, comes φεγγ in φέγγος; φα is further formed into φαλ in φαληρός, Doric φαλαρός, φαληριόωντα Il. XIII. 799; *fari, fama, fanum, fatum, Bonifatius*, compare Εὐφήμιος, *fatuus, fas, fateor, fetialis, a speaker* = *herald, infitias* (*ire*), *infitiari, fabula, praefica, facundus, facetus; fax, facies.*

φα—φεν—φατός, πέφαται, πέφανται, πεφάσθαι, πεφήσομαι, πρόσφατος, ὀδυνήφατος, ἀρηίφατος, μυλήφατος; ἔπεφνον, φόνος, φοίνιος, = φονϳ with epenthetic ι on account of the retention of it in the following syllable; O. H. G. *pano, a murderer*; (?) E. *bane.*

φερ, Skr. *bhar*,—φέρω, φέρτε without tach-vowel = *ferte*, φέρετρον, φαρέτρα, φόρος, φόρτος; *fero, ferculum, Feretrius, fertilis, ferax, fors, fortuna, fortuitus;* Gothic *bairan;* O. H. G. *piru = fero, purdi = bürde;* Gothic *gabaurths;* O. H. G. *bâra*, H. G. *bahre, bar*, in composition; E. *bear, birth.*

φηγός, *fagus;* Gothic *bôka;* O. G. *pouchà*, H. G. *buche;* E. *beech*, Sec. 13, 2.

φλα—φλάζω, παφλάζω, φλασμός; φλε—φλέω; φλι—φλιδή; φλυ—φλύω, φλύαρος; φλοι—φλοῖσβος, ἀφλοισμός,

Sec. 9, 5; *flare, flos, floreo, fluo;* Gothic *uf-biesan;* O. H. G. *plâsan;* Gothic *blôma;* O. H. G. *pluomo,* H. G. *blume,* E. *bloom;* O. H. G. *pluohan,* H. G. *blühen.*

φ λ ε γ—φλέγω, φλόξ; *flagrare, flamma, flamen; fulgeo, fulgur, fulmen.*

φ ρ α κ—φράσσω = φρακjω, φράγμα; *farcio, farcîmen, frequens;* Gothic *baurgs;* O. H. G. *puruc,* H. G. *berg, burg;* E. *borough.*

φ ρ ά τ ω ρ, φρατήρ, φράτρα, Ionic φρήτρη, φρατρία; *fråter,* Gothic *brothar;* O. H. G. *pruodar,* H. G. *bruder;* E. *brother.*

φ ρ έ α ρ, Sec. 37, 1; Gothic *brunna;* O. H. G. *prunno,* from *brinnan, to burn.*

φ υ—ἔφυν, φύω, φυή, φύσις, φώς = *the breeder*(?) , φιτύω; *fu—fuam, fui, fore; fi —* in *fio = fuio* compare Æolic φυίω, *fieri,* anciently *fiere, fierem* not a passive form; *fe —fev—fētus, effētus* from *feo, fevo; fēcundus, fēmina, fīlius, fēlix, fēnum, fēnus* see above Sec. 24, θα; Gothic *bauan, to dwell;* O. H. G. *pim,* H. G. and E. *bin.*

φ υ γ—φυγή, φυγεῖν, φεύγω; φύζα = φυγjα, πεφυζότες Il. XXI. 6, φυζακινός Il. XIII. 102; *fuga, fugio;* Gothic *biugan;* H. G. *biege.*

φ ύ λ λ ο ν; *folium;* O. L. G. *blad,* O. H. G. *plat,* H. G. *blatt;* E. *blade.*

Root Consonants. 49

B. SEMI-VOWELS. PERSISTENT SOUND OF CONSONANTS.

1. LIQUIDS.

XXVI. THE NASAL AND DENTAL LIQUID N.

The Greek ν is primitive and radical, answering to the Latin *n*, and in the following roots, stems, and words corresponds to the *n* of the other Indo-Germanic languages:—

ἀν—ἄνεμος ; *animus, anima.*

ἀνήρ, stem ἀνερ, ἀνδρεῖος, for the δ in ἀνδρός Sec. 34, 6, ἠνορέη, ἀγήνωρ, ἄνθρωπος *the countenance of man.*

ναϝ—ναυ—ναῦς, Epic and Ionic νηῦς, νήϊος, Doric νάϊος ; *navis, nauta, nausea.*

νε—νέω, νῆμα, νήθω, χερνῆτις Il. XII. 433; *neo;* O. H. G. *nâan.*

νεϝ—νέος, νεότης, νεοίη Il. XXIII. 604, νεαρός, νέατος, νείατος, νείαιρα, νεοσσός, νεανίας, νεβρός = νεϝρ. with hardened digamma ; *novus, denuo, nūper.*

νεκ—νέκυς, νεκρός, νεκυία ; *neco, nex.*

νεμ—νέμω, νόμος, νομίζω, νέμεσις *"imputatio;" Numa, numerus, nummus.*

νεσ—νε—νέομαι, νίσσομαι, νόστος, Νέστωρ.

νιφ—*niv—nigv*—νίφω, νίφα acc., νιφάς, νιφετός ; *nix = nigs*, gen. *nivis = nigvis, ningit*, nasalized = *nigvit;* Gothic *snaivs*, O. H. G. *sneo*, H. G. *schnee*, E. *snow.*

νυ—νεύω, νεῦμα ; *nuo, nūmen, nūtus.*

ὄνομα = ὄγνομα from the root γνο, Sec. 20, compare Sec. 9, 5, Ionic οὔνομα, Æolic ὄνυμα, ἀνώνυμος, νώνυμνος ; *nomen* from *gnomen*, compare *cognomen, ignominia ;* Gothic *namo*, H. G. *namen*, E. *name.*

4

ὄνυξ, *unguis ;* H. G. *nagal, nagel,* E. *nail.*

ὦνος, ὠνέομαι, Greek root ϝων, hence the syllabic augment in ἐωνούμην ; *vēnum eo, do, vēneo, vendo.*

Changes of ν before *mutes:*

ν, which is a nasal and also a dental liquid, is affected before the mutes according to the classes to which they belong; it remains unchanged before the dental mutes in κεντέω, σπένδω, λανθάνω ; is changed into the labial and nasal liquid μ before the labial mute in κάμπτω, ἄμφω, λαμβάνω, nasalized from λαβ ; and becomes a guttural before a guttural mute, ἄγκυρα, ἄγγελος, λαγχάνω, a nasalized present form of the root λαχ.

XXVII. THE NASAL AND LABIAL LIQUID M.

This is original and fundamental in :

ἀμ—ἀμάω, ἄμητος; *meto, messis, messor ;* H. G. *mât,* E. *math.*

ἀμ—*sam*—ἅμα, Æolic ἅμυδις, ὁμοῦ, ὁμός, ὅμοιος ; *simul, similis, simultas ;* H. G. *sam, sammt ;* E. *same :* Sec. 30.

ἀμείβω, *moveo,* Sec. 22.

ἀμύνω, μύνη Homeric; *munio, moenia, murus.*

μα—μάομαι, μῶμαι, μέμαμεν, μαιμάω, ματεύω, ἀπροτίμαστος Il. XIX. 263.

με—*ma*—μήν = μηνς, Ionic μείς, μήνη, = *the measurer,* μέτρον, μιμέομαι, thence *imitor, imago* = *mimago ; mensis, metare, metiri, modus, mos, nimis,* = *ni-m-is* comparative adverb, *without measure ;* Gothic *mena, menoth,* O. H. G. *manot,* H. G. *mond, monat,* E. *moon, month.*

μεγ—*mag*—μακ—μέγας, μακρός, μῆκος, ἀμαιμάκετος ; *magnus, major, magis, macto, macte.*

Root Consonants. 51

μ ε ν—μαν—μνα—μένω, μένος ; μαίνομαι, μανία ; μέμνημαι, μνήμη ; *maneo, memini, mens, comminiscor, moneo.*

μ ε ρ—μαρ—μέριμνα, μερμηρίζω ; *memor, memoria.*

μ έ σ ο ς, μέσσος, μέσσατος, μεσσάτιος, μεσσηγύς ; *medius, dimidius, meridies,* euphonic substitution of *r* for *d;* H. G. *mitte,* E. *mid(dle).*

μ ή τ η ρ, Doric μάτηρ ; *māter ;* O. H. G. *muotar,* H. G. *mutter,* E. *mother.*

μ ι γ—ἐμίγην, μίγδην, μίγνυμι, μίσγω = μιγσκω, μίξις ; *misceo, mixtus, mistus;* O. H. G. *miskiu,* H. G. *mischen,* E. *mix.*

μ ι ν—μινύω, μινύθω, μίνυνθα, μείων ; *minuo, minor, minister ;* Gothic *minnists = minimus,* E. *mite.*

μ ο λ—μολεῖν, βλώσκω = μβλωσκω, compare βροτός and Sec. 34, 6, μέμβλωκα, compare ἄμβροτος.

μ ο ρ—μαρ—βροτός = μβροτος, *mortuus,* ἄμβροτος, ἄβροτος = ἀμρ. ; μαραίνω ; μέροπες (?), rather root μαρπ(τω) ; *morior, marcesco.*

μ υ—μύω, μύστης ; *mutus, musso.*

XXVIII. THE LINGUAL LIQUID Λ. *l.*

ἀ λ—ἄναλτος Homeric ; *alo, alumnus, coalesco,* also *cōlesco,* compare *cōgo* from *coago, alvus ;* so too *ol—*in *olēre, olesco, olus, abolitus. adultus = adolitus, exolesco, prōles* from *pro-olo, suboles.* The root ἀλ is extended to ἀλδ— ἀλθ—in ἀλδαίνω, *I nourish,* ἄλθομαι, ἀλθαίνω, *I heal;* H. G. *alt,* E. *old, elder.*

ἀ λ—ἄλη, ἀλᾶσθαι, ἀλέη, ἀλέομαι, ἀλευάμην, ἀλεείνειν ἀλεωρή, ἠλεός, ἠλίθιος, ἀλιτεῖν, ἀλείτης, ἀλιτήμων, ἀλιτήμενος, ἠλάσκειν, ἠλασκάζειν, ἀλάστωρ.

γάλα, stem γαλακτ = γλακτ, γλάγος, γλακτοφάγος Il. XIII. 6, γυλαθηνός, see θα Sec. 24; *lac*, stem *lact*.

Ϝελ—Ϝαλ—*to throng*, εἴλω, ἐάλην, ἀλείς, ἔελμαι, εἶλαρ, ἴλη, ὅμιλος; ἅλις, ἀλία, ἀλίζω, ἡλιαία, ἁλής, ἀολλής, ἀελλής, ἀολλίζω.

Ϝελ—ἐλύω *I revolve*, εἰλύω *I enwrap*, εἰλυφάω Il. XI. 156, εἰλυφάζω, ἰλλάς Il. XIII. 572, ὀλοοίτροχος, *a rolling stone*, ib. 137 (οὐλαί, οὐλοχύται, ἀλέω, *I grind?*); ἐλίσσω, ἕλιξ, ἑλικῶπες; for the digamma compare Il. XVI. 569; *volvo;* O. H. G. *wellan*.

λα—λῆμα, λιλαίομαι, λελίημαι, λίαν, λώϊον, λῷστος, λαρός; *lascivus;* λαϜ—λάων, λάε = λαϜ. Od. XIX. 229; λαυ — ἀπολαύομαι, λεία, ληΐς; *lucrum;* H. G. and E. *lust*.

λαός, λήϊτος, λειτουργία; O. H. G. *liut*.

λεγ—λέγω, λόγος, λέσχη; *lego* etc., also *legūmen, diligens, neglego, intellego, religens, God-fearing,* compare ἀλέγω Il. XVI. 388, opposed to *neglegens, religio,* or from *ligare* = a chained conscience (?).

λεῖος, λειότης, λειαίνω; *lēvis, levigare*.

λέχριος, λέχρις, λικριφίς Il. XIV. 463, Od. XIX. 451, with suffix φι—φιν and *s* of the plural, compare Latin—*bus*, λοξός; *obliquus*, stem *lic, luxus, disjointed;* H. G. and E. *link*.

λιχ—λείχω, λιχμάω, λίχνος, ἐπιλίγδην; *lingo, ligurio;* O. H. G. *lecchon*, E. *lick, lickerish*. Sec. 23.

λυ—*to loose*, λύω, *solvo* = *seluo, luo, I expiate;* λυ —*to rinse*, λῦμα, λυμαίνομαι, λούω from λοέω, thence λοέσσαι, λοῦται contracted from λοεται or λούεται; *lu*—in *polluo, diluo, adluo, alluvies;* *lav*—in *lavere, lavare, lautus; lustrum*.

Root Consonants. 53

λ υ κ—λύχνος, λευκός, λεύσσω, σσ from κj, ἀμφιλύκη, λυκάβας, *light-path* = *year;* *lux, luceo, lucidus, diluculum, lumen* = *lucmen,* luna = *lucna;* O. H. G. *lioht,* H. G. *licht,* E. *light.*

λ ώ β η, *lābes, fall, shame, stain, lābor, lăbarc,* compare Sec. 8, 1.

ὅ λ ο s, οὖλος Ionic, *entire, compact,* οὖλε = *salve,* οὐλή *a healed wound;* ὀλοόφρων Odyss. from ὀλοός, *of sound mind; salus, salvus,* anciently *sollus* = *entire, safe, sollers, solidus;* H. G. *salig, selig,* E. *silly,* O. E. *seely.*

σ α λ—σάλος, σαλεύω ; *salum.*

σ φ α λ—σφαλῆναι, σφάλλω; *fallo;* H. G. *fallen,* E. *fail, fall.*

XXIX. THE LINGUAL LIQUID P. *r.*

ἀ ρ—ἀρόω, ἄροτος, ἄροτρον, ἄρουρα ; ἔρα, ἔραζε (?) ; *aro, aratrum, armentum, arvum ;* Gothic *arjan,* O. G. *erran* (*arare*) ; Gothic *airtha,* O. H. G. *erda,* H. G. *erde* (?), E. *ear,** *earth, year.*

ἀ ρ—ἄρα, Homeric ῥά, ἄρ, ἄρηρα, ἀραρεῖν, ἀραρίσκω, ἐριήρης ; ἄρτι, ἄρτιοϲ, ἀρτύω ; ἀρείων, ἄριστος, ἀρετή, ἀρι— e.g. in ἀριδείκετος ; ἁρμός, ἁρμόζω, ἁρμονίη, Homeric, *a fastening ; arma, artus, ars, iners.*

ἐ ρ—ἐρέσσω, ἐρέτης, ἀμφήρης ; ἔριθος *a hired servant* (?); *remus, remex, remigium, ratis,* E. *row.*

Ϝ ε ρ—ἐρέω, εἴρω, εἴρηκα = ἐϜρ., ἐρρήθην = ἐϜρ., ῥήτρα, εἰρήνη, ὀαρίζω (?) ; *verbum;* Gothic *vaurd,* H. G. *wort,* F. *word.*

* The young oxen that *ear* the ground.—Isaiah, ch. v.

54   *An Introduction to Greek and Latin.*

εἴρομαι, ἐρέσθαι, *to ask*, are different from this, and have no trace of the digamma.

ἐρ—σερ—ἕρμα, ὅρμος, σειρά, εἴρω, thence ἤειρεν Il. X. 499, with the lengthening of the syllabic augment to η to compensate for the absence of the consonantal beginning, ἑερμένος; *sero, sera, sertum, series, servus.*

ὁ ρ—ὄρωρα, ὦρτο, ὄρσο, ὄρσεο, ὄρνυμι, ὀρίνω, ὀρούω, οὖρον *a stretch*, Od. VIII. 124, δίσκουρα Il. XXIII. 523; *orior, ortus, origo;* variation ἐρ in ἔρχομαι = ἐρσκ.

ὁ ρ—Ϝορ—*to watch*, ὅρονται Od. XIV. 104, οὖρος, ἐπίουρος, ἔφορος, φρουρός = προορος, τιμάορος, τιμωρός, πυλᾶωρός = πυλάορος with varying quantity, πυλωρός, θυρᾶωρός, θυρωρός, ὥρα, ὁράω, ἑώρων, instead of the digamma, οὐδενόσωρα Il. VIII. 178, δυσωρήσωσιν X. 183; H. G. *wart, warten*, E. *ward.*

ρ ε π—Ϝρεπ—ῥέπω, ῥοπή, ῥόπαλον, makes the foregoing syllable long by position Od. IX. 319, ῥίπτω, καλαῦροψ, *a shepherd's crook*, Il. XXIII. 845; *rĕpens.*

ρ ι γ—Ϝριγ—ῥῖγος, ῥιγέω, ἔρριγα, ῥίγιον, καταριγηλός in which the second syllable is long by position on account of the digamma Od. XIV. 226, ι is universally long; φρικ —φρίξ, φρίσσω; *frīgus, frīgeo, frīgidus;* on the other hand *rĭgor, rĭgeo, rĭgidus;* H. G. *friusan, frieren* (?), E. *freeze, frore.*

ρ υ—ῥέω, ῥεύσω, ἐρρύην, ῥύμη, ῥεῦμα, ῥοή, ῥώομαι, ἐρωή, ῥυθμός; *ruo*; O. H. G. *stroum* points to an original root σρυ, H. G. *strom*, E. *stream.*

Only a few Greek roots which begin with ρ correspond with roots which begin with *r* alone in kindred languages. The roots which in those languages begin with *r* have in

Root Consonants. 55

Greek a vowel often prefixed to the ρ, compare e.g. ἐρεύγω, *ructo;* ὀρέγω, *rego,* see Sec. 9, 5. The Greek roots which begin with ρ have for the most part a digamma at the beginning as ῥέζω, see Sec. 20 Ϝεργ—Ϝρεγ, ῥήγνυμι, *frango,* ῥιγέω, ῥέπω, or a σ, as ῥέω, ῥώομαι, *I stream.* Hence the ρ is doubled in the augment, ἔρρεε, ἐρρύην, ἔρρηξα. Compare for *str* instead of *sr* the Old Latin *stlis, slis,* whence *lis,* H. G. *streit,* E. *strife.*

Interchange of the Lingual Liquids r *and* l.

This change, which is caused by the weakening of *r* to *l,* is not confined to Greek, but takes place also partly between Greek and Latin, and partly between one of these and the Teutonic languages.

1. Within the limits of Greek: ἀρκ—ἀλκ—in ἀρκέω, ἀλκή etc., see Sec. 16; ἁμαρτάνω, ἤμβροτον, ἤμπλακον; ἀμέργω, ἀμέλγω, *mulgeo,* H. G. *milch,* E. *milk;* βρύω *I swell,* βλύω, *I bubble out,* compare φλυ, Sec. 25; κυρ—κυλ in κυρτός, *curvus* and κυλίω, κύκλος, compare *circus;* κάρχαρος, καρχαρόδους Il. X. 360, καρχαλέος, *rough, sharp;* μορύσσω, μολύνω *I defile;* χηραμός *a cleft,* χηλαμός* name of a mountain; Σείριος, σέλας; ἐρ—ἐλ in ἔρχομαι, ἐλθεῖν.

2. Between Greek and Latin: βάρβαρος, *balbus, balbutio;* κύκλος, *circus* see above; σέλας, *serenus;* χελιδών, *hirundo.*

3. Between Greek and Latin on the one side and the Teutonic languages on the other: μάρμαρος, *marmor,*

* Liddell and Scott say this is a corrupt form.

H. G. *marmel*, E. *marble;* μορμύρω, H. G. *murmeln*, E. *murmur;* πλατύς, H. G. *breit*, E. *broad;* χρυσός, Gothic *gulth*, O. H. G. *kold*, H. G. and E. *gold*, see Sec. 23 ; *lis* from *slis, stlis*, stem *stlit*, O. H. G. *strît*, H. G. *streit*, E. *strife*. Compare ἀλφ—*arbeit* Sec. 25.

2. ORIGINAL SPIRANTS. Σ (SPIRITUS ASPER). F. JOD.

XXX. THE SIBILANT Σ AND ITS SUBSTITUTE THE ROUGH BREATHING.

1. The original *s* is retained in Greek at the end of words, before mutes at the beginning and in the middle of words, less often before a vowel at the beginning.

α. At the end, so far as the Greek laws of termination permit, compare Sec. 35 : e.g., in μένος, stem μενες, Skr. *manas*, γένος ; as suffix of the nom. sing. masc. and fem. πόσις = ποτις, *patis*, ὄψ = Ϝοπς, and of the genit. sing. —ος.

β. At the beginning and in the middle generally before mutes :

Root ἐς, *to be;* 2 sing. ἐσσί Homeric; 3 sing. ἐστί ; 1 pl. ἐσμέν, 2 pl. ἐστέ ; imp. ἴσθι = ἐσθι, ἔστω etc., impf. dual ἦστον, ἤστην, 2 pl. ἦστε connected with ἦτε; Latin *sum* = *esum, est, estis*, etc. ; Gothic, H. G. *ist*, E. *is*.

ἐς—Ϝες—*vas*, Latin *ves* in *vestis*, ἕννυμι = Ϝεσν. with assimilated σ, σ is retained in ἔσσο, ἔστο pluperfect, as also in ἐσθής, *vestis*, see below, Sec. 31 ; instead of the assimilation of σ there is a compensatory lengthening in καταείνυσαν or -είνυον Il. XXIII. 135.

Root Consonants.

στα—ἵστημι, where the σ has disappeared at the beginning of the reduplicated syllable, εἱστήκειν = ἑσε-στηκειν, see Sec. 17 ; στορ—in στορέννυμι Sec. 17 ; ἑστία, Sec. 31.

γ. At the beginning before a vowel:

σάος, σῶς, σαόω, σώζω, etc.; *sanus;* O. H. G. *gasunt*, H. G. *gesund*, E. *sound*.

σαφής, σοφός; *sapio, sapor, sapiens, sucus;* O. H. G. *saf*, H. G. *saft*, E. *sap;* s has disappeared in ὀπός, *sap*, E. *opium*.

σέβομαι, σέβας, σεμνός = σεβνος.

σέλας, σελήνη; *sol, serenus*, root *svar*.

σιγάω, σιγή, σῖγα, Cretan ἴγα; H. G. *swigen, schweigen*, the Greek σ here = the original *sv*, for which the rough breathing ' was used in Greek, compare ἱδρώς, Sec. 21 and below.

σῦς, connected with ὗς; *sus*, Gothic, *svein*, O. H. G. *sû*, H. G. *sau*, E. *sow, swine*.

2. Instead of the original and Latin *s* in the beginning before a vowel, Greek for the most part used the rough breathing ', often interchanged with the smooth breathing.

ἄδην, ἅδην, ἅδδην, ἅδος, ἀδηκότες Il. X. 98, also ἄμεναι, ἆσαι, ἄσασθαι Il. XIX. 307, from ἄω; *satis, satur, satias, satio;* Gothic *saths*, H. G. *satt*.

ἅλλομαι, ἅμα, Homeric aorist with the smooth breathing ἄλσο, ἄλτο, = ἕαλτο, ἐπάλμενος; *salio, saltus, salto*.

ἅλς, ἅλμη, ἁλμυρός; *sal, salio, salsus, insulsus*, compare H. G. *sulza, sulze;* H. G. *salz*, E. *salt*.

ἅμα, ἄμυδις, ὁμοῦ, etc.; *simul;* H. G. — *sam, sammt,* see Sec. 27.

ἅπαξ, root ἁ = *sa,* ἁπλοῦς, *semel, simplex.*

ἐδ—*sed*—in ἕδος, ἕζομαι; *sedes,* etc., Sec. 21.

ἑκυρός, *socer,* Sec. 16.

ἔνος in ἔνη καὶ νέα, *senex,* etc., compare O. H. G. *siniskalkus, seneschalk,* E. *seneschal.*

ἕξ, ἕκτος; *sex;* Gothic *saihs,* H. G. *sechs,* E. *six.*

ἑπτά, ἕβδομος; *septem;* Gothic *sibun,* H. G. *sieben,* E. *seven.*

ἑπ—ἕπομαι, *sequor;* σ before a mute is retained in σπεῖν, compare ἔσπετε, see Sec. 19, 2.

ἕρπω, *serpo;* εἷρπον = ἔσερπον, see Sec. 18.

ἡδύς, *suavis,* ' = *sv;* not aspirated ἦδος, ἄσμενος, see ἁδ, Sec. 21.

ἥλιος, ἠέλιος, *auselius* (= *Aurelius*); as ὕλη, *silva, sila.*

ἡμι—ἥμισυς, *semi*—, *semis;* O. H. G. *sâmi*—.

ἱδρώς, *sudor,* not aspirated ἴδος, ἰδίω, see Sec. 21.

ὁλκός, ἕλκω, having lost the rough breathing ὦλξ, acc. ὦλκα, Doric ὦλαξ, Attic ἄλοξ; *sulcus.*

ὅλος, not aspirated οὖλος Ionic; *salvus,* anciently *sollus,* Sec. 28.

οὗ, οἷ, ἕ, pronoun stem ἑ, ἑός, ὅς, *suus; sui, sibi, se,* originally *sve,* σϝε, hardened into σφέ, *suus;* ἴδιος = (σ)ϝιδιος.

υἱός, Gothic *sunus,* H. G. *sohn,* E. *son.*

ὑπό, ὑπέρ, ὕπτιος, ὕπατος; *sub, super, supinus, supremus, summus.*

ὕπνος, *somnus* = *sopnus, sopor;* the Gothic *slêpan* differs from this, O. H. G. *slâfan,* E. *sleep.*

Root Consonants. 59

ὁ, ἡ, article, a form with the rough breathing from the original pronominal stem *sa*, see Pronouns.

3. σ has disappeared :

α. In the beginning of words before vowels, besides the cases of change from the smooth to the rough breathing noticed above, in ἄλοχος, also ἀδελφός; the so-called copula ἁ = ἁ in ἅπας, ἅπαξ, ἅμα = *sa, sam*, Sec. 27, instead of this also ὁ, compare ὁμοῦ, ἅμα, in ὅπατρος = ὁμοπατρος, ὀγάστωρ; ἐχ—σεχ in ἔχω, Sec. 23 ; ἔσταλκα = ἐστ. = σεστ.

β. At the beginning before liquids : μικρός, σμικρός, Ionic and Old Attic ; νέω = σνεϝω, *I swim*, thence the Homeric impf. ἄνεον Il. XXI. 11; νευρά, O. H. G. *snuor*, νυός, *nurus*, O. H. G. *snur ;* νίφα, *nix*, O. H. G. *sneo*, E. *snow ;* ῥυ = σρυ in ῥέω, thence ἐρρύην, H. G. *strom*, E. *stream*, Sec. 29, compare *lis*, Sec. 29 ; compare the disappearance of *st* in *locus*, anciently *stlocus*.

γ. In the beginning before mutes : πτύω, *spuo, speien, spit*, Sec. 18 ; πένομαι, πόνος, compare σπάνις ; κεδάννυμι—σκεδ., κίδναμαι—σκιδν.; τέγος, *tectum*, στέγος; ταῦρος, H. G. *stier*, E. *steer ;* the *s* disappearing in *tabula*, root *sta*.

δ. In the middle of a word before μ : εἰμί = ἐσμι, for compensatory lengthening, Sec. 9, 2, compare εἶμαι = ἔσμαι, or directly from the Æolic ἔμμι by the preceding assimilation of the σ; σμ is moreover a common collocation of sounds in the middle of words, compare πέπεισμαι.

ε. In the middle of a word between vowels, see Sec. 9, 1, c ; with regard to the change of the Latin *s* between vowels into *r*, Sec. 11, 3.

The repugnance of Greek to σ is especially shown

before vowels at the beginning of words, and between vowels in the middle of words. There is found also a partial and cautious abandonment, even in the Old Æolic and Ionic dialects, of the *h*-sound, which frequently took the place of σ, by weakening it into the smooth breathing.

XXXI. THE LABIAL, SEMI-VOWEL SPIRANT ϝ, corresponding to the Latin *v*, sporadically represented by the rough breathing in Greek, at the beginning of a word.

1. The Greek ϝ has disappeared, or is turned into the vowel υ, and is only now to be recognized by the traces it has left, and by comparison with kindred languages, Sec. 11, 2.

ἀ ϝ—ἄημι, ἄητο, ἄητος, ἀήτης, δυσαής, ἀήρ, ἄελλα, αὔρα ιὐλή; αὔω *I call*, αὔσας, ἀϋτή, ἀϋτέω, thence the Homeric, ἴνεως = ἀναϝος, ἰωή with reduplication; ἀέσαι *to sleep*, ἰαύω reduplicated present; ἄισθω *I breathe out;* ἀϋτμή, H. G *âtum, athem ; ventus*, Gothic *vinds*, E. *wind*.

ἀ ϝ—*au*—ἀίω = ἀϝιω, αἰσθάνομαι, probably also ἐπητής. Od. XIII. 332, ἐπητύς XXI. 306 ; οὖς, ὠτός, οὔατα Homeric ; *audio, oboedio, auris, ausculto ;* Gothic *auso*, H. G. *ohr*, E. *ear*.

αἰεί = αἰϝει, locative form, αἰών, ἀΐδιος, ἐπ-ηε-τανός; *aevum, aetas = aevitas ;* Gothic *aivs, time*, O. H. G. *ewâ, law, wedlock*, E. *ever*, H. G. *je, nie = ni·aiv*, E. *never*.

ἔαρ = ϝεαρ, ἦρ ; *ver*.

ϝερ—ἔρρω, ἔρρε, ἐρρέτω, ἔρρων, Homeric ἀπό-ερσε ; ἐρύω, etc. ; *verro, I sweep*.

Root Consonants. 91

Ϝι—*vi*—ἰτέα, *willow, vitis, vimen, viētus, pliant, withered*,
O. H. G. *wid*, H. G. *weide ;* thence οἶνος, *vinum = voinum, vinea ;* H. G. *wein*, E. *wine*.
Compare Ϝιδ—*vid*—in ἴδμεν, οἶδα, ἵστωρ, *video*, Sec. 21.
ἐλύω, *volvo ;* οἶκος = Ϝοικ., *vicus ;* ἔργον = Ϝεργ., H. G. *werk*,
E. *work ;* Ϝεπ in ἔπος, *vox ;* ἐμέω, *vomo ;* ἴον, *viola ;* ἰός,
virus ; ἴς, ἶνες, with suff. ἴφι, thence adj. ἴφιος, *vis ;* Ϝ in the
middle of a word : ὄῑς = ὄϜις, *ovis ;* ᾠόν = ὠϜιον, *ovum ;* νέος
= νεϜος, *novus ;* πλέω = πλεϜω root πλυ, *pluo = pluo, pluvia*.

2. Original Ϝ, Latin *v*, is represented by sp. asp. ':
Ϝεσ—*ves*—ἕννυμι = Ϝεσνυμι, εἷμα, Æolic ἔμμα = Ϝεσμα,
ἀνείμων Od. III. 348. The digamma is traceable in
καταείνυσαν, ἐπιειμένος, ἕσσατο ; ἑᾱνός, εἱᾱνός subst., εἱᾱνός
pliant ; vestis, vestio ; ' has disappeared in ἐσθής.
Compare ἕσπερος, *vesper ;* ἑστία, Ion. ἱστίη, ἑστιάω, Attic
imperfect ἑστίων = ἐϜεστ., *Vesta*, root *vas*, *us* in *uro*,
Sec. 33 ; ἵστωρ, connected with ἵστωρ = Ϝιδτορ, ἱστορία
from Ϝιδ, *vid*.
ὑδ—*ud*—*vad*, Sec. 21.

3. For the change of Ϝ to a vowel see Secs. 9. 11.

XXXII. THE PALATAL, SEMI-VOWEL SPIRANT JOD has
disappeared in Greek, and is retained as the Latin
j, English *y, g*.
See Secs. 9. 11. 34, for examples of *j* becoming a
vowel, for its disappearance, assimilation, and amalgamation with other letters.
The original *j* as the beginning of a root is represented
in **Greek**:

62   An Introduction to Greek and Latin.

1. By the mixed sound ζ, which has arisen from *dj*, *gj*:

ζυγ—*jug*—ζυγόν, ζεύγνυμι, ζώννυμι; *jŭgum, jungo, jūmentum, jūgis*, united together, therefore lasting, *juxta* a superlative form = *jugista*; Gothic *juk*, H. G. *joch*, E. *yoke*; original root *ju* in *jus, right = bond*. Perhaps identical with this is:

ζυ—*ju, to mix = to bind together*, in ζύμη *leaven*, ζωμός, *jus, soup*.

ζεσ— = *jas* in ζέω *I seethe*, ἔζεσμαι, ζέσις; O. H. G. *gerjan*, also *jesan*, H. G. *gischt*, compare *jäst*, E. *yeast*.

Ζεύς = δjευς, *Juppiter* = *djup*. from the root *dju, div*, Sec. 21.

δίζημαι reduplicated form = διδjημαι, so too δίζω Il. XVI. 713, probably also διφάω ibid. 747; root ζα, ζη = *dja =ja, to go, strive, seek*, ζητέω.

ζα Æolic in composition = δja = διά: ζάθεος, ζάκοτος, ζαμενής, ζατρεφής, ζάχολος, ζαχρηής; ἀζηχής = ἀδιεχης (?).

2. By δ alone instead of δj in ζ:

δα = the above-named ζα for δια in δάσκιος, δαφοινός, δάπεδον; δή = *dja* in *jam*.

3. By the rough breathing ' in ἧπαρ, *jecur*, Skr. *yakrt*, Sec. 6, 3, Sec. 19, 2; ὅς, ἥ, ὅ = *yas* relative and demonstrative pronoun, see below.

ἑ—*ja*—ἵημι reduplicated = *jijami*, causative form of *ja, to go*, see above impf. ἵην, 2, 3 sing. ἵεις, ἵει according to the analogy of contracted verbs, Epic aorist ἕηκεν with syllabic augment instead of the *j* at the beginning of the root; εἷμεν with augment, ἕμεν, ἀφέτην without augment,

Il. XIX. 402 ἔωμεν = ὦμεν; thence ἦμα, ἤμων Il. XXIII. 886, 891.

4. By the smooth breathing, or it disappears in ἰάπτω reduplicated = *jij*. compare *jacio*, an extension of the root *ja* to *jap*, Latin *jac*.

XXXIII. GREEK PURE VOWEL ROOTS.

α ὑ—εὐ—αὔω *I burn, I dry*, ἄζω *I wither*, εὕω, εὔω *I singe*, αὖος, αὐαλέος, αὐστηρός, αὐχμός; ἕως, ἠώς, αὖως Æolic, αὔριον, ἦρι, ἠέριος; *us*—in *uro* = *ouso, ussi, ustus, aridus, aurora* = *ausosa*; original root *vas* = *us* in *Vesta*, ἑστία, Sec. 31, 2.

ἠ—in ἠμί, 3 sing. ἠτί Doric, pret. 1 sing. ἦν, 3 sing. ἦ; *ajo* = *agjo, adagium, nego*.

ἰ—εἶμι, 1 pl. ἴμεν, 3 pl. ἴασι, imperf. ἤια, Att. ἤειν, ἤειμεν with temporal augment, εἴσομαι, εἴσατο, ἰτός, ἴθμα, οἶτος, οἶμος, οἶμα, οἰμάω; *imus, itum; eo, eam, eunt* with assimilation of the radical vowel *i* before *o* and *a* to *e*, *iter, indutiae* = *induitiae*, compare the archaic *induperator* = *imperator*; from the root *i* in the last instance certainly also αἰεί, *aevum, aetas*, Sec. 31.

XXXIV. CONSONANTAL LAWS OF SOUND.

These relate to the changes which take place in consonants under the influence of other consonants. They are as follows:

1. Assimilation (*a*) regressive, of the preceding sound to that which follows: σ to the following ν, μ, in ἕννυμι

from ϝεσν., ἔμμι Doric = ἐσμι, εἰμί ; of the originally existing spirants σ, ϝ to ρ in ἐρρύην, περίρρυτος from ρυ, σρυ, ἄρρηκτος = ἀϝρ; of the labials to μ, τέτριμμαι from τρίβω, κομμός = κοπμ., γράμμα = γραφμα ; of the dentals to σ or σσ (for the most part to one only): ποσσί, ποσί = ποδσι, ἧσατο = ἥδσ., δώμασι = —τσι, ἄνυσις = —τσις, κόρυσι = —θσι, δαίμοσι = —ονσι ;

(*b*) Progressive, of the following sound to the preceding : ϝ, *j* in ξέννος Æolic from ξένϝος Doric, τέτταρες from τετϝ., ἵππος = ἰπϝος, ἰκϝος, *equus*, Æolic κέννος, κτέννω from κενjος, κτενjω, μᾶλλον = μαλjον from μάλα, compare *melius*, ἄλλομαι = ἀλj. compare *salio*, ἄλλος = ἀλj. *alius*, στέλλω = στελjω ; ττ = τj : ἥττων = ἡτjων, originally ἡκjων, compare ἥκιστα ; ἐλάττων = τjων, originally ἐλαχjων, compare ἐλαχύς ; instead of the assimilation of the σ of the first aorist to λ μ ν ρ preceding, a compensatory lengthening of the syllable takes place : ἔστειλα, Æolic ἔστελλα, from ἐστελσα, ἔφηνα = ἐφανσα, ἤγγειλα = ἠγγελσα, ἐγείνατο, Æolic ἐγέννατο, from ἐγενσατο.

2. The approximation (*a*) of the foregoing sound to the following: before τ and σ only a *tenuis* (λεκτός from λεγ, λέξις = λεκσις, δεκτός from δεχ), before δ a *medial* (γράβδην from γραφ), before θ an *aspirate* (ἐλέχθην). The dentals δ, τ, θ change into the spirant σ before μ, ἤνυσμαι (ἀνυτ), πέπεισμαι (πιθ) ; on the other hand ἴδμεν Ionic, connected with ἴσμεν, ὀδμή, κεκορυθμένος ; the gutturals κ, χ into γ, δόγμα from δοκ, τέτυγμαι from τυχ, like ἴκμενος, ἀκαχμένος (reduplicated root ἀκ) Ionic ; τ before ι in the endings of stems and inflexions, except in Doric, changes

into σ, φησί, Doric φατί, on the contrary τι of the 3 p. sing. is retained in ἐστί; φέρουσι, Doric φέροντι, τιθεῖσι = τιθέντι, φασί, Doric φαντί, εἴκοσι, Doric Ϝίκατι, γερουσία = γέροντια, ἀναισθησία from ἀναίσθητος, πλούσιος from πλοῦτος, σύ, Doric τύ. (*b*) Of the following sound to the preceding, σχίζω, from σκιδ, *scindo, scidi* (from the aspirated tenuis, under the influence of the preceding spirant σ), πάσχω from πασκω, παθσκω, ἔρχομαι = ἐρσκ. after the disappearance of the σ.

3. The blending of two sounds in one mixed and hissing sound : δ*j*, γ*j* into ζ; at the beginning of a root, Ζεύς, ζα—Æolic, Sec. 32, 1; in the beginning of a word, ἔζομαι = ἐδ*j*., *sed* —, σχίζω = σχιδ*j*ω, τράπεζα = τετραπεδ*j*α, ἀργυρόπεζα; ἄζομαι = ἀγ*j*., ἅγιος, κράζω = κραγ*j*ω, στίζω, Sec. 17, μείζων = μεγ*j*ων, μέγας, *magnus*; on the other hand, ἔρδω from Ϝεργ*j*ω instead of ἐρζω, by metathesis ῥέζω, Sec. 20. τ*j*, θ*j*, κ*j*, χ*j*, into σσ (assibilation); λίσσομαι = λιτ*j*., compare λιτέσθαι, λιτή; μέλισσα = —τ*j*α, ἱμάσσω = ἱμαντ*j*ω, where the ν disappears before σ, ἐρέσσω = — τ*j*ω, ἐρετμός; κρείσσων = κρετ*j*ων; κορύσσω = — θ*j*ω, βάσσων = βαθ*j*. from βαθύς; πέσσω = πεκ*j*ω from πεκ (*coq*) connected with πεπ, Sec. 19; πίσσα = πικ*j*α, *pix*; ὄσσε = ὀκ*j*ε (*oculus*), so too ὄσσομαι; ὄσσα = ὀκ*j*α (*vox* Sec. 19, 2); ἥσσων = ἡκ*j*ων, γλύσσων from γλυκύς; πλήσσω from πλακ, πρήσσω, πράσσω from πρακ, φράσσω from φρακ (κ weakened to γ in ἐπλήγην, πέπραγα, ἐφράγην), φρίσσω from φρικ, ἄνασσα = ἀνακ*j*α; ἐλάσσων = ἐλαχ*j*ων, βράσσων = βραχ*j*. from βραχύς, *bre*(*g*)*vis* (not βραδύς), θάσσων from ταχύς. A single instance of σσ = δ*j* occurs

in πρόφρασσα Homeric feminine of πρόφρων = προφραδjκα instead of the expected ζ as in ἀργυρόπεζα.

4. Dissimilation to avoid identity of sound: change of dentals before τ and θ into σ; ἴστωρ from ϝιδτ., ἀνυστός = ἀνυτ-τος, πίστις, πιστός = πιθτ., πεισθῆναι = πειθθ.; the same also happens when the ν disappears before σ; κεστός from the stem κεντ, πέποσθε for πεποστε for πεπονθτε.

5. Phonetic law of the aspirates: avoidance of aspirates at the beginning of two syllables which follow each other: ἐτέθην, ἐτύθην, from the roots θε, θυ, σώθητι for σωθηθι, compare ἀμπέχω, ἐκεχειρία; on the other hand, ἐχύθην, φάθι. When according to the laws of sound a θ loses its aspirate at the end of a root it is transferred to a at the beginning of a root, τριχός — θρίξ, τρέχω — θρέξομαι, ταχύς — θάσσων = ταχj., on the other hand when san aspirate if retained at the end of a root before θ, θ still stands at the beginning instead of τ; ἐθρέφθην.

6. Insertion of a sound: between νρ, μρ, μλ in ἀνδρός = ἀνρος,—notice however the remarkable shortening of the first syllable in ἀνδροτῆτα Il. XVI. 857. XXIV. 6, which takes no notice of the consonant which is inserted,— γαμβρός = γαμρος, μεσημβρία = — μρια, ἄμβροτος, shortened into ἄβροτος Il. XIV. 78, = ἀμροτος from μρο = mor (morior); ἤμβροτον = ἠμροτον, by metathesis from ἤμαρτον, thence ἀβροτάξομεν Il. X. 65, compare ἤμπλακον; μέμβλωκα = μεμλ. from μολ, μλο, μέμβλεται,

Consonantal Laws of Sound. 67

μέμβλετο Homeric = μεμλ. = μεμέληται, ἐμεμέλητο. In the beginning βρ, βλ, instead of μρ, μλ; βροτός = μροτ., βλώσκω = μλωσκω, μολεῖν. ὑπεμνήμυκε with epenthetic ν, Il. XXII. 491, as in νώνυμνος, is an exception.

7. The loss of consonants: σ between vowels see above; between consonants τέτυφθε = — φσθε; of τ in κέρως = κέρατος, stem κερατ, φέρει = φερετι, see below; of ν between vowels in μείζους from μείζονες, before σ in φέρουσι, with compensatory lengthening of sound, κεστός from κενστ; of ντ, νδ in γέρουσι = — ντσι, σπείσω = — νδσω, Sec. 9, 2; 11, 3.

8. Change of position, or metathesis of the root consonants: θαν — θνα in θανεῖν, θνήσκω, θρα — θαρ in θράσος, θάρσος; δέδορκα, ἔδρακον, see Variations of Roots, Sec. 37, 4.

9. Law of reduplication: Of two consonants at the beginning of a word the first only is reduplicated; of the aspirates the first only of their component parts—the corresponding tenuis κ, τ, π,—γέγραφα, πέφυκα, πέφνον = πεφενον, κεχώρηκα; present reduplication with the vowel ι, ἵστημι = σιστ., τίθημι, κίχρημι. For further details see below on Present and Perfect Stems; the metathesis of the reduplication ἔμμορε = μεμορε, is like that in stems which begin with ρ.

XXXV. The Laws of the Ending.

1. The Greek language dislikes consonantal endings. No word ends in a mute, except οὐκ from οὐχί, and ἐκ from ἐξ = ἐκs, but semi-vowels only ν, ρ, σ (ψ, ξ) close the word. Other consonants are discarded, or changed into ν, σ; ἔφερε(τ), ἔφερον(τ), λέγοι(τ), λεγέτω(τ), δός = δοθ = δοθι, γάλα = γαλακτ, παῖ vocative = παιδ, γύναι = γυναικ, ἄνα = ἀνακτ, γέρον = γεροντ; τ disappears in the neuter pronoun τί = τιτ, compare *quid;* τ at the end of a word is changed into s in the neuter participle, εἰδό, from εἰδοτ, and in adverbs in ως, originally ωτ. So σ disappears before consonants at the end of a word; in οὕτως ἀτρέμα, ἄχρι; in φι as suffix of the plural, on the other hand compare λικριφίς, *nobis.*

2. Greek endings do not allow every combination of the final σ with the foregoing consonant; ποῦς from ποδς, ἐσθής = ἐσθητς, τέρας = τερατς, δαίμων — ονς, φέρων — οντς, εἰδώς = — Fοτς, μήτηρ — ερς, ποιμήν — ενς, εὐμενής — εσς, τιθείς = τιθεντς, a compensatory lengthening; on the other hand, however, φάλαγξ, λύγξ, φλόξ, κόλαξ, ὄψ, ἅλς.

3. The original *m* in 1st pers. sing. and acc. sing, becomes ν or is discarded; ν in person-endings from μ. ἔφερον; ἦν, connected with ἦα, ἔα, ἦ, compare *eram* from *esam;* in the optative of verbs in μι εἴην; φέρω(μι); compare δῶ from δομ, γέγονα(μι), οἶδα, Æolic Fοίδημι, ἔδειξα(μ); πατέρα, original form *pataram;* compare δέκα, *decem.*

4. The so-called *ephelkystic* ν, or ν suffixed, is not original, but a supplementary extension of a word ending with a vowel by taking ν to avoid the elision and strengthen the final syllable; in ἔλεγεν the ν appears after the τ which originally ended the word is discarded. This ν becomes fixed in 1st pers. plur. of the *verb* — μεν, from the original μες = *mas, masi*, after the disappearance of the *s;* φέρομεν from φέρομε, original and Doric φέρομες.

5. Latin is less capricious in its endings. It allows the guttural and dental tenues even in combination with other consonants, *lac, hunc, sunt, est*, and differs from the Greek in admitting *m, d, l*. It avoids only the labial tenuis, as well as the combination of two mutes, *lac* instead of *lact; d* is discarded in the ablative singular and adverb, *patred, facillumed*, but retained in the neuter pronoun *quid, id;* with regard to the disappearance of *s* see Sec. 11, 3; and in case-endings, Sec. 47.

PART II.

FORMATION OF ROOTS AND STEMS.

XXXVI. CONCEPTION OF ROOTS AND THEIR FORMATION—REDUPLICATION—PRIMARY AND SECONDARY ROOTS.

1. A root is the simplest combination of sounds which contains a meaning without the help of any elements of grammatical relation. It expresses an idea without any sort of close and concrete definition or application.

It has no pronominal suffix—this first appears in forming stems and words to express the noun and verb; it is therefore in itself neither nominal nor verbal, but expresses indifferently the sense of naming or of affirming denoted by the noun and verb; it is purely abstract.

For example, the primitive root *da* is the common source of the verbs δίδωμι, *do*, of the nouns δοτήρ, δοτός, δόσις, *dator, datus, dos, donum*. Apart, therefore, from those noun and case endings which go to form the stem, and simply by reason of its general signification, it can designate, though in a non-differentiated and vague manner, *the giver, the recipient,* and *the gift.* Deprived, however, of the predicative verbal suffixes it can mean nothing so precise as "*he gives*," etc. The bare root can no more contain such a synthesis of a subject with a predicate denoting *a judgment*, than it can imply the distinction between the thing done and the doer of it, or the definitions of sex and case.

2. Since the root is unable to express relation or concrete definition, it follows that it is not admitted by itself, as a mere root, into developed language. By linguistic analysis, it is artificially discovered and made clear, so that

(α) From a word can be subtracted not only all elements of grammatical relation, or pronominal suffixes, but also their influence on the sound of the root, as conditioned by the laws of sound.

(β) The root-vowel also, which has been lengthened or increased, can be traced back to its simple and short fundamental vowel.

(γ) Lastly, a sound which has been in any way lost at the end or from the body of a word can be supplied through the comparison of fuller and more original root-forms of the same or cognate languages. Compare for example, ἐστί, root ἐς; τίθημι θε; ἵστημι στα; ζεύγνυμι ζυγ, *jungo jug*, Ζεύς, *Jupp. div, dju* (*ju, jov*); ἔζομαι *sed;* ἵημι ἐ, *ja*; πέποιθα, πίστις πιθ; εἶμι, οἶτος ι; εἰμί, εἴην, ἔα ἐς, κρείσσων κρετ, βάσσων βαθ, πάσσων παχ; μακρός, μάσσων, μῆκος, *magnus, major* μακ, *mag;* ἕαδα, ἡδύς, ἦδος, *suavi sva;* ἰδίω, ἰδρώς, *sudor, sveiz svid;* ὄψ, *vox* Fεπ, *voc;* ῥέω, ἐρρύην, O. H. G. *stroum*, E. *stream* from ῥυ, σρυ, etc.

3. Closely connected with the lengthening and increase of the root-vowel is a further amplification of the root in order to express relation. This also must be removed in order that the pure root may be reached, and is called

REDUPLICATION.—It consists of a full or partial iteration of the root in order to express a more intensive meaning, and is found both in the noun and in the verb. In the noun, for example in ἀκωκή root ἀκ, ἀγωγή root ἀγ, διδαχή root δακ, ἰωγή root Ϝαγ, ἰωή root ἀϜ, ἴονθος, not Homeric, from the root ἀνθ; partly with increase of the vowel in the root-syllable, as in ἐτήτυμος, partly with the reduplicate vowel weakened to ι, compare *ciconia, cicatrix*, analogous to the verbal present reduplication, partly with both; without this in μάρμαρος root μαρ, κάγκανος root καϜ, κάρχαρος root χαρ in χαράσσω, with which compare *furfur;* lastly in nouns such as λαῖλαψ, δαιδάλεος, παιπαλόεις, ἀμαιμάκετος with diphthongal reduplication.

The verbal reduplication is partly variable, and so to speak transitory, attaching to individual tense stems. In the present tense it expresses duration, in the perfect, conclusion of the action, in the aorist it simply intensifies the meaning. Partly it is stable, and in one sense goes back to the root itself, as especially in certain Latin verbs; *bibo* root πι in πίνω, *po* in *potus*, Sec. 18, *coquo* reduplicated root *coc*, compare πεκ, πεπ, Sec. 19, 2, *vivo* reduplicated root *gvig*, *vig* in *vixi*, compare *quicken*, originally *gi* = βι in βίος, *vi* Sec. 22. The Greek verbal reduplication on the other hand, except for example in ἰάλλω, ἰάπτω, ἰαύω, is almost peculiar to certain tense-stems, ἵστημι, ἕστηκα, as compared with ἔστην, root στα; κίχρημι, as

Primary and Secondary Roots. 73

compared with ἔχρησα root χρα; πίπτω, πεσεῖν, root πετ; πέποιθα, πεπιθεῖν, πείθω.

4. PRIMARY AND SECONDARY ROOTS.—Other extensions of the original root exist in guttural, dental, and labial affixes to the original vowel-ending, which have coalesced more or less firmly with the root, and are universally or partially retained in the verbal inflexions.

These are the so-called root-determinatives, which stamp with greater distinctness the idea of a root. Compare ζυγ, ζυ Sec. 32, πτακ, πτα Sec. 18, δακ in διδάσκω from the original δα in δίδαε Sec. 21, μαθ, παθ in μαθεῖν, παθεῖν from the original μα, πα, πλα, πλαθ in πίμπλημι, πλήθω, πλῆθος; *tud* in *tundo, tutudi* and τυπ in τύπτω, lead back to a common primitive form *tu*, τυ, which combined the idea of thrusting and striking.

The shortest form of the root is the most original, and also of the most general meaning: compare *i, to go, ed, to eat, da, to give, ju* in *jus, law* and *jus, broth* = *to bind* and *mix*, ζυγ, *jug, to bind together*.

All polysyllabic so-called roots are derivatives, compare ἀλειφ in ἀλείφω and λιπ in λίπα, ἔλαχ in ἐλαχύς, etc., and *leg* in *lēvis* from *legvis*. The present stem is very frequently a root which has been extended by reduplication accompanied by a nasal sound and a verbal suffix, for example: γίγνομαι from γεν, λαμβάνω from λαμβ from λαβ with suffix αν, λαγχάνω λαχ, *rumpo, rup*.

XXXVII. Marks and Peculiarities of the Root.

1. Generality of meaning.

The root is a pure abstraction, Sec. 2, 2, of vague and indefinite signification, capable of further extension, often difficult to bring under a precise and single expression.

The root begins to differentiate itself as soon as it enters into the use of actual language, so as to denote essentially different and distinct objects and modes of action. Examples: root πετ, *pet;* the general idea is that of *hasty movement through empty space,* thence, (1) πέτομαι, *I fly, penna (petna),* (2) *peto, I strive,* (3) πίπτω, *I fall.*

Root φα, *fa* (secondary root φαν, φαϝ); the general idea is of *giving knowledge,* thence (1) φημί, *fari,* etc. (2) φαίνω, φῶς, *fax,* etc.

Root ἀρ, ἐρ, *to plough, to row;* the general idea is of *labour in a yielding substance;* taken together with ὀρ, the general idea is of *stirring up.*

Root θυ, *fu, to roar, to bluster, to smoke, to sacrifice,* in θύω, θυμός, θύος, *fumus;* the general idea is that of *violent movement.*

Root *ter,* in τείρω, τερέω, *tero, terebra, to rub* and *to bore;* the general idea is that of *friction.*

Root φρυ, φυρ in (1) φρέαρ = φρεϝαρ, Gothic *brunna,* H. G. *brunnen,* (2) in O. H. G. *brinnan, to burn,* (3) πορφύρω *to wave,* (4) πορφύρα *purple;* the fundamental meaning comprises in it the general idea of *to well, to wave, to burn, to shimmer.*

Root ζυ, *ju* in ζυγόν, *jungo, jus;* root τυ, *tu* in τύπτω, *tundo,* see above.

Classification of Roots.

2. The root is always and unconditionally a monosyllable, and the vowel is short, Sec. 7 : *i, to go ; es, to be, da, do, to give; ed, to eat; bi, pi, po, to drink; vi,* βι, *to live; vid, to see; ves,* ἐs, *to clothe; sta, to stand; aiθ,* originally ἰθ *to kindle; vas, us* (εὖ), *to burn; pet, to fly, to fall;* φυ, *fu, to become;* θε (*dha*), *to place, to do; sed, to sit; fa, to speak, to shine; mor, mro, to die ; dic, to show ; stor, ster, stra, to strew ;* Fop, *ver, war, to wait; spec,* σκεπ, *to spy; vart, ver, to turn; torc,* τρεκ, τρεπ, *to twist; plu,* πλυ, *to flow;* ρυ, σρυ, *to stream; scand, to climb; scid, to cleave; ta, ten, to stretch; er, to rub, to bore; tud,* τυπ, *to strike; ar,* ἀρ, *to plough;* etc.

3. Roots may be classed according to their function as (α) verbal and (β) pronominal, or roots which express ideas and relations, also termed predicative and demonstrative, or material and formal. These two classes of root sometimes do not differ in form; as in *i, to go,* which is also demonstrative, κι in κεῖμαι, *quies,* also interrogative and indefinite in *quis,* τις = κις, *ta, to stretch,* also demonstrative = *he.*

4. Varieties of form in a root, occasioned not only by the change of the primitive vowel *a* into *e* and *o ;* but also by

(1) Metathesis or change in the position of the sounds, ἀϜ in ἀήρ, *va* in *ventus ;* ἀλφ, *lab,* ἀλφάνω, *labor ;* ἀρδ, ῥαδ Sec. 21 ; βαλ, βλα in βαλεῖν, βέβλημαι; ἐρ — *ra* in ἐρέσσω, *ratis ;* γεν, γνα in γένος, γνήσιος, *gnascor ; gna, gno,* in *gnosco, gnarus,* Gothic *kannjan ;* θαν, θνα in θανεῖν, θνήσκω ; θαρ, θρα, Sec. 34, 8 ; καμ, κμα in καμεῖν, κεκμηώς,

ἀκμής; κρι, *cer, cre* in κρίνω, *cerno, crevi; men,* μνα, *mens,* μένος, μνήμη; μολ, μλο; *mor,* μρο, Sec. 34, 6; ὀπ, πε, reduplicated πεπ, in ὀπτός, πέπτω, πέπων, Sec. 19, 2; πετ, πτα in πέτομαι, ἔπτην; *spec,* σκεπ, Sec. 16; στορ, *ster, stra,* Sec· 17; τλα, ταλ; τεμ, ταμ, τμα; τερ, τρα Sec. 17; φλεγ, *fulg* in φλέγω, *fulgeo.* φρυ, φυρ, see above.

(2) By the change of consonants into vowels and the hardening of vowels; ἀϝ, αὐ, ἀήρ, ἀύω, ἰαύω; *dju, div, to gleam,* Secs. 21. 32; γαυ, γαϝ, Sec. 20; ι, *to go,* thence *ja* in ἵημι = *jijāmi* causative, *jacio;* λαϝ, λαυ; λυ, *lu, lav, to scour, to wash,* Sec. 28; ὑδ, *ud, vad,* Sec. 21; *us, vas,* εὐ, αὐ, Sec. 33.

(3) By change of consonants: ἀλκ, ἀρκ, Sec. 29; τυπ, *tud,* Sec. 36, 4; *vi,* βι, Sec. 36, 3; ἐρ, ἐλ in ἔρχομαι, ἐλθεῖν; displacing the aspirate in ταφ, θαπ, θαμβ, Sec. 17; weakening the tenuis into a medial in πλακ, πρακ, ῥακ, φρακ, φρικ, Secs. 18. 20. 29. 34, 3.

(4) By strengthening the consonant or extending the root, κτα, κτεν in κτάμεναι, κτείνω; τα, τεν, *ten;* ζυ, *ju,* ζυγ, *jug,* compare Sec. 36, 4; φα, φεν, Sec. 25; φα, φαλ, Sec. 25; θε, *fac,* Sec. 24; στα, σταθ, *stal, stla,* Sec. 17.

(5) By taking away the original consonant at the beginning, in ἐχ = σεχ, ἐπ = σεπ, ἐρπ = *serp,* Secs. 18. 19. 23, compare ϝραγ, ῥαγ, *frag,* Sec. 20, σρυ, ῥυ, Sec. 29.

XXXVIII. Stems of Words.

1. The root, in its further construction into a word, passes generally, but not necessarily, through the stem, as a middle stage. By certain definite extensions of the

Stems of Roots. 77

root, which are in part nominal, and in part verbal suffixes, the stem shows a tendency towards becoming either a noun or a verb. It is therefore not indifferent to the distinction between noun and verb, but is not as yet a complete word.

Considered analytically, the stem of a word is that which remains after the removal of the nominal and verbal inflexional endings of the declensions and conjugations. Yet it is not the simple root, but has the stamp on it of either noun or verb—e. g., ὄρνυμι root ὀρ, inflexional ending μι, νυ verbal suffix of the present stem, verbal stem ορνυ; πόσις, *drink*, root πο, s suffix of the nominative, noun suffix σι = τι, nominal stem ποσι; φά-τι-ς.

2. The stem may however coincide with the root, on the one hand in the case of primitive or root verbs, φαμέν, ἴμεν, on the other hand in the case of nouns which have the naked root for a stem, or at least differ from it only in the quantity of the vowel, *vōx*, *dŭx*, so that a particular suffix is not necessary to the formation of the noun.

Such primitive nominal stems, which have no nominal suffix, are entirely independent of the difference between the categories of *nomina agentis* and *nomina actionis*, as they are of that between genders, *voc-s* fem. *duc-s* masc.

3. When root and stem are different the distinction between nominal and verbal stems is shown by the function of particular suffixes which find their place between the root and the inflexion. These are partly pronominal

roots, partly syllables, or even mere letters, whose meaning cannot be fixed. They take part, however, in the formation of nouns and verbs alike, as, for instance, the pronominal stem *ta* serves both to stamp the nominal stem, οἶτος, δοτός, and, in a weaker form, makes the third person singular of the verb. The suffixes *ja*, *αν*, *να*, etc., appear both in verbal and nominal stems. Compare ἅγιος, δίκαιος, τιμάω = τιμαjω, μανθάνω, ἱκανός, δαμνάω, κεδνός.

4. Besides these pure roots, many nominal stems are also direct verbal stems. In these the present stem alone takes a special stem-forming verbal suffix. This is usually *ja* in its many changes conditioned by the laws of sound. The rest of the tense-stems show the pure nominal stem. See below, Sec. 39, 2.

XXXIX. (1) Verbal Stems.

1. Stem or root verbs containing only the root-stem and tense-stem. This last includes the present stem, and, generally, the extension of the root by means of the reduplication which for the most part takes place in the present stem. The end of the root is strengthened by the verbal stem-suffixes, and the vowel is strengthened.

Pure root verbs in μι: φημί, εἶμι, εἰμί, with present reduplication ἵημι, τίθημι compare ἔθεμεν, ἵστημι compare ἔστημεν, δίδωμι compare ἔδομεν, δείκνυμι, ζεύγνυμι compare ἐζύγην.

Root verbs in ω with tach-vowel ο, ε: vowel forms, ἄω *I satiate*, δίω, θύω *I sacrifice*, τίω, χράω; consonant

Verbal Stems. 79

forms, ἕδω, λέγω, φέρω, etc.; with lengthening of the vowel or extension of the root in the present; φεύγω, τήκω, λείπω, compare *dīco, dūco;* δάκνω, τύπτω; suffix *ja* forming ι in ἐσθίω, δαίομαι; βάλλω (λλ = λj̯), κρῑ́νω, τείνω; σσ = κj̯ λεύσσω, πέσσω, πλήσσω, φρίσσω; σσ = τj̯ λίσσομαι; ζ = δj̯, γj̯; ἕζομαι, ἅζω, κράζω, ῥέζω. For further details see below, under Present Stem. Compare Latin verbs in *io, fugio, rapio* in the third conjugation.

2. Nominal verbal stems, with unaltered and unformed nominal stem,—which is not a mere root. In these the present stems alone take suffix *ja;* all the other tense stems are pure nominal stems: verbs in ζω, σσω; ἐλπίζω = δj̯ω, ἤλπισα — δσα, stem ἐλπιδ as in ἐλπίς, so also ἐρίζω, stem ἐριδ, φροντίζω; παίζω, παίξομαι, connected with ἔπαισα, stem παιγ in παίγνιον, παιδ in παῖς; μαστίζω — γj̯ω, stem μαστιγ, μαστίξω, ἁρπάζω, stem ἁρπαγ, Homeric future ἁρπάξω, σαλπίζω, stem σαλπιγ; σσ = θj̯ in κορύσσω, κεκορυθμένος; = κj̯ in κηρύσσω, stem κηρυκ, φυλάσσω, stem φυλακ; = τj̯ in ἱμάσσω — αντj̯ω, stem ἱμαντ in ἱμάς, ἱμάντος; = χj̯ in μειλίσσω — χj̯ω, stem μειλιχ in μείλιχος. Verbs with nominal stems in ες, τελείω from — εσj̯ω, stem τελες in τέλος, so also νεικείω; in αν; μελαίνω — ανj̯ω, stem μελαν in μέλας, μελάνει Il. VII. 64; in αρ; καθαίρω — α j̯ω, stem καθαρ, τεκμαίρομαι, stem τεκμαρ; in λ; ἀγγέλλω (λλ = λj̯) stem ἀγγελ.

3. Denominatives, derived from nouns with formed nominal stems ending with a vowel. These retain the vowel stem-ending of the noun in the inflexions of the verb, as a verbal extension of a complete nominal stem.

In other forms, therefore, than the present, they exhibit, besides the root, the vowel elements which betray their nominal derivation.

The so-called contracted verbs, from the original *ajω*, *ejω, ojω = ajami*, formed by the syllable or auxiliary verb, *ja*, with causative meaning, or meaning of duration, come under the head of denominatives; they are also sometimes intransitive, τιμάω = τιμαjω, from the nominal stem τιμα, φορέω, ὀχέω, from the stems φορε φορο, ὀχο, βιόω, ὀρθόω, from the stems βιο, ὀρθο. Compare *amo = amajo, moneo = monejo, statuo = statujo*, nominal stem *statu;* verbs in ιω with ι persistent in all tense-stems; ἰδίω from the root ιδ = σϜιδ in ἶδος, ἴδισα, κυλίω, μηνίω, κονίω = ιjω (ι = ιj), compare Latin verbs of the fourth conjugation with contracted *i* as *sapio — ijo*, opposed to the conjugation of *fodio, cupio*, etc. To this head belong also verbs in αζω, οζω, ιζω (so far as ζ is a mere extension of *j*), νω, ενω, ονω: ἀγαπάζω, ἁρμόζω, stem ἁρμο in ἁρμός, ὑβρίζω, νεμεσίζω, δακρύω, ἰθύω, ἰσχύω, ἀριστεύω, κολούω stem κολο, κολοϜ = κολουjω. Lastly, verbs in αινω, υνω: λειαίνω, θαρσύνω, ἡδύνω. Latin desideratives in *turio* from the *nomen agentis* in *tor, turus: ēsurio = edturio, parturio* from *partor*.

4. Manifold interchanges in flexion between forms of primitive and derived verbs; κυρέω existing by the side of κύρω, ἔκυρσα; γηθέω, γέγηθα; δοκέω, ἔδοξα; αἴδομαι, αἰδέομαι; ἔμαθον, μαθήσομαι; ἐγενόμην, γενήσομαι; γοάω connected with ἔγοον, μηκάομαι connected with μέμηκα, μυκάομαι connected with μεμύκει. Compare the Latin

fugio, cupio, video, juvo juvare by the side of *fugi, cuperem, vidi, juvi; lavo, lāvi, lăvavi; saepio, saeptus.*

XL. (2) NOMINAL STEMS, including Participle and Infinitive.

The nominal stem = the root; there is then no nominal suffix, but there is, on the contrary, a change or increase of vowel in many possible ways: ὄψ—Ϝεπ, φλόξ—φλεγ, Ζεύς — Δjευ (*dju, div*), χέρ-νιψ — νιβ, ἀπόρρωξ root Ϝραγ, *vōx* — *voc* = Ϝεπ, *nex* — *nec, lēx* — *leg, dux* — *duc, pāx* — *pac, rēx* — *reg.*

Suffix *a, o* in A- and O- stems, to denote an agent as well as a thing: ἀγός, ταγός, ἔργον — Ϝεργ, φόρος, φορά, — φερ, φυγή — φυγ, ζυγόν — ζυγ, λοιπός — λιπ, ἀκωκή, reduplicated, — ακ; *vadum* stem *vado, fīdus, jugum, coquus, vīvus, dīvus, deus* = *dēvos, deivos* from *div; toga* — *teg, advena, collēga.*

Suffix *v, u:* ὠκύς (ακ), βαρύς, πλατύς; *acus;* in Latin u- stems are transferred to the *i* declension, *levis* — ἐλαχύς, *brevis* — βραχύς, *suavis* — ἡδύς. — Suffix *ja:* ἅγιος, μοῖρα = μορja, ὄσσα = ὀκja; *eximius, conjugium, ingenium; ja* is a secondary suffix and denotes the feminine: δίκα-ιος, ἀλήθεια = — σja, φέρουσα = — οντja, λελοιπυῖα = — υσja, μέλαινα, δότειρα.

Suffix *va* — *vo, van* = Ϝο, Ϝον: αἰών = αἰϜων; *aevum, aetas* = *aevitas,* root *i to go; arvum* (*ar*), *alvus* (*al*), *vacuus.* — Suffix Ϝεντ: χαρίεις, χαρίεντος, χαρίεσσα = — Ϝετja. Suffix Ϝοτ: εἰδώς = — Ϝοτς, λελοιπώς.

6

82 An Introduction to Greek and Latin.

Suffix *ma, mo, mon, mat, meno*: τιμή, θυμός, τλήμων, εἶμα = Fεσματ, ὄμμα (ὀπματ); *forma, animus, sermo(n)*. Middle participles, διδόμενος compare *alumnus, ferimini* (sc. *estis*). Inf. ἔδμεναι, with locative ι as in χαμαί. Suffix *ra — la:* λαμπρός, κυδρός, λαρός, στήλη ;. *ruber, scala (scandla), ala, tela, telum, velum,* Sec. 17, *querela*.

Suffix *an — ana — na:* τέρην (ενς), *pecten;* ὄργανον, ἱκανός, ἡδονή. Infinitive — ναι, εναι, λελοιπέναι, στῆναι, δοθῆναι with locative ι, φέρειν = φερενι — εναι; *donum, somnus (sopnus)*. Gerund-suffix *ondo, undo, endo*.

Suffix *ta, to,* Sec. 38, 3, *tat* in adj., subst., part. pass., and verbal adjective: πολίτης; κοῖτος, *secta, noxa (cta); κλυτός, γνωτός, status, potus;* νεότης (νεοτητ), *civitas*.

Suffix *tar, ter, tor, tra,* etc., in words expressing kindred and *nomina agentis:* πατήρ, φράτωρ, σωτήρ, ἴστωρ, ἰατρός, ῥήτρα; *pater, victor*. Part. fut. stem — *turo*. Denominative verbs in — *turio,* Sec. 39, 3. Feminine *nomina actionis: sepultura, usura*.

Suffix *ti, si, tu,* etc., in *nomina actionis:* μῆτις (μα), φάτις, φύσις, βρωτύς, μνημοσύνη; *messis (met-tis), vectis, potis, compo(t)s, dos (dots), mens, superstes (stit);* further extension in *statio, initium, justitia;* supine in *u — um; casus = cadtus;* further extension in *tuo — tua, mortuus, statua, tut* in *servitus, altitudo*.

Suffix *ant, ent, ont,* in part. act. pres., fut., aor.: ὤν = ἐσοντ, ἐοῦσα = ἐσοντja, ἱστάς = ἱσταντ, θείς = θεντ, λύσων = — οντ, λύσασα = — αντja; *praesens* from *esent* from the root *es; ient, eunt (iens, euntis),* from the root *i;* further extension *praesentia, prudentia*.

Suffix κα, *co:* θήκη (θε), secondary φυσικός, compare

under perf. in κα; *cloaca, fecundus, locus,* anciently *stloc* from *stla, stal,* further extension from the root *sta;* secondary *civicus,* etc.

Suffix *es, us, os:* γένος (γενες), μένος, ψευδής (ες); *genus, corpus, opus* anciently *opos, foedus, robur* anciently *robus, vetus — veteris;* masculine in *ōr = os: sopor,* etc., *aurora = ausosa,* change from *s* to *r* between vowels in Latin; *sedes, caedes, labes,* the other cases as in *i*-stems.

The Latin infinitive active in *ere* was originally *erē,* perhaps the shortened dative of a noun in *es; vehere = vehesei, fieri* anciently *fiere,* not a passive form, *= fiesei, esse,* root *es = es(e)se, esse* root *ed = edse, ferre = ferse, velle = velse, fore = fuse, ire = eise,* root *i,* present stem *ī, ei.* Inf. perf.; *esse* is added to the perfect stem in *-i, peperi-sse, dixisse = dicsi-esse,* the archaic *dixe* being formed by the apocopated *esse* attached to the bare root, compare *dixim.* Inf. pass. *dici* from *dicier,* by metathesis = *dicise, dici* dative of a noun, from the bare root *dic, se* perhaps a reflexive pronoun; *amari, amarier = amasise,* inf. act. in *i* instead of the original *ē, ei,* with the addition of the reflexive *se* (?).

The Greek infinitive middle in σθαι comes from the original suffix *dhjai* = θjαι, whence σθαι was formed by assimilation and dissimilation.

XLI. COMPARATIVE AND SUPERLATIVE STEMS.

(a) The original comparative suffix was *jans.* The *s* disappears in Greek, and *j* becomes a vowel or is blended with the preceding consonant of the adjective-stem into σσ (ττ), ζ, Sec. 34, 3; κάκιον, stem of the comparative and neuter, masc. fem. κακίων = κακιονs, compare δαίμων, ποιμήν, ἡδίων from ἡδύς from the root ἁδ, svad; μείων fron the root μιν μι, Sec. 27; ἀρείων, χείρων, Epic χερείων, from which σ has disappeared, from the stems ἀρες, χερες in χέρης, Sec. 23; the comparative formation in ζ from δj is wanting; on the other hand μεῖζον = μεγjον with epenthetic ι, Sec. 9, 1, b, ὀλίζων = ὀλιγj, Il. XVIII. 519; ἐλάσσων, ἥσσων, βράσσων, πάσσων, βάσσων Doric, κρέσσων Ionic = κρετj; θάσσων, μάσσων (μακ, Sec. 27), γλύσσων connected with γλυκίων, ἆσσον = ἀγχjον, Sec. 34, 3. In Latin without nasal strengthening *ios — ior*, neuter *ius* with original *s; suavior = svadvios*, anciently *melios, meliosem, lĕvior = legvior* (ἐλαχύς), *mājor = magior, pējor, minor = minior;* so too *ius* is shortened into *us* in *minus;* to *is* in *magis = magius*, adverb connected with *majus = magius* neuter, weakened *mage;* the same shortening takes place by the paring down *io iu* to *i* in the comparative suffix *is* of *satis, nimis, tantisper; plus = plo(e)jus* = πλεῖον, root *ple, to fill; plures* anciently *pleiores*, then *plerique, the most part*, where *que = qued* abl. of the indef. *qui = somehow*, a generalizing signification.

(β) The original suffix *ra, tara:* ἔνεροι, *superus, inferus;* τερο in γλυκύτερος, χαριέστερος, μελάντερος, φίλτερος by the side of φιλαίτερος; in adjective-stems in ες, ἀληθέστερος, so too εὐδαιμονέστερος; the same suffix appears in πότερος, Ionic κότερος; *uter = quoteros*. Compare *dexter, inter, terrestris, pedestris; sinister, minister, magister,* doubly comparative forms from *is + ter*.

Comparatives and Superlatives. 85

Superlative. (α) Original suffix *ta*, doubled *tata*, το, τατο : το in ordinal numbers πρῶτος, *quartus, quotus;* τατο in μέσσατος, by assimilation from μεστ, μεσσότατος, μεσαίτατος, δεύτατος, τρίτατος Epic ; the regular superlative to the comparative in τερο, φίλτατος to φίλτερος, by the side of φιλαίτατος; το is added to the comparative suffix ις = ιονς compare Latin *is*, in superlatives of which the comparatives end in ιον : κάκιστος, ἥδιστος, φίλιστος, Soph. Aj. 842, φιλίων Homeric, ὀλίγιστος, βάρδιστος Il. XXIII. 310, ἥκιστα of ἥσσων, ἥκιστος of the adverb ἧκα Ib. 531. Compare *juxta = jugista, exta, the entrails = exista* connected with the comparative form *exterus, extra; praesto = praeis-to.*

(β) The original suffix *ma, mata* — μο, ματο : ἕβδομος, πύματος, compare the noun-formations κάλλιμος Homeric, ὄρχαμος ; *minimus, infimus, primus, septimus, summus (supm.), dextimus, plurimus = plus-imus.*

(γ) Suffix *tama*, Latin *tumo, timo, simo: maximus = magt., optimus, veterrimus*, from — *ersimus, pulcherrimus, simillimus, facillimus* from — *lsimus*. Compare the adjectives *maritimus, finitimus, legitimus;* in *doctissimus, levissimus*, the superlative ending *simus* is added to the comparative stem *is* from *ius*.

XLII. STEMS OF THE NUMERALS.

Cardinal numbers. 1. εἷς = ἑνς, Doric ἧς, stem and neuter ἕν (οὐδέν) = ἐμ in ἅμα = the original *sam* in *semel, simplex, simul, singuli*, compare ἅπαξ (ἁ = *sa*), Secs. 27. 30, 2. Feminine μία, μιᾶς = σμια = *samja, ja* being the feminine suffix; on the other hand the Homeric ἴα, dative masculine ἰῷ, so too οἶος, *unus*, stem οι-*no* with suffix *na*, Gothic *ains* from the demonstrative *i*. 2. δύο from *dva*, Sec. 21. 3. Stem τρι, *tri*, τρεῖς, *tres ;* Gothic *threis*, H. G. *drei*, E. *three*. 4. τέσσαρες, *quatuor*. 5. πέντε, *quinque*, Sec. 19, 2. 4. 6. ἕξ, *sex*. 7. ἑπτά, *septem*, Sec. 30, 2, compare Sec. 35, 3. 8. ὀκτώ, *octo*, Gothic *ahtau ;* ὄγδοος = ὀγδοϝος, *octavus*. 9. ἐννέα, *novem*, Sec. 9, 5. 10. δέκα, *decem*, Secs. 21. 35, from an original *dakan = dva-kan =* 2 × 5 (?). εἴκοσι, Sec. 9, 5. Sec. 16. Sec. 34, 2. *viginti =* *dviginti, dvidecenti*. Fundamental form *dvidakati =* 2 × 10. ἑκατόν, Sec. 16. The same syllable *ko = ka*, shortened from δέκα, has the meaning 10 in the tens, but in the hundreds, where it springs from ἑκατόν, it has that of 100. There is no common Graeco-Italian word for 1000; χίλιοι and *mille* are both obscure.

Ordinals have generally the superlative forms, Sec. 41. The comparative suffix τερο is kept in δεύτερος; ὄγδοος see above, with weakening of the tenuis to a medial as in ἕβδομος.

PART III.

WORD-FORMATION OR INFLEXION.

XLIII. THE WORD.

The stem is not, like the root, an abstract of indefinite meaning, neither is it a complete and finished assemblage of sounds which can express a concrete conception, or a judgment including the synthesis of subject and predicate. It is made into a true word by the addition of the elements of relation—the inflexional endings.

Every real word expresses the idea of a thing existing by itself in a state of rest, or of an action taking place in time. It contains either an appellation or an assertion, a conception or a judgment, is either a noun, or name-word, or else a verb, or time-word. It has, therefore, besides the vague nominal or verbal suffixes which form the stem, nominal or verbal inflexion-endings.

A nominal inflexion expresses an attributive relation to the noun, and is the case-ending; a verbal inflexion expresses a predicative relation, betokening the subject of an action, and is the personal ending—along with the tense-stem and mood-element, Secs. 55-57: these two are the factors of word-formation.

These inflexional suffixes, both of the noun and of the

verb, contain original pronominal or demonstrative forms and stems.

Adverbs, particles, and prepositions are also originally case or verbal forms.

Interjections, (so far as they are not verbal forms, embodying an imperative), and vocatives—the mere noun-stem in form of an interjection—are not real words. They express mere indefinite feelings and emotions without concrete relations, and have therefore no suffixes.

I. THE NOMINAL INFLEXION. DECLENSION.

XLIV. Elements.

The inflexional endings of the noun denote more distinctly a thing which the nominal stem describes indefinitely.

1. According to its sex as a person, or as a thing which may be regarded according to the analogy of the difference of sex—a tree for instance, as a fruit-bearing thing, presents itself to the mind as female,—or expressly as wholly destitute of sex, that is neuter.

2. According to number as unity or plurality.

3. According to its relation to an action or motion expressed by the verb.

The inflexions consist of signs of gender, case, and number. The dual is a variety of the plural. The vocative is not a case, but a mere nominal stem, and in the neuter and plural = the nominative. No alteration of the root or stem takes place in the inflexions of the noun, except such as the laws of sound demand when the inflexional suffix is added to the stem.

The declensions of the pronouns show essentially weaker forms than those of the nouns.

XLV. Signs of Gender.

Gender, originally not denoted by any variation of sound, is designated by secondary expedients in consonant stems, in diphthong stems, and in *i* and *u* (*v*) stems, —*e.g.*, ὁ πατήρ, ἡ μήτηρ, ἡ ναῦς, ἡ πόλις, ὁ νέκυς. In stems in the original *a*, the so-called O and A-stems, where Latin *u* = o, *a* is lengthened in the feminine to ā, ᾱ, η, Sec. 7, ἀδελφός, ἀδελφή; in Latin also the final *a* of the feminine stem was originally long, compare *āi ārum, ābus*.

Forms also of the A-stems do duty as masculines with lengthened endings, as πολίτης. In Latin the final *s* is dropped as in the ancient form *parricidas*, and the original ā is shortened in *advena, terrigena* as in ἱππότᾰ from ἱππότης. On the other hand the A-stem is used as feminine without the stem (in o or *u*) being lengthened, as ὁδός, ἄλοχος; *humus, mālus*.

Certain case-suffixes are appropriated to the expression of only a particular gender. The genitive singular masculine and neuter of the A and O-stems—the so-called second declension—has the original ending *ojo*, Sec. 47, while the feminine has the simple genitive suffix *s*. The neuter differs from the masculine and feminine in the singular by the want of the nominative form, instead of which it employs either the form of the accusative, or the bare stem, *damnum*, δένδρον, μέθυ; though in Latin many neuters take the *s* of the nominative, as *vulgus, virus*, and it takes the suffix *a*, originally *ā*, in the nominative and accusative plural; the rest of the cases have similar forms for the neuter and masculine. In the declension of pronouns the neuter has the original suffix *t*, the masculine and feminine s, τι, *quid* = *kit;* τις, *quis* = κις. Certain stem forms are fixed also for the feminine; thus stems in *ja*, φέρουσα = φεροντja, δότειρα —ερja by the side of the older stem-form used as masculine δοτήρ = δοτερς, ἡδεῖα feminine of ἡδύς; in ιδ in δεσπότις, αὐλητρίς like the masculine δεσπότης, αὐλητήρ; compare also πρόφρων, πρόφρασσα; the Latin stem in *ic* in *victrix* with the masculine *victor*.

XLVI. Declensions

Difference of declension is conditioned by the final sound of the nominal stem. This is either a consonant or a vowel, which latter may be divided into hard vowel sounds, in α, ο; weak vowel sounds, in ι, υ; and diphthongal, in αυ, ευ, ου.

Consonant stems: 1. Consisting of a mere root, or unformed nominal stem, without any stem-forming suffix; ὄψ, *vox*, root ὀπ, *voc*, κῆρυξ, stem πηουκ, πούς = ποδς, with compensatory lengthening, *pēs* stem *ped*, ἐλπίς, stem ἐλπιδ, θήρ. 2. With stem-suffix originally *as*, Greek *os*. ες, Latin

Declension. 91

os, us, is ; μένος, δυσμενής ; *genus* genitive *generis = genesis, genesos, cinis, arbos (r), vetus ;* in Greek the ς at the end of a stem is thrown away before the case-suffix which begins with a vowel; *s* is original and belongs to the stem also in the fifth so-called Latin declension, *dies, spes,* genitive *diei = diesis,* it disappears in the oblique cases; for the transition in the so-called E-declension, Sec. 47. 3. With stem-suffix in *n ;* ποιμήν — εν, τέκτων — ον, δαίμων ; *nomen, sermo (n), homo* stem *homen.* 4. With stem-suffix in dentals οντ, *ent,* ғοτ, ατ, αδ ; γέρων, φέρων, εἰδώς = ғοτς, σῶμα, λαμπάς ; *ferens.* 5. With stem-suffix in *r* in δοτήρ, πατήρ (ερ), ῥήτωρ, *dator, pater.*

Vowel-stems : 1. A and O-stems, capable of no transition into the consonant declensions; ἵππος, ζυγόν ; *equus = equ(o)s, jugum = jugo(m)* ; feminine χώρα, *equa.* 2. Weak vowel J and U-stems and diphthongal stems, passing into the consonantal declensions, in single caseforms by changing vowels into consonants ; φύσις, πόλις, *avis, ovis ;* νέκυς, ὀφρύς, σῦς ; *fructus ;* ναῦς, βασιλεύς, βοῦς.

XLVII. CASE-ENDINGS.

1. *The nominative, accusative, and vocative, both of the singular and plural,* are cases of the subject and immediate object, of the starting point and goal of an action or motion. These cases are identical in the neuter. Suffix *s* or *m,* or none.

The nominative singular masculine and feminine suffix *s,* the sign of personality, of something conceived as living, is the relic of a pronominal root *sa*, in Greek ὁ, ἡ. When this falls away the vowel is long by compensation, Sec. 9, 2, πατήρ from πατερς. It is lost in feminine A-stems, χώρα—compare masculine ἱππότα—a is shortened after consonants, γλῶσσα. Latin *materia* coexists with the form *materie-s; pes = peds, mors = morts*, root *mor* suffix *ti; s* disappears after *r* and *l, acer* by the side of *acris, vigil(s)*.

Nominative plural masculine and feminine, — ες, originally *as;* δυσμενεῖς — εσες, γλυκεῖς = εϝες, πόλιες Ionic, πόλεις from πολεjες, lengthened in the Homeric πόληες, νῆες = ναϝες. The weaker form in O and A-stems, ἵπποι, χῶραι, οἱ, αἱ, the older τοί, ταί, compare τώς, where the stem widened by *j*, with suffix *as*, is cut down to οι, αι. In Latin *hostes, hostīs, hosties* compare πόλιες, *hosteis*, πόλεις; according to the analogy of the J-stems, also all consonant stems, *vocēs* from *vocies; fructūs* from *fructues*, compare νέκυες. O and A-stems are analogous to the Greek; *equi* from *equei, equoi (oe), equois; equae*, anciently *equai*, from *equais;* anciently *magistreis, filis* from *filieis;* in the so-called fifth declension *dies, species = dieses*.

Dual nominative and accusative ε, originally *a*, a weakening of the plural form —*as;* δυσμενῆ from — εσε, πόλεε from — εjε. In O and A-stems the original *a* of the case-endings coalesces with o, a of the stem-ending into ω, ᾱ, ἵππω, ζυγώ, χώρα. The only Latin duals are *duo, ambo*, compare *octo*.

Accusative singular originally — *am*, or, when the stem ends in a vowel, *m; ν* occurs instead of *m* according to the Greek law of sound, Sec. 35, and *a* when the stem

Case Endings. 93

ends in a consonant ; πατέρα by casting off the ν, for α is a tach-vowel, = *pataram*. Neuters have no case-suffix, φέρον = φεροντ. Ναῦν from the vowel stem ναυ, Homeric νῆfα from the consonant stem ναf ; πόλιν vowel stem, by the side of the Epic πόληα from πολεjα, consonant stem, compare νηός, πόληος, and Sec. 9, 2 ; εὑρέα Homeric, stem εὑρύν.

S of *the accusative plural masculine and feminine* is affixed to the accusative singular. Neuters have *a*. Νῆfας, ναῦς (ναυνς) ; πόλεις = πολεjας, Homeric πόληας, compare from πολύς the Homeric πολέας = πολεfας, by the side of πολλούς, Ionic πόλιας = ανς, *ams ;* ἵππους, Doric ως, = ονς, τούς = τονς, χώρας = ανς, *fructūs = fructuns*, *equos = equons, equas = equans*.

The vocative, as distinguished from the nominative, has no suffix, and leaves the stem unaltered : εὐμενές, δαῖμον, αὦτερ, πόλι, πρέαβυ, ναῦ ; yet in consonant-stems the nominative often serves as vocative, φύλαξ ; on the other hand, the ending of the stem is thrown away in accordance with the laws of endings, in ἄνα = ἀνακτ, παῖ = παιδ ; in O-stems the original ἄ is weakened into ε, ἵππε ; χώρα, γλῶσσα are the same as the nominative ; νύμφη, vocative νύμφἄ Homeric; in masculines in ης, ἄ : πολῖτα, δέσποτα.

2. The other cases denote partly the relations between one object and another, expressed by a noun, partly an attachment of one object to another by motion from the one to the other. These endings were originally local in their signification, and often interchanged their functions.

The ending of *the genitive singular* was originally *as*,

Greek ος, often lengthened into ως in J- and U-stems treated as consonant-stems, and in diphthong-stems, in consequence of the disappearance of *j* and ϝ and the change of quantity thence resulting; ναῦς, consonant-stem ναϝ, genitive ναϝος, ναός Doric, νηός Epic Ionic, νεώς Attic, so Epic βασιλῆος, Attic βασιλέως, ἄστεως = ἀστεϝος, on the other hand γλυκέος = — εϝος; πόλις is treated as vowel-stem, πόλιος Ionic, but was originally a consonant-stem, πολεjος, thence πόληος Homeric, πόλεως Attic; in χώρας the a of the genitive coalesces with the ending of the stem. The genitive of the O-stems ended originally in οσjο (οjος?) thence οjο, Homeric ἵπποιο, Attic ἵππου, from ἵπποο; compare Il. II. 325, Od. I. 70, ὅο = οὗ more correct than ὅου, compare Πετεῶο Il. IV. 327; πολίτου according to the analogy of the O-stems instead of the original αο (αjο, ασjο), Homeric — αο, along with — εω, where there is a change of quantity, whence ω. The Latin *os*,—archaic in *senatuos*, becomes — *is*, *us*, as *generis* = *genesos*, *fructus* = *fructuos*, by the side of the archaic *fructuis*, *senatuis*, also *senati* according to the analogy of the O-stems. The terminal *s* disappears in O- and A-stems: *equi* from *equeis*, *equois* compare *illius*, *istius*; the ancient *filiai*, *aquai*, *familiai* modify *ai* into *ae*, as *aquae*; there was an old form with *s*; *familias*, *terras*. Just as *s* of the stem disappears, so also does *s*, in genitive forms in *ei* of the so-called 5th declension, as *diei* by the side of the old form *dies* as a genitive, instead o *diesis*; in the so-called E-declension the transition into *ie* — *ies* (*materies*) exists by the side of the form *ia*; *materiei* compare the old *familiai*.

Case Endings. 95

The original form of the *genitive plural* was *am, sam,* Greek ων, in A-stems originally σων, χωρῶν = χωρασων; old Greek and Homeric αων, εων, Doric ᾶν; Latin *um* in consonant-stems, *generum = genes-um, ium* from the original J-stems, as well as those treated as such; in O- and A-stems, *rum* from *som, equarum = asum*, by the side of forms without *s* as *agricolûm*.

The dative and locative singular. The dative proper, the case of the more remote object, betokens a relation of interest, the entrance of a person or thing into the sphere of operation of an action; the locative betokens rest in a place. In Greek the two cases have for the most part coalesced, since the dative relation was originally considered also as locative. The dative ending was originally *ai, ei*, the locative ending was the demonstrative root *i ;* πατρί with short ι being locative, *patrī* dative. The true Greek dative is found only in O- and A-stems ἵππῳ = ἵππωι, χώρᾳ = ᾱι, from *aai.* The former have special locative-forms as adverbs, οἴκοι, ποῖ, οἷ; the single example of a locative feminine is χαμαί. The difference of meaning between the pronominal locative "whither" and the nominal locative "where," is not original. True Latin datives are *senatui = uei, patri* old form *patrei, diēi* connected with *diē = diesei ;* O- and A-stems *equo = equoi,* old form *populoi, cui = quoi, equae = equāi.* The only Latin locative in *i* used adverbially coalesces with the genitive in O- and A-stems, in consequence of the disappearance of the *s* of the genitive ending as *humi, domi, belli, Corinthi (i = ei =* οι, compare οἴκοι); *Romae* locative = *Romai,* as χαμαί, only occasionally = genitive originally *Romais;* further adverbial locative forms are *heri, ruri, peregri, postri-diē* from *diei, temperi.* By per mutation of *e* and *i* the Latin locative has been confused with the ablative form which has lost its original *d; rure* = *rured*, an ablative like *peregre.*

The ablative singular originally ended in *at, t.* In Greek this termination is retained only in the endings of adverbs in — ως, ταχέως, πάντως, ὥς, τώς, πῶς, Ionic κῶς, originally *kat.* The Latin *d* is archaic in *senatud, hosteid, sententiad,* but was cast away at a later period, and the ablative in consonant-stems thenceforward ended in *ĕ*. The Latin adverbs in *ē* were originally ablatives, compare the archaic adverb *facillumed; ante* = *antid* in *antidhac, post* = *postid* in *postidea,* thence *postea, extrā, suprā, itā* = *itad,* etc., enclitic *que* in *quisque, usque, plerusque,* etc. from *qued* the ablative singular of the indefinite pronoun *qui* with the meaning *somehow, in which way,* thence. Sec. 41, 1.

Locative dative plural. Greek in σσι (σfι), σι: πόδεσσι, ποσσί, ποσί (ποδσι), πόλισι Ionic, πολίεσσι Homeric. O- and A-stems were lengthened by the phonetic or resonant ι, Sec. 9, 3: ἵπποισι, χώραισι, thence ἵπποις, χώραις, Epic and Ionic ῃσι, ῃς (η = originally ā); old forms without this ι are Ὀλυμπίασι, Ἀθήνῃσι, θύρᾱσι. This case does not exist in Latin.

The ablative singular and plural suffix φι(ν) = *bhi*, a descriptive case formation, with local, copulative, instrumental, or ablative function, for singular and plural, ὄχεσφι, ναῦφι, Ἰλιόφιν, βίηφι, κλισίηφι, θεόφιν; Doric and Homeric τείν = τεφιν, compare *tibi*. Latin pronoun

Pronouns. 97

dative singular *tibi, sibi; ibi* locative of the demonstrative *i, alibi, utrobi; mihi = mibhi*. Dative and ablative plural in *bos, bus*, with the *s* of the plural, anciently *bios, fies*, as in λικριφίς, Sec. 28; *acubus, ovibus, ambobus; nobis, vobis* are weaker but original forms. In A- and O-stems *b* disappears; *equis* from — *eis, ois (obios)*; *mensis — eis, ais (abios)*; compare *deabus, filiabus*, and *rēbus, diēbus*. Closely connected with this case are the

Greek dative and genitive dual. The suffix φιν, with φ lost and contracted to οιν, αιν from οφιν, αφιν, in O- and A-stems, passes into the other stems; ποδοῖιν, πολέοιν.

XLVIII. Pronouns and Pronominal Declension.

1. Personal and reflexive pronouns without difference of gender: ἐγώ, ἐγών; Skr. *aham;* *ego;* Gothic *ik;* thoroughly independent of and different from *ma*, the 1st personal verbal pronoun; σύ, weakened from τύ, Doric, coexisting with τύνη; *tu* stem *tva;* compare the possessive τεός. The accusative forms ἐμέ, μέ, σέ, Doric τέ (= τϝε), reflexive ἔ, Homeric ἑέ, Æolic ϝέ (= σϝε), Latin *se = sve*, with no sign of case, show the real stems of these pronouns, *ma, tva, sva*. Locative and dative ἐμοί, σοί (= τϝοι); οἷ, compare οἴκοι; Doric ἐμίν, Homeric τεΐν, Æolic ἐΐν, from ἐμεφιν, etc., compare *mihi, tibi, sibi,* ablative *me, te, se = med, ted, sed* also used as accusative. Genitive ἐμεῖο,— from original case-suffix σjo,—ἐμέο, ἐμεῦ, ἐμοῦ; τεοῖο, σεῖο, σέο, σεῦ, σοῦ; ἕο, ἕο, εὖ, οὗ (for σϝεο), without elision and hiatus, as in Od. IX. 398, making the foregoing syllable

long by position, so also the possessive ὅς; *mei, tui, sui*, genitive of the personal pronoun. Plural nominative Æolic ἄμμες, ὔμμες, accusative ἄμμε like the singular; ἡμεῖς, ἡμᾶς, etc., treated as J-stems. The dative ἡμῖν has arisen from the locative — φιν. *Nobis* with *bi*, as in *tibi*, and the *s* of the plural. Dual nominative and accusative νώ from the stem νο, νῶι according to the analogy of the dative; σφώ, σφῶι from τϝω; σφωέ; genitive and dative νῶιν, νῷν; σφῶιν, σφῷν; σφωΐν with suffix φι.

The possessive pronoun is derived from the stem of the personal pronoun: 2nd person Doric and Epic τεός = τϝος, *tuus*, in Ionic Attic weakened into σός. 3rd person ὅς, ἑός Homeric = σϝος, hardened into σφός Doric, *suus*, makes the preceding syllable long by position as οὗ, Il. VIII. 406. XVI. 542. Plural ἁμός, ὑμός, σφός, Homeric Doric, ἄμμος, ὔμμος Æolic.

2. Demonstrative pronouns with difference of gender: ὁ, in later language, and sometimes in Homer, employed as an article, = *sa*, see for the rough breathing, Sec. 30. 2, instead of σος the final *s* of the nominative masculine being dropped; ἡ = *sā ;* neuter τό = τοτ, the τ at the end of the word having disappeared as in τί, compare *istud, illud*. The rest of the case-forms ending in a dental are derived from the pronoun-stem *ta*, etymologically the same as the German article *der, den ;* besides οἱ, αἱ we find τοί, ταί, older forms, Doric and also Homeric; τούς = τονς ; from both forms ὅδε, τόδε, τοῖςδεσσι. Homeric, with inorganic case-ending. The pronominal stem *ta*, or in its less common form *sa*, is the foundation

of the article, and both stems are the basis of the demonstrative forms. The forms of the article beginning with τ were used in the Ionic dialect, and by the Attic tragedians, who also employed this form as a relative, to avoid a hiatus. Different from this is the

Relative pronoun ὅς, ἥ, ὅ = *jas, jā, jat* from the pronoun *ja*, root *i*; this also was originally demonstrative, compare the Attic ἣ δ' ὅς, καὶ ὃς ἔφη, ὃς καὶ ὅς. Compare Sec. 32, 3.

The indefinite interrogative is τίς = κις, τί = *kit, quis, quid*, Sec. 19, 4; the same *d* which = *t*, belonging to the pronoun-stem *ta*, is found in other neuter forms of the declension of pronouns: *id, illud, quod, aliud* = ἄλλο(τ);. *qui* ablative = *quo* compare *alioqui, nequiquam*.

The Latin demonstrative *is* comes from the pronominal stem *i*; *ea, ejus*, arise from the modification of *i* into *e* before *a, o, u*, compare *eo, eam, eunt*, from the verbal root *i, deus* from the root *div*, coexisting with *dius* = δῖος. *Hic* from the pronominal stem *ho*, suffix *i* and *ce*; if *ne* follows the *e* is changed into *i, hicine, hoc* = *hodce*; *haec, quae* feminine and neuter = *haice, quai* with the demonstrative pronoun *i*, thence without it *aliqua, si qua*, compare *antehac*. The archaic *ibus, hibus* = *eis, his*; *hoc* archaic for *huc*.

XLIX. ADVERBS AND PREPOSITIONS.

1. Adverbs are nominal or rather pronominal word forms. They are employed originally to designate relations of place, and afterwards those of manner and time. They

are undeclined, formed partly from pronominal stems and partly from those of nouns both substantive and adjective. They are petrified case-forms, standing alone, and for the most part declare themselves by their endings as definite cases of nouns or pronouns. E.g., pronominal adverbs from the stem of the demonstrative ὁ, τό, of the relative ὅς, of the indefinite πος = Ionic κος, are ὧδε, ὡς, τώς, πως, ablative forms; οἶ, ποῖ locative;—compare the Homeric adverbs ἀνιδρωτί, ἀναιμωτί, etc., with locative ending τι used in a modal or instrumental signification— οὗ,ποῦ genitive, with local suffix θι,θεν,δε; the ending of the temporal adverb ὅτε, τότε, πότε, Doric ὅκα, etc., is identical with τε, *que;* compare καί, Secs. 16. 19. For adjectival adverbs in ως, ω, Latin in ē (*ed*), see, under the ablative, Sec. 47. For substantive adverbs with local suffix ι, see under the locative, θι, θεν, δε Sec. 47. Modal suffix α, η in the pronominal ᾗ, πῇ, τῇ, πάντη; ᾰ in ἅμα, μάλα, τάχα, etc. Many adverbs are identical with the accusative singular and plural of neuter adjectives.

2. Prepositions are in fact adverbs, and as such contain case-elements. In Homer they are still used in their original adverbial character; they were afterwards united to verbs and nouns as prefixes, and finally came to govern certain cases. E.g., ἐπί, ἐνί, ἀντί, ἀμφί, παραί; *prae* = *prai* are locatives; *pro* = *prod, ante*(*d*), *apud* are ablatives; πάρος is a genitive; compare *coelitus, antiquitus;* for the so-called instrumental adverb in α, as ἀνά, παρά, ἄντα, see above under Adverbs.

Inflexion of Verbs. 101

3. The whole of the many forms of the infinitive, Sec. 40, are also to be considered as petrified forms of *Nomina actionis* (locative or dative), just as participles and verbal adjectives are *Nomina agentis*, or declinable nominal-forms from verbal-stems with the nominal stem-suffix added.

II.

THE INFLEXION OF VERBS. CONJUGATIONS.

L. Elements.

1. The idea of action or motion is expressed only in an abstract form by the verbal stem. It receives its closer definition and formation into a word,

α. Through the reference to definite persons, as sub jects of the action or motion; this is expressed in the personal endings.

β. Through the indication of the mode in which something is done or has happened, in its relation to fact either as what has really occurred, or as what is merely thought of and willed; this is expressed in the mood-elements. The indicative is the objective mood, without special mood-elements. The subjective moods are the conjunctive and optative with special mood-suffixes.

γ. Through the relation of the action to a definite time, as well as its indication as lasting, momentary, and finished—the last difference is thoroughly carried out in Greek only; this is expressed in the tense-stems.

2. Genus Verbi. The action which is expressed by the verbal stem may regard the subject which is designated in the personal ending as a more immediate or more distant object.

This reflexion of the action on the subject, which thereby bears a receptive passive relation to the action, is denoted by the middle forms of inflexion, whose reflex signification is shown by more extended and stronger person-endings. They differ from the verbal forms of the active, which express an exclusively active relation of the subject to an action.

But since this mixed, middle, partly active, partly passive relation of the subject to the action may be also considered as exclusively passive, the middle verbal form serves secondarily also to express the passive—*mediopassivum*.

3. The forms of the passive show a tendency towards new formations. This occurs primarily in Greek, where only the compound aorists and the future passive are peculiar forms of passive meaning differing from the middle, but also in Latin, which has no original middle voice. In Latin, the passive forms,—which, in the so-called deponents, simply perform the office of a middle voice,—are produced by affixing the reflexive pronoun to the active personal endings, and by the passage of the reflexive into the passive signification.

1. PERSONAL ENDINGS.

LI. PRIMARY AND SECONDARY PERSONAL ENDINGS. AUGMENT. IMPERATIVE.

1. The synthesis of a subject with a predicate, which is essential to a verb in order to give it predicative force, is accomplished by the amalgamation of the pronominal stem, serving as a subject, with the predicate, a stem implying meaning in its simplest verbal form. Weakened forms of the pronominal stems in the three persons of the singular without reference to gender, appear in the personal endings as enclitics at the end of the verbal stems. By means of the accent of the word they make up with the root or the verbal stem the unit called a word. They are *ma*, compare ἐμέ accusative of the personal pronoun; *tva*, compare *tu*, Doric τύ, σύ; *ta*, compare το, stem of the article.

Root *as, to be, mi* weakened from *ma, I, as-mi, = being I, I am.* Root *da, to give,* pronominal stem *ta, that, he; da-ta, giving he, he gives ; da-tva, giving thou, thou givest.* Weakened form of the pronoun in the personal endings; *mi, si, ti.* The endings of the plural consist of a combination of two pronouns of the singular. Personal endings: 1st plural *masi = matvi, I and thou = we;* 2nd plural *tvasi = tvatvi, thou and thou = ye ;* 3rd plural *anti, nti,* either a strengthened form of *ti*, or compounded with the pronominal stem *an = he and he, they.* E.g. *asmasi, we are; astasi, ye are; asanti, they are;* compare the doubling of the pronominal stems in another, that is to say, a constructive—see Sec. 53—sense in the personal endings of the middle voice.

These so-called primary personal endings are found in the tense-stems of the present, future, and perfect (in this last case the primary personal ending is smoothed away in consequence of the reduplication), and in all forms of the conjunctive.

2. A further shortening and weakening of the personal endings takes place under the influence of the augment in the historic tenses—imperfect, aorist etc.—and in all the forms of the optative. These are the so-called secondary personal endings—1st pers. *mi* to *m*, *v* according to the Greek phonetic law, 2nd pers. σι to s, 3rd pers. to τ, which disappears at the end of a word; 3rd pers. plural *v* from *nti*.

The augment consists of the syllable *a*, in Greek ε, a pronominal stem having reference to distance. It is prefixed to the root as a particle relating to past time, and thus differs from the suffixes of the personal endings which denote the subject. It also coalesces with the following word into one sound. It differs in meaning from the reduplication of the perfect because it does not, like the reduplication, denote completion, but past time only, it differs also in its looser relation to the tense-stem. Thus it does not, like the reduplication, coalesce with the whole tense-stem, but only with the indicative, and, as in Homer, does not necessarily attach itself even to this. The original form of the verb with augment is as follows,— root *da*, *adam*, *adadam*, instead of *adami*, *adanami*. Greek ἐδίδων instead of ἐδιδωμι.

On syllabic and temporal augment see the grammars. A syllabic augment where there is a vowel at the beginning of the root, and a temporal augment where this is lengthened to ει instead of η, point to a rejected consonant at the beginning of the root ϝ, j, σ: examples, Sec. 11, 2; Sec. 21 ἰδ—ϝιδ; Sec. 20, ϝαγ, ϝεργ; Sec. 23, ἐχ, σεχ; Sec. 30, 2, Sec. 31, Sec. 32, 3, ἑ; a syllabic augment with doubling of the ρ, points to a rejected ϝ or σ before ρ, ϝραγ Sec. 20, ῥυ, σρυ Secs. 29. 30, 3.

3. The imperative, a verbal interjection (by which the subject expressed in the personal terminations is to be considered as a vocative), is in the 2nd pers. singular of many primary verbs in -μι characterized by aspiration of the personal termination, θι from *dhva = tva*, compare θ in 2nd pers. singular; see below for the remaining personal terminations of the imperative.

LII. PERSONAL ENDINGS OF THE ACTIVE.

Here we have first to consider the difference of the inflexional forms, in the present and the strong aorist. These differences exist between (α) the primitive verbs, the so-called verbs in μι, which have, with the exception of εἰμί = ἐσμι and ἧμαι = ἥσμαι, exclusively a vowel rootending and a monosyllabic original stem (to which also as far as regards the inflexion of the present stem belong verbs with a stem-suffix νυ added to the bare stem or to the root, as δείκνυμι, ζεύγνυμι), and which affix the personal ending immediately to the root, and (β) verbs ending in the 1st sing. in ω, which insert between the root and the personal ending a tach-vowel, originally α in the

Greek, uniformly interchangeable with the vowels ε and ο (1st sing. ω, see below). The latter class of verbs, by far the most numerous, contains, besides consonantal root-verbs in ω, as ἄγω, πλέκω, βλέπω, πέτομαι, μένω, also a considerable number of roots with vowel-endings, so-called 'verba pura' as τίω, δύω, λύω, θύω, φύω, in which however the irregularities in the quantity for the most part, or the length of the root-vowel in the present, even though it only occurs sporadically, indicate the loss of a *j* which served to lengthen the present, and has fallen out from its place between the vowel root-ending and the person-endings: φύω, Æolic φυίω, so θῦ'ω = θυιω compare λῦ'ει Od. VII. 74. Other verbs in -ω whose roots end in vowels, as ζέω, νέομαι, τρέω, see Secs. 32. 26, imply the loss of σ; or F, λάε, φάε, Secs. 25. 28, and appear as consonant-root verbs in ω with spirant rejected. So while the existence of original present forms of primitive verbs in ω with vowel root-ending but without any lengthening of the presen is doubtful, the existence of the so-called tach-vowels, as phonetic intermediaries between consonant root-endings and personal endings, which later on were introduced in the case of stems with vowel-endings, must be regarded as certain. Forms such as *est, volt, fers, ferris,* see below, are the rem nant of an inflexion without tach-vowels in Latin.

The primary form of the 1*st person singular* is μι, from the original *ma.* The original form from the root *as* is *asmi,* thence εἰμί = ἐσμι, Æolic ἔμμι; in εἶμι the vowel is strengthened from the root ι; Æolic μι also appears in the contracted conjugation φίλημι, ὄρημι. The μι disappears after

Personal Endings. 107

a consonant root-ending, or after a tach-vowel (*a-e-o*) which is added to the verb-stem, τιμαj in τιμάω = τιμαjω, and the tach-vowel itself is intensified into ω; λέγω = *legomi* instead of *legmi*, Latin *lego*. Perfect — a from αμι, λέλοιπα from λελοιπαμι, compare the Æolic Foίδημι. In the conjunctive the original personal endings are retained in the Homeric forms ἴδωμι Il. XXII. 450 ἴδωμαι(?), ἐθέλωμι, εἴπωμι. In the optative, which elsewhere shows a secondary personal ending, the 1st singular primary form in μι has been introduced, as φέροιμι, older forms with secondary ending τρέφοιν, etc.; ν on the other hand, appears in the optative of the verbs in μι, εἴην, τιθείην compare φιλοίην. The secondary form is ν for μ in the ending of the imperfect, without tach-vowel in ἴστην, with tach-vowel affixed to the stem in ἔφερον. The ν for μ is dropped and a tach-vowel is found in the first aorist in α, as ἔδειξα = ἐδεικσα(μ).

In Latin the *m* of the original *mi* is kept in *sum* = *esum-esm*, *esmi* = εἰμί, in *inquam*, in the imperfect in *bam* (see below), *eram*, in the conjunctive-optative *veham*, *sim* = *siem*, *esiem*, compare εἴην = ἐσjην; elsewhere the termination is *o* : *fero* = *ferom*. Derived verbs with stem-ending *a*, *ama*, *voca*, contract this *a* with the *o* of the termination; *voco* = *vocao*, *vocajo*, as τιμῶ from τιμαω, τιμαjω.

In the *2nd person singular* the pronominal stem is *tva*; with expulsion of *v*, *ta* as in the Latin imperative in *to*; θι aspirated in κλῦθι imperative, θα in οἶσθα = Foιδτα with dissimilation and aspiration of the τ under the influence of the spirant σ; ἦσθα with radical σ; through assibilation we get from this, *swa*, *swi*, *si*, *s*.

In Greek we find the primary form σι in ἐσσί Ionic = original form *assi*, from which comes the Homeric εἶς, the personal ending being entirely lost in the Attic form εἶ, *thou art*, and = *thou wilt go*. φέρεις, φέρῃς from φερεσι, φερησι, with transposed or epenthetic ι. Moreover we find the termination σθα in the Homeric conjunctive in ἐθέλησθα, in the Epic and Æolic indicative τίθησθα, φῇσθα, δίδοισθα, ἔχεισθα, in the optative βάλοισθα, in the imperfect ἦσθα, ἔφησθα, ᾔδησθα Attic—compare Latin perfect 2nd singular and plural *sti, stis*, and 1st plural μεσθα for μεθα, where σθ represents the simple aspirate. The secondary form is s as in ἔφερες, φέροις, as also in ἵστης, τίθης, δίδως. Perfect λέλοιπας. In Latin *legis* = *legesi*, the optative *sis* = *sies ; es, thou art* = *ess, essi, assi ; ēs, thou eatest* = *eds*, root *ed ; vis* = *ves, vels*, compare the conjunction *vel*, originally an imperative. The 2nd singular perfect is *sti*, compare above, σθα.

Imperative θι : ἴθι, ἴσθι = ἐσθι, ἴσθι = ϝιδθι, dissimilation from the root ϝιδ, γνῶθι, ὄρνυθι, ἴληθι, ἄνωχθι, στῆθι, ἔσταθι by the side of θές, δός, for θετι, δοθι, ι being rejected and s instead of θ at the end of a word ; τίθει, δίδου, ἵστη instead of ἱσταθι after the analogy of the so-called contracted verbs, Homeric δίδωθι. θι disappears in verbs which have a tach-vowel : λέγε, τίμα = τιμαjε, compare *lege, ama*. The bare stem appears in the Latin imperatives *dic, duc, fac, fer*, compare the conjunction *vel*, originally an imperative. The emphasised form in Latin in *to, esto, memento*, is an imperative perfect from *tod* = *tat* reduplicated. The 3rd person pronominal stem is used for the 2nd and 3rd persons.

Personal Endings. 109

The demonstrative pronoun of the 3rd *person singular* is *ta*—compare τό, τοί, Sec. 38, 3, and in Latin *tum, tam, talis, tantus*—is weakened into *ti* and mostly softened to *si*. The original form *asti, he is, dadâti, he gives*, becomes ἐστί, δίδωσι. τι is retained in ἐστι compare πίστις, and in the Doric δίδωτι, τίθητι, ἴσατι; σι is found in φησί, τίθησι, εἶσι, ζεύγνυσι, and in the Homeric conjunctive ἄγῃσι, εἴπῃσι, ἐθέλῃσι, δῷσι, δώῃσι, with transposed or epenthetic ι in the preceding syllable (and hence the ι subscript is to be retained). The indicative of verbs in ω is as ἔχεισι. Forms in ησι as ἔχησι are doubtful. The termination is dropped in φέρει from φερειτι, φερετι, φερεσι with ellipsis of the σ between vowels (?), and in the perfect γέγονε. In the secondary forms of the historic tenses and optative τ must be dropped according to the law of final sounds: ἔβη, ἐδίδω, ἔφερε, ἦε, φέροι, εἴη. Imperative τω from τωτ, ἱστάτω, perfect ἐστάτω, τιθέτω, compare the Latin—*to*. In Latin the *t* of the secondary personal ending is retained, as *est, legit = leget*(*i*), *amat, erat, pepigit*, compare πέπηγε. And though in Latin the *t* of the 2nd person is softened to the spirant *s*, the *t* of the 3rd person has kept its sound as a dental tenuis.

The original 1*st person plural* was *masi = matva, matvi*, see above, whence *mas, ma*, original form *asmasi, we* (*I +
thou*) *are*. From the Doric μες in εὕρομες, we find μεν in Ionic and even in Æolic, with the spirant dropped, originally *ma*. A nasal sound was afterwards introduced to strengthen the ending: ἐσμέν, ἴμεν = *imasi, imatva;* φέρομεν, with a bare and therefore short tach-vowel. Latin *legimus* from *legumus*, compare *sumus = esumus*, so *volumus, quaesumus.*

The 2nd *person plural* was *tvasi, tasi*, see above, original form *astasi, you are*. In Greek a bare τε remains, as in ἐστέ, ἴτε dropping entirely the sound of the 2nd person pronominal stem, which is weakened first to σι, then to ς, and finally altogether abandoned. The Latin *tis* shows a trace of the 2nd person pronominal stem, *legitis* = *legetes*, λέγετε(ς). The imperative shortens into *te, legite* = *legete*, emphatic—*tote*. ἄνωχθε, by the side of ἀνώγετε, ἐγρήγορθε. The dual originally = 2nd person plural τον from *tasi*, as the 1st person plural μεν from *masi*.

The 3rd *person plural* was *anti, nti*, see above. In Greek the primary form is αντι, ντι, original form *asanti, they are*, thence ἔᾱσι Ionic instead of ἔσαντι, Doric ἐντι, and finally εἰσί = ἐσ-ντι, ἴᾱσι from ἰαντι, φᾱσί from the Doric φαντί, ν being dropped and α lengthened, Attic διδόασι, τιθέασι, δεικνύασι = τιθεαντι, διδοαντι, ἱστᾶσι = ἱστααντι; the Homeric τιθεῖσι, ἱεῖσι, διδοῦσι, ῥηγνῦσι, are from the Doric τίθεντι, δίδοντι; φέρουσι is from the Doric φέροντι, compare γερουσία from γεροντια. The Latin *sunt* = *esonti, ferunt* = *feronti, tremunt* archaic *tremonti*. The secondary form is *ant, nt*, τ being dropped in the Greek termination, ἦσαν = ἦσαντ, ἔφερον, the optative εἶεν = ἐσjεντ, φέροιεν. In Latin *t* is retained as *erant;* the termination σαν in ἔφασαν, ἔδοσαν, etc., equals ἔσαν, shortened, and without the augment; so ἱσταίησαν, connected with ἱσταῖεν, is a form composed with σαν = *asant;* εἴησαν, by the side of εἶεν, is a compound of the root *as*, ἐς with itself; ἴσασι = ϝιδ-σαντι, so εἴξασι = εἰκσαντι; with the primary form in σαντι, *asanti* compare *dederunt* from *dedisonti*. Imperative οντων with the addition of ν, compare *legunto;* τωσαν

Middle Passive. 111

is a late form from τω of the singular and σαν shortened from *asant*.

The primary form of the 3rd person dual is τον, the secondary form in the historic tenses is την : ἦστον, ἤστην, compare ἦστε with the σ of the root retained, connected with ἦτον, ἤτην, compare ἦτε.

LIII. Greek Middle-Passive.

The personal endings of the middle voice are lengthened active forms which have a reflexive force. Original forms *mai, sai, tai*, from *mami, tvatvi, tati* = *I myself*, or *to myself, thou thyself*, or *to thyself, he himself*—the constructive combination of two personal pronouns acting as subject and object, which is either nearer or more remote, in distinction from the copulative combination, *I and thou, thou and thou*, in the plural active.

The primary form of the 1*st person singular* is μαι from *mami;* the secondary μην from *mam;* τίθεμαι, φέρομαι, φέρωμαι; ἐφερόμην, φεροίμην, ἐτιθέμην.

The primary original form of the 2*nd person singular* is σαι from the original *tvatvi, svasvi, svai;* the secondary is σο with the 2nd pronoun entirely lost.

α. Forms with the sibilant retained in conjugations in μι and in the perfect; τίθεσαι, ἵστασαι; δύνασαι, ὄνοσαι Homeric; imperfect ἐτίθεσο, ἵστασο; imperative τίθεσο etc., ἐπίστασο.

β. Forms where σ is dropped without contraction of the vowels : λιλαίεαι, δίζηαι Od. XI. 100, ὄρηαι XIV. 343; secondary: ἐμάρναο, ὠδύσαο Od. I. 62 ; imperative μάρναο, παρίσταο; aorist ἔθεο, θέο, θεῦ from the Homeric θέσο; on ὄρσο, δέξο, vide Sec. 63, 3.

γ. Forms without σ with contraction of the vowels in the 'tach-vowel' conjugation: φέρῃ, Attic φέρει from φερεσαι, Epic φέρεαι; the secondary form ἐφέρου from ἐφερεσο, Attic imperfect of the μι conjugation ἐδύνω, ἠπίστω, Homeric ἐκρέμω; imperative ἐπίστω; aorist ἔθου, ἔδου Attic; imperfect φέρου, aorist θοῦ, δοῦ from θεσο, δοσο.

The primary form of the 3rd person singular is ται from *tati*, secondary το from *tat*, imperative σθω from ττω, by doubling the τω of the active; the σ is due to dissimilation and the aspirate θ to the influence of the breathing, φάσθω.

The 1st person plural is μεθα, μεσθα, from *madhai* = *matvai*, *matasi* = *I thou thyself*. The 2nd person plural σθε from *stvai* contains the pronoun of the 2nd person in three forms = *thou thou thee*. The 3rd person plural, *antai*, *ntai*, from *antati* = *he he him*, with ν dropped becomes *atai*. In Epic and Ionic αται, ατο, α is an original element of the personal ending; κέαται, κέατο, βεβλήαται, ἔαται, old Attic only after a consonant ἐφθάραται; elsewhere primary νται, secondary ντο.

LIV. LATIN MIDDLE-PASSIVE

In the place of the lost primitive middle-forms come new formations and periphrases, compare Sec. 50.

α. New formations—by adding to the verbal stem with a tach-vowel the accusative of the reflexive pronoun *se* (*sva*), here joined to the 1st and 2nd persons as well as to the 3rd, reduced to *s, r*. 1st person singular *legor* from *lego-se*. 2nd person singular *legeris* from *legesi-s(e)*, *legere = leges-se*. 3rd person singular *legitur* from *legeti-s(e)*. 1st person plural *legimur = legimus-se*. 3rd person plural *leguntur = legunt-(u)-se*. Imperative *amare = ama-se*, *legere = lege-se*.

β. Periphrases—in the 2nd person plural by the participial middle-stem in *mino* in the plural, *estis* being omitted, as *amamini*, *legimini*. This participial form takes also inorganic characteristics of mood and tense in *legamini = legimini sitis*, *legemini = legimini eritis*.

2. MODAL ELEMENTS.

LV. Greek Conjunctive and Optative.

The subjunctive mood in Greek is formed by the simple insertion of the modal suffix, or by intensifying the vowel which comes between the verbal stem and the personal ending.

In Latin the subjunctive is generally formed by compounding the verbal stem with a suitable conjunctive form of the auxiliary, Sec. 67. The mood of objective reality, *i.e.*, the indicative, is characterised by the lack of a special modal element, and by the immediate junction of the verbal stem to the personal ending.

The conjunctive is the mood of fact, conceived as happening or likely to happen, indicated in the present as a continuous, in the aorist as a momentary action. The original suffix was *a*, or in combination with the tach-vowel ā. So the radical form, *asāmi, I may be*, from indicative *asmi, asāsi* from *assi*, etc. In Greek the primary personal terminations are ω or η for ā. The conjunctive also of the primary verbs in μι—without a tach-vowel in the indicative—is formed after the analogy of the verbs in ω with a lengthened tach-vowel, which is amalgamated with the final vowel of the root. ὦ, Ionic ἔω from ἔσω = *asāmi*, ᾖs, Ionic ἔῃs from ἔσησι = *asāsi*, ᾖ, Ionic ἔῃ, ἔῃσι, ᾖσι = *asāti*. 3rd person plural ὦσι, Ionic ἔωσι, Doric ἔωντι from ἔσωντι = *asānti*. φῶ = φαω, φῇs = φαῃs (with η instead of ā), ἰῶ = ἰεω, τιθῶ = τιθ-ε-ω, ἱστῶ = ἱσταω; so the aorist θῶ, Epic θέω, θείω; δῶ, δώω, δῶμαι = δοωμαι. The Homeric dialect still exhibits isolated remains of ormations with short vowels of the conjunctive of primary verbs, which in the indicative were destitute of a tach-vowel. ἴομεν Homeric conjunctive passes into ἴμεν, later ἴωμεν, after the analogy of the forms with the tach-vowel. In the O-conjugation the 1st person singular conjunctive does not differ from the indicative, φέρω from *bharāmi*. 2nd person singular φέρῃs from φέρησι, 3rd person singular φέρῃ = φερητι, 1st person plural φέρωμεν from *bharāmasi*, 3rd person plural φέρωσι, Doric φέρωντι = *bharānti*.

The optative is the mood of wish and of mere conception of fact, a verbal stem strengthened by the verbal suffix *ja, to go*, serving as an auxiliary verb with the idea of effort —compare the verbal periphrases *venum ire, amatum iri*. Original form *as-ja-m ;* in the Greek the modal suffix is ιη ι, ιε. Secondary personal ending εἴην = ἐσjημ, εἴης = σjηςs, εἴη = ἐσjητ (by the side of ἔοις, ἔοι Ionic and Epic), after the analogy of the conjugation with tach-vowel, see below, εἴημεν, εἶμεν = ἐσ/ημες, εἶεν = ἐσ/εντ; so ἰείην, τιθείην, ἱσταίην, διδοίην from present stem ἰε, τιθε, ἱστα, διδο; 3rd person plural ησαν, as εἴησαν, etc., vide Sec. 52; the simple aorist is like the present, δοίην root δο, θείην root θε, σταίην root στα. Optative of the so-called contracted verbs τιμῴην from τιμαο-ιη-ν, connected with τιμῷμι = τιμαο-ι-μι as in the O-conjugation; lastly, the conjugation with the tach-vowel has for modal element only ι, which is contracted with the tach-vowel into the diphthong οι. 1st singular primary personal endings, Sec. 52: φέροιμι with older form φέροιν, otherwise secondary endings; middle φεροίμην. ἰοίην, optative of εἰμι, unites the tach-vowel o and the suffix ιη, besides ἰείη II. XIX. 209 (ἰείη?), ἴοι as in the O-conjugation. The strong aorist of the O-conj. ends like the present, λίποιμι, λάβοιμι for λαβοιν. The compound aorist retains a, λύσαιμι, λυσαίμην; the passive follows the conjugation in μι which has no tach-vowel, λυθείην = λυθε-ιη-ν, φανείην from φανε-ιη-ν.

LVI. LATIN CONJUNCTIVE-OPTATIVE.

1. The Latin conjunctive, as the only subjective mood, is fused with the optative, since the distinction of meaning between the various forms of the conjunctive and optative in Greek, became obliterated in Latin. The forms of the conjunctive and optative thus mixed with one another are also applied to the expression of the future.

2 The forms of the Latin conjunctive mood in *a* correspond with the Greek conjunctive in ω, η. With the original conjunctive suffix *a* are made the conjunctive forms of the 3rd, 2nd, and 4th conjugations. 1st singular *legam*, differs from the indicative *lego;* so also the archaic forms *fuam, creduam, perduam; doceam, audiam; legāmus* = λέγωμες, *legātis* = λέγητε.

3. Remains of the optative forms in Latin. The mood forms with $\bar{\imath}$, $\bar{e}$, from the original modal suffix *ja*, *ia*, by contraction *ie*, $\bar{\imath}$, $\bar{e}$, are optative in form and in origin.

Forms in *i: sim* = *siem, esiem,* ἐσjημ, εἴην; so *sīs, sit,* the *i* was afterwards shortened, *sīmus, sītis, sint* from *siēs* = εἴης, *siēmus* = εἴημεν, *sient* = εἶεν from ἐσjεντ. So *velim, edim* = *ediem*, besides *edam, duim* = δοίην by variation of the root *da* to *du* = δο, besides *duam,* compare the archaic forms *perduim, creduim,* along with the conjunctive forms *perduam, creduam; dederim* = *dedi-sicm*, with a strange shortening in the plural *dederĭmus; faxim* = *facsisim*, Sec. 69, 2.

Forms in $\bar{e}$: the so-called future of the stem-verbs or the so-called 3rd conjugation was in the 1st singular in the older language *dicem, legem* (*e* from *ai* = the Greek οι, *o* tach-vowel, *ι* modal element); this $\bar{e}$ was retained by the later language in the other persons *dices, dicemus* etc., which are to be considered as pure optative forms. The so-called conjunctive present of derived verbs in *o* = *ao, ajo,* of the 1st conjugation, *amem* from *ama-i-m*, compare τιμῴην = τιμω-jη-ν, is an original optative form.

4. Where both forms in $\bar{a}$ and in $\bar{e}$ are found, as in *legamus, legemus, audiamus,* only the conjunctive form in *a* has the signification of the subjective mood, the optative form in *e* retaining the signification of the future, that is for the 3rd and 4th conjugations. The optative 1st singular form *legem, audiem* was however displaced by the conjunctive form *legam, audiam,* which was then changed into the expression of the future. The 1st person singular conjunctive present, and the 1st person singular indicative future in conjugations 3 and 4 have consequently one and the same form which is used for the double purpose of denoting a wish and expressing futurity.

3. TENSE-STEMS.

LVII. IDEA AND CLASSES OF TENSE.

1. The tense-stem of a verb is that which remains of a given verbal form after taking away the personal terminations and the characteristic of the mood. It coincides with the root present forms in the case of root-verbs which contain the simple root without any sort of amplification or any intensification of vowels to express the present, e.g., ἴμεν, φαμέν, λέγομεν; and also in the unaugmented forms of the strong aorist, λάβω, λάβοιμι, λίπε. In the one case the form is marked as a present by the absence of the usual elements for the formation of other tense-stems; in the other case as an aorist by the want of the amplification of the present of the given verb

which belongs to the tense-stem (λείπω, λαμβάνω). In all other cases the tense-stem is distinguished from the root and consists of the root, plus reduplication, vowel-intensification, and additions to the termination.

2. A tense-stem can therefore be formed (α) from a simple — amplified or non-amplified — root, uncompounded with any other secondary verbal root, that is to say, without auxiliary. The simple tense-stems are the *Perfect* formed by reduplication of the root; the *Simple or Strong Aorist*, bearing usually the stamp of the simple root in contradistinction to the various amplifications expressive of the present, and characterised by a demonstrative adverb referring to past time, that is, the augment in the indicative, as well as by secondary personal terminations belonging to the tense. The *Present* is characterised by various extensions of the root, at the beginning, at the ending, and in the middle, as well as by primary personal endings. The *Imperfect* is derived from the present by means of the augment and secondary personal endings. The above are the Indo-Germanic and also the Greek simple tense-stems.

(β) By compounding the verbal root with the root *as*, ἐs, *to be*, which serves as an auxiliary verb; the *Compound tenses* include the *Compound or Weak Aorist, Future*, and *Pluperfect*, to which also belong certain forms of the perfect resulting from other combinations, as well as of the aorist passive.

3. Greek, however, in the first-named tense-stems, the

Greek Perfect and Pluperfect.

perfect, aorist, present, and imperfect, has retained more simple forms than Latin, and has preserved a more primitive character in the formation of tenses. In Latin the present is the only tense which is formed simply throughout; in the perfect active it fluctuates between the two kinds of tense formation; it has lost the aorist with the exception of a few uncertain traces; its imperfect is a later formation by means of an auxiliary verb. On the Latin future, see Sec. 56, 3. 4, and under Compound Tense-Stems.

(1) SIMPLE TENSE-STEMS.

LVIII. THE GREEK SIMPLE PERFECT* AND PLUPERFECT.

1. The root is lengthened at the beginning of the word by means of reduplication. Reduplication was originally the doubling of the root or the compounding it with itself, with the view of intensifying and enhancing the verbal notion, and in its weaker form as the reduplication of the perfect, it is a sign to denote an action finished and completed at the present moment, while the augment denotes a momentary action in past time. The original form of the root is *da*, *sta*, thence *dada*, *stasta*.

The first root is shortened in the final sound, as in

---

* This is inserted here as the first tense-stem, because, with the omission of reduplication and vowel-intensification, it exhibits the pure verbal root, while the present stem in so many formations departs further from it, and the simple aorist betrays a secondary character in the augment and secondary personal endings.

λέλοιπα; in the commencing sound, as πέπληγα; the aspirate is dropped, as πέφηνα; the first sound of the reduplication is dropped, as ἔκτονα; instead of the root-vowel ε is the vowel of the reduplicated syllable. The so-called Attic reduplication in verbs which begin with α, ε, ο is partly the doubling of the whole root, as ὄδωδα, ὄπωπα, in simple root-verbs; and partly the doubling of the first part of the verbal stem, as ἀλήλιφα (ἀλιφ secondary root of ἀλείφω), εἰλήλουθα stem ἐλυθ, ἀγήγερκα, ἀκήκοα, ἀρηρομένος Il. XVIII. 548, ἐρηρέδαται XXIII. 284, compare ἀραίρηκα Ionic; further see the Grammars and Sec. 34, 9.

2. The root-vowel is lengthened sometimes in the first, sometimes in the second stage, Sec. 8: as λέληθα from the root λαθ; ἔᾱγα, Ionic ἔηγα = Ϝεϝαγα, ϝαγ; ἔκτονα, κτεν; ἔοργα = Ϝεϝοργα, ϝεργ; πέφευγα, φυγ; ἔρρωγα, ϝραγ; οἶδα, ϝιδ; the lengthened vowel is dropped in the plural, ἴδμεν, ἴσμεν; ἔοικα from εἰκ, ϝικ, dual ἔϊκτον: compare the pluperfect plural ἐπέπιθμεν from πέποιθα and the shortened plural forms of the perfect βέβᾰμεν, τέθνᾰμεν, τέτλᾰμεν, ἔστᾰμεν, δέδῐμεν from the singulars τέτληκα, δέδοικα, etc., syncop. ἄνωγμεν.

3. Stem termination α: γέγονα(μι), οἶδα, Æolic ϝοίδημι; shortened personal endings under the influence of the reduplication, as in the compound aorist; 3rd plural ασι = *anti*, primary ending; 3rd plural middle Epic and Ionic αται for the original ανται, Sec. 53, also in vowel root-endings. Consonant root-endings are in part aspirated, ἔρχαται (εἴργω), ἐτετάχατο.

4. A later peculiarity of the perfect stem, unknown as yet to Homer, is the aspiration of the final consonant of the root in one class of verbs; δέδηχα from root δακ; εἴλοχα for λέλογα from λεγ; πέπρᾶχα, transitive, and intransitive πέπρᾶγα; κέκοφα, by the side of an older Homeric κεκοπώς from κοπ.

The simple Greek pluperfect which expresses the idea of completeness in past time is formed from the perfect stem with the augment and secondary personal endings. This formation is found in the active only in isolated instances, and is confined (a) partly to plural forms which themselves differ from those of the perfect in augment only, under the influence of which the lengthened vowel also disappears, as ἐπέπιθμεν from the perfect πέποιθα, ἐδείδιμεν, ἐδείδιε, with ending σαν in the 3rd person plural, as ἐτέθνασαν, without augment μέμασαν; (β) partly to forms from the 1st person singular with the secondary personal ending ον in analogy to the imperfect; as ἐμέμηκον from the perfect μέμηκα, from root μακ in μηκάομαι, ἤνωγον from ἄνωγα, which is not to be regarded as an imperfect from ἀνώγω a present formed from ἄνωγα; on ἠνώγεα, ἠνώγει, ἀνώγει, see Compound Pluperfect; compare this form of the pluperfect from the compound perfect ἐπέφυκον; dual forms εἴκτην, ἐκγεγάτην. The middle always has, on the other hand, simple forms of the pluperfect in the 1st person singular μην from the perfect in μαι, with secondary personal endings and augment, as ἐλελύμην from λέλυμαι.

LIX. Latin Simple or Strong Perfect.

In Greek only, where the aorist exists side by side with the perfect for the purpose of expressing momentary action in past time, the perfect serves exclusively to express completion in present time. In Latin, since there is no aorist, the perfect serves a double office, to indicate the completion of an act in present time—the perfect proper; and its momentary occurrence in past time—historic or aorist perfect. The chief method of formation is here also originally the reduplication of the root to express immediate action, which is then at once removed to the past. The reduplication is only partially adopted.

The stem-ending or tach-vowel is *i* (*ei*). 1st singular *i* (*ei*) for *eim*, as *fero* from *feromi*. 2nd singular and plural *sti, stis;* compare the combination σθ in the Greek personal endings φῆσθα, τίθησθα, 1st person plural middle μεσθα, infinitive σθαι. 3rd singular *it* from *eit* with original lengthening of the *i*, which is shortened in the 1st person plural *imus;* *i* is elided in syncopated forms as *dixti, scripsti* from *dicsi-sti, scripsi-sti*. The long *i* in the 3rd person singular is retained in *vixit, vendidit, dedit*, etc., in Old Latin, and in part by the later poets. 3rd plural *ērunt, ēre, dederunt* from *dedi-sont*, compounds with *esonti*, compare ἴσασι, Sec. 52,—where the *i* is transformed into *e* by the influence of the *r* which takes the place of *s* between two vowels.

Latin Perfect. 123

1. Perfect forms in which the reduplication is retained. The root-vowel retained in the reduplication: *tutudi*, root *tud, pupugi, poposci, momordi, didici* from *disco = dic-sco*, compare *doceo*, root *dic*, as *dak* in διδάσκω,—and the archaic forms, *peposci, memordi*.

Reduplicated vowel *e*, especially when the root-vowel is *a* or a vowel derived from *a* through intensification or weakening: *dedi* from *da, cecini, pepigi, cecīdi, fefelli, tetigi, peperi, peperci, tetini* archaic; *cecīdi* from *caedo* (*ae = ai*), *tetuli* archaic *tuli*, from root *tol* in *tollo = tal*, τλα in τλῆναι; *pepuli* from *pello*, compare πάλλω. Where the root begins with *st, sp, sc*, the root-syllable loses the *s* and retains only the mute: *steti* root *sta* for *stesti* (dissimilation), so also *spopondi, scicidi* archaic form in connection with *scidi;* compare the reduplicated present *sisto = ἵστημι, sistāmi*.

The reduplication is for the most part found only in simple verbs; it is dropped in compound ones, as *expuli*, yet it is retained in verbs derived from *do, sto: abdidi, abstiti;* syncope occurs after the prefix *re*, as *reppuli = repepuli, rettuli, rettudi, repperi*, where there is no assimilation arising from the original *red*.

The vowel of the root-syllable. The vowel of the present *a* becomes *e*, or *i*, before two consonants and before *r: fefelli, peperci, peperi, cecini*. The present-vowel *e* becomes *u* before *l* as *pepuli*, but compare *tetendi*. Roots ending in *a* lose the root-vowel in the root-syllable: *da — dedi, sta — steti*, after monosyllabic prefixes the vowel of the reduplication becomes *i; abdidi, condidi*. Compare the change of the root-vowel in the compound verbs, *caedo, occīdo, cecīdi; pango, impingo, pepigi; cado, incĭdo, cecĭdi; cano, occino, cecini.* The influence of the reduplication as well as of the prefixes weakens the vowel because the accent is thrown back.

The amplification of the present is dropped in the reduplicated perfect: *tutudi, pupugi,* present *pungo, pepigi pango, peperi* the *i* in *pario* being dropped, which belongs to the present stem only, Sec. 39, *momordi* by the side of the denominative present form *mordeo, pepuli,* in which the second *l*, which originated in *i, j,* is dropped.

2. Perfect forms in which the reduplication is dropped: *tuli, scĭdi,* from *tetuli, scicidi; fĭdi* from *fid, findo;* in compounds as *comperi,* see above; as well as in those perfects whose stem coincides with the present, as *fui, plui, pandi, cudi* (*cūdo*), *verti, scandi, prehendi,* these probably arose from reduplicated forms such as *fufui, veverti.*

3. Perfect forms in which the vowel of the root-syllable is lengthened to compensate for the dropping of the reduplication; *ā* from *ă: lavi, cavi, favi, pavi; ē* instead of *ā* from *ă: feci = fefici, cepi, fregi, jeci, egi, pegi; ē* from *ĕ: veni, sedi* (from original stem-verbs, *venĕre, sedĕre,* compare *sido; venio, sedeo* are presents with denominative stem forms, *legi, edi, emi; ī* from *ĭ: vidi* root *vid* (*video* denominative), *vici, liqui; ū* from *ŭ: fudi, fugi, iuvi, rupi; ō* from *ŏ: fodi, movi, vovi.* The length of the

vowel of the root-syllable is occasioned by the dropping of the first consonant: *jēci=jejici, ēgi=egigi, lēgi=leligi.* All simple perfects therefore have originally sprung from reduplicated ones. The reduplication was either retained with a shortened root-vowel or dropped and the root-vowel lengthened instead.

LX. Greek Simple or Strong, so-called Second, Aorist.

The stem of the strong aorist is, with a few exceptions, the same as the simple verbal root. This in its unmodified state, as distinguished from the present stem, expresses momentary and transient action. Further formative materials are, for the indicative mood, the augment expressing past time inserted as a prefix before the root, and, through its influence, secondary personal terminations. An aorist form, like ἔβην root βα, coincides, as in ἔφην, with the imperfect of a verb, which in the present also shows only the bare root; but this is, like βῶ, βαίην, etc., in distinction from φῶ, φαίην, to be recognised as an aorist from the fact, that from the root βα no present form with naked root, such as βημι, is in use; ἔβην therefore, coexisting with the present βαίνω, is used as an aorist, while ἔφην with an original durative signification is used as an imperfect. The Homeric dialect frequently employs the reduplication in an intensive signification, with or without the augment, in order to form the strong aorist: πέπιθον, ἔειπον = ἐϝεϝεπον, ἔπεφνον with syncope of the root-vowel, root φεν; ἐσπόμην = σεσεπ., Epic and Attic εἶπον = ϜεϜεπ., ἤγαγον ἀγαγεῖν; ἠνίπαπον, ἠρύκακον reduplicated Epic aorist with repetition of the final consonant instead of the first root consonant.

1. Forms from the root-ending, without a tach-vowel, are almost entirely confined to roots with vowel-endings: ἔβην, ἔφθην, ἔσβην, ἔτλην, ἔγνων, ἑάλων stem ἁλω, ἐβίων, ἔδυν, ἔφυν, 3rd person singular ἔκτα, οὖτα, 1st person plural ἔθεμεν, ἔδομεν, 3rd person plural ἔβαν; ἔθεσαν in composition, Sec. 52. Conjunctive-optative, Sec. 55, θῶ = θεω(μι), θῇς, θείης = θεησι, θείην, etc. Imperative τλῆθι, κλῦθι, πῖθι, reduplicated κέκλυθι, Sec. 52. Middle ἐθέμην, ἐφθί'μην, optative φθί'μην, 3rd singular πλῆτο, λύτο, σύτο, χύτο, ἄμπνυτο. Epic middle forms from verbs with consonantal root-endings without a tach-vowel: γέντο, δέκτο, λέκτο, πάλτο, ἄλσο 2nd singular, ἆλτο 3rd singular, ὦρτο, μῖκτο, πῆκτο. Infinitive πέρθαι = περθ-σθαι, λέχθαι, ὄρθαι, δέχθαι. Participle ἄλμενος, ἄρμενος, δέγμενος, ἄσμενος, Sec. 21, used adjectivally with σ from δ. Imperative λέξο, δέξο, ὄρσο, Sec. 63, 3.

2. Forms with tach-vowel: ἔλιπον, ἔφυγον, ἔλαβον. Middle ἐλιπόμην. The moods correspond to those of the present. For reduplicated forms, see above. To these forms with unaltered short root-vowel (λιπ, φυγ), the ear itself attaches the idea of momentary action, whereas the lengthened present-imperfect form by its sound and length expresses the idea of duration, compare ἔλιπε, ἔλειπε.

3. Forms with change of vowel—with syncope of the radical vowel or metathesis, as in ἔπραθον from πέρθω, a special change of the root in the strong aorist—in order to distinguish the aorist from the imperfect: ἔκτανον, root κτεν, ἔτραπον, imperfect ἔτρεπον.

The aorist formation has been lost in Latin through the want both of the augment and of the distinction between primary and secondary personal endings. The following verbal forms are regarded as sporadic remnants of the simple aorist; *parentes, parents*, in meaning = οἱ τεκόντες, in contradistinction to the strengthened present form *parientes* = οἱ τίκτοντες; the archaic indicative *tago, tagit* with the present *tango*, compare the Homeric reduplicated aorist τεταγών; *pagunt* with the present *pango*, root *pag*, compare πήγνυμι, passive aorist ἐπάγην. An aorist form distinct from the present cannot exist in Latin except where the present stem is strengthened by *i, j*, or by the introduction of nasal sounds, the omission of which makes the recognition of the aorist possible.

LXI. Greek and Latin Present Stems.

The present stem comprises a very numerous series of forms. These are caused by the addition of vowels and consonants to the root, by lengthening the root at the beginning, in the middle, and at the end, and they often differ very widely from the root. Each of these forms has its peculiar meaning, denoted by the suffix or the infix, which need not here be more fully specified—intensive, durative, inchoative, iterative, desiderative, causative, intransitive, passive. The present is distinguished by the primary personal endings both from the imperfect, even where this latter has no augment, and from the strong aorist, and especially from the latter by its lengthened root.

1. Present stems identical with the simple root, to which is added the personal ending. (α) Forms without tach-vowel. Vowel-root ι, φα: plural ἴμεν, ἴτε, ἴασι = *imasi, itasi, ianti;* φαμέν, φατέ,—φᾱσί = φαντί Doric, with compensatory lengthening—φάθι. In the singular the root-vowel is lengthened, εἶμι, φημί, etc. There is a change of quantity between the singular and plural in such primitive forms; the stem is strengthened in the singular where the termination is lighter, but lightened in the plural, the terminations of which were originally heavier. Compare Perfect, Sec. 58, 2. Consonantal root ἐς, thence εἰμί = ἐσμι, Æolic ἔμμι, Sec. 52. Latin *sum*, etc., Sec. 52. From the root *i*, *to go*, the supine *itum* shows the bare root; *ed*, *to eat*, for the 2nd singular, see Sec. 52, 3rd singular *est* = *edt*, dissim. = *edti*, so *volt, fert, dat, stat;* 1st plural *dămus, dătis;* passive *dătur;* so *se* is joined immediately to the root in the infinitive in *esse, to be, esse, to eat* = *edse, ferre* = *ferse, velle* with progressive assimilation = *velse, volse*, Sec. 40. (β) Forms with a tach-vowel: τίω, τίομεν, compare ἴμεν, φέρω, λέγω. Latin root *i, to go*, in 1st singular *eo* = *io*, 3rd plural *eunt* = *iunt*, conjunctive *eam* = *iam*, participle *iens*, with inflexion of the tach-vowel (*i* is changed to *e*, except in *iens*,—but on the other

Present Stems.

hand compare *euntis*,—before all endings beginning with a vowel); *veho, lego*.

2. The vowel of the simple root is strengthened (α) where there is immediate addition of the personal ending. Sporadic strengthening occurs in the indicative singular of primitive verbs: root ι, present stem ει, thence εἰμί, εἶς, εἶ = εἶσι, εἶσθα, 3rd singular εἶσι. Conjunctive and optative ἴω, ἴοις, are inflected with a tach-vowel; ἴομεν, ἰοίην, Sec. 55. Root φα, present stem φη, φημί, φῇς, φησί. Latin root *i*, strengthened to $\bar{i} = ei$: *īs, īt, īmus, ītis*, (compare on the other hand *ĭmen*,) passive *ītur*, imperative *ī, īte*, infinitive *īre*. Compare *dās, stāmus, stātis, stāre; fāmur, fāri*. Also in Greek, η remains in the plural of verbs in ημι, which are secondary forms of verbs in εω, as the Æolic ὄρημι, φόρημι, αἴτημι. (β) Where inflexion with the tach-vowel occurs the strengthening of the vowel is universal: φεύγω, φυγ; λείπω, λιπ; λήθω, λαθ; τήκω, τακ; τεύχω, τυχ; τρώγω, τραγ; τίω, also with ῐ, τι. Verbs in εω, as ῥέω, χέω, πλέω, from a root in υ, ῥυ, χυ, πλυ, had in the present an original vowel-strengthening from υ to ευ, but the υ changed into ϝ afterwards disappeared, compare γλυκύς, genitive γλυκέος from εϝος; further strengthening in πλώω, ῥώω, χώομαι, besides the more frequent Epic πλείω, Latin *dūco* from *dŭc* in *dux, dŭcis; dīco* from *dĭc* in *indĭcare, causidĭcus, veridĭcus, maledĭcus; fīdo* from *fĭd* in *fĭdes, perfĭdus; nūbo* co-existing with *pronŭba*.

3. Reduplication of the root with the vowel ι of the

present-tense reduplication, which has an intensive-durative signification, while the vowel of a root which ends in a vowel is lengthened in the singular: root δo, present stem διδο, singular διδω, δίδωμι; στα, ιστα, ιστη, ἵστημι; θε, τιθε, τίθημι; ἐ, ἰε = ἰέ, ἰη, ἵημι = *jijāmi*. Compare δίζημαι, Sec. 32, with ζ = δj. Plural without lengthening, δίδομεν, ἵσταμεν, τίθεμεν, ἵεμεν. Root δε, *to bind*, δίδη imperfect Il. XI. 105, διδέντων Od. XII. 54; root βα, βιβάς; root χρα, κίχρημι. Nasalised reduplication πίμπλημι, πίμπρημι from πλα, πρα in πλήθω, πρήθω.

Reduplicated present stems with a tach-vowel: γίγνομαι root γεν = γιγεν., πίπτω = πιπετω, μίμνω = μιμενω; ἵζω root ἑδ, *sed* = ἱεδjω, compare *sīdo* = *sisedo*, see also (by reason of the suffix *ja*) see under 5 below; λιλαίομαι, γιγνώσκω, διδράσκω, τιτύσκομαι, πιφαύσκω with suffix σκ. The present reduplication may be retained in other tense-stems: ἰαύω root ἀF, Sec. 31, ἰάπτω, ἰάχω = FιFαχ, ἰάλλω, τιταίνω, διδάσκω; compare future διδώσω Od. XIII. 358. Diphthongal reduplication in δαιδάλλω, παιπάλλω, παιφάσσω, ποιπνύω, δείδω, δειδίσκομαι; the simple root-vowel is repeated and nasalised in παμφαίνω. More uncertain and irregular reduplication in παπταίνω from root πτα, πτακ in πτήσσω, ἀραρίσκω, μαρμαίρω, μερμηρίζω, Sec. 27, καχλάζω, παφλάζω Il. XIII. 798, root φλα, Sec. 25, πορφύρω root φυρ, Sec. 37, ὀπιπεύω root ὀπ, Sec. 19, 2, δενδίλλω Il. IX. 180, τηλεθάω root θαλ, ἀπαφίσκω stem ἀπαφ, aorist ἀπαφεῖν, root ἀφ, νηνέω from νέω in παρενήνεον Od. I. 147.

Latin *gigno* = *gigeno*, as γίγνομαι, *sido*, *sisto*, compare the perfect reduplication *steti* Sec. 59, 1, *sero*, *I sow*,

Present Stems. 131

= *seso, siso,*—with *e* before *r* for *i* as *dederunt = dedisont,*—
root *sa, sătum,* compound perfect *se-vi.* Verbs with
original and stable reduplication, *coquo* Sec. 19, 2; *bibo*
= *pipo,* root *pi,* πι in πῖθι compare *potus* Sec. 18; *vivo*
Greek root βι Sec. 22; *dedo*₁ according to the analogy of
the perfect reduplication.

4. Present stem with consonantal suffixes: νυ with intensification of the root-vowel, ζεύγνυμι, δείκνυμι, ῥήγνυμι, πήγνυμι; without intensification, ὄρνυμι, ἕννυμι, in which the first ν is assimilated from σ, ὄλλυμι from ὀλν, with progressive assimilation; στορέννυμι = στορεσν. stem στορεσ, etc. These are all denominative. Suffix να: δάμνημι, κίρνημι (κεράννυμι), σκίδνημι by the side of σκεδάννυμι, πίλναμαι; also with the suffix *ja*: ἱκνέομαι, κυνέω (ἔκυσα), δαμνάω (ἐδάμην). Suffix ν: πίνω (πιεῖν, πῖθι), τίνω, κάμνω, δάκνω, τέμνω, φθάνω, φθίνω. Suffix αν: ἱκάνω compare ἱκανός, κιχάνω, αὐξάνω, ἁμαρτάνω; with nasal infix λαγχάνω, λανθάνω, λαμβάνω, θιγγάνω, μανθάνω, χανδάνω, compare θάμβος, θαμβέω, τάφος, ἔταφον, root ταφ, nasalised θαμβ.

Latin *lino, le-vi, sino, sī-vi, sĭtum, cerno, cre-vi, sterno, stra-vi, sperno, spre-vi, pōno,* from *posno, posino, po-sĭ-tus.* Present stem with nasal strengthening without suffix: *tango (tag), findo, fundo, rumpo, scindo, tundo.* The nasal consonant grows into the root and becomes fixed in *fingo, finxi, pingo, jungo,* by the side of *figulus, pictum, jugum.*

5. Suffix *ja, j, i,* according to the different changes determined by the laws of sound. *J* vocalised δαίομαι root δα, ἐδασάμην; ἰδίω with fixed ι Sec. 39, 3 '*j* thrown

back as *i*, βαίνω = βανjω root βα, suffixes ν and *j*, φαίνω, τείνω, πείρω (περ, ἔπαρον, πέπαρμαι), εἴλω = ἐλjω (ἀλῆναι), κρῖνω = κρινjω future κρῐνῶ, κρινέω, aorist participle κρῐθείς, πλῡνω πλῠνῶ, κλῑνω κλῠνῶ, ἐκλῐθην; *j* as a mixed sound according to Sec. 34, 3 : ὄζω — ὀδj., ἔζομαι — ἐδj., φράζω aorist πέφραδον, κράζω root κραγ; τάσσω root ταγ, τακ, πτήσσω root πτακ, πτύσσω root πτυχ, φρίσσω root φρικ, λίσσομαι root λιτ; *j* assimilated in ἅλλομαι compare *salio*, βάλλω, θάλλω (τεθηλώς, θάλος), πάλλω, σφάλλω, ἀγγέλλω, στέλλω, ὀφέλλω Homeric, connected with ὀφείλω, as εἴλω with ἴλλω; *j* is dropped between the vowels in ὀπύω, by the side of ὀπυίω, also φύω, Æolic φυίω, θύω. Compare Latin verbs in *io* of the 3rd conjugation with *i* syncopated as *cupio cupĭmus, capio, fugio, fodio, morior, patior, gradior*, as opposed to the fixed *j* contracted to *ī* in the 4th conjugation; *ero* = *esjo, erunt* = *esjunt*, as ἔσσομαι = ἐσj., which is a present with future signification. J is dropped in derived verbs in *uo*, as *statuo, tribuo*, in verbs in *eo* as *moneo*, in *ao*, or *o*, as *amo* for *amajo, amas* = *amais*. J is assimilated in *pello* compare πάλλω, *percello, fallo* compare σφάλλω, *vello, curro*.

6. The suffix σκ has generally an inchoative signification which may easily be recognised,—compare the diminutive suffix ισκο in νεανίσκος and *adolescens;* βάσκω, φάσκω, θνήσκω, reduplicated γιγνώσκω, διδράσκω, πιφαύσκω, μιμνήσκω; it is found with a subsidiary vowel ἀρέσκω, ἀλίσκομαι, ἀραρίσκω, εὑρίσκω, ἐπαυρίσκω; in denominalives γηράσκω. One of the root consonants is sometimes dropped before σκ, as διδάσκω from stem διδαχ.

Present Stems. 133

root δαχ, δακ, see δα Sec. 21, δειδίσκομαι root δικ, εἴσκω root ἰκ, τιτύσκομαι root τυκ, τυχ Sec. 17, λάσκω root λακ; σκ is aspirated in πάσχω root παθ or πα; instead of σκ we find χ in ἔρχομαι from ἐρσκ root ἐρ = ὀρ in ὄρνυμι, connected with ἐλ in ἐλθεῖν; κ is weakened to γ in μίσγω, compare *misceo* root μιγ, *mic*, Sec. 27. An iterative signification of this suffix appears in the Epic and Ionic iterative forms of the imperfect and aorist to denote that a continuous action is repeated or that an action is begun in time past; ἔχεσκον, δόσκον. Compare Latin *nascor, pasco, nosco, cresco, disco = dicsco, posco = porcsco* root *porc, proc, prec* in *precor, procus*, Sec. 18; *apiscor, adipiscor, paciscor, proficiscor, revivisco*, nasalised *nanciscor;* of denominatives *obdormisco, concupisco, obliviscor, inveterasco, aresco, maturesco, delitesco*.

7. The dental suffix *ta* or further formation of the root by means of the determinative *t*—compare *t* in passive participles and verbal adjectives—is mainly found after labials; τύπτω root τυπ, κρύπτω compare κρύφα, ῥάπτω compare ῥαφή, θάπτω ἐτάφην, βάπτω βαφή, ἅπτω ἀφή, βλάπτω ἐβλάβην βλάβη, ἰάπτω, Sec. 32, 4, ἐγχρίμπτω nasalised; after gutturals, τίκτω τεκ, πέκτω πεκ; after a vowel ἀνύτω connected with ἀνύω. Compare *pecto, necto, flecto;* *t* is weakened to *d* in *tendo, -fendo* root θεν Sec. 24.

8. The aspirated suffix or root determinative θ is found in πρήθω, πλήθω, Sec. 36, 4, φθινύθω, ἔσθω ἐσθίω by dissimilation from the stem ἐδθ, αἴσθω, βαρύθω, θαλέθω, lengthened Homeric forms ἠγερέθονται, participle with

present reduplication, βιβάσθων, ἔσχεθον from aorist ἔσχον, imperfect ὀρέχθεον Il. XXIII. 30, of ὀρέγω, μετεκίαθον Od. I. 22.

9. In Greek and Latin the present stem very generally exhibits the form of derived verbs, the other tense stems that of primitive verbs, Sec. 39, 4; but the inverse relation also exists, e.g., in πέτομαι πετήσομαι, *petĭmus petīvi petītum, cupĭmus cupīvi*.

LXII. GREEK IMPERFECT.

The imperfect, which expresses duration in past time, is formed by annexing the prefix of past time to the present stem which conveys the idea of duration, as well as to stem-lengthenings, expressive of this idea and its modifications, with secondary personal endings. (a) Formation without tach-vowel: ἐτίθην, ἐδίδων, ἵστην, ἵην, ἐδείκνυν; ἔφην Sec. 60. Root ἐς 1st sing. ἦν with the σ dropped, ἦ with the ν rejected, ἦα, ἔα Ionic, 2nd sing. with the radical σ, ἦσθα, ἔησθα; 3rd sing. ἦν, ἦε(ν), ἔην, ἦην. 1st plural ἦμεν, Doric ἦμες; 2nd plural ἦτε, ἦστε, compare dual Sec. 52; 3rd plural ἦσαν from ἤσαντ, without augment ἔσαν, but retaining the σ of the root: on the other hand the Ionic present is ἔασι: early imperfect with a tach-vowel ἔον.

Εἶμι, Epic imperfect ἤια, Attic ᾖα, ᾔειν, Attic plural ᾔειμεν with augment and present-tense intensification by the side of Epic ἴτην, ἴμεν, ἴσαν; Epic ἤομεν, ἤιον by the side of ἤισαν Sec. 52, with transition to the tach-vowel conjugation. Compare Latin *eram* from *esam*, *asam*, with *m* in the 1st person singular as in *sum*, *inquam*, and in the compound imperfect in *bam* from *fuam*, a formation which, in default of the augment, and different primary and secondary personal endings, the language readily adopts. For the conjunctive optative of the imperfect *eram*, *essem*,—*sem*,—*rem* in composition, see Sec. 72.

(β) For the inflexion with tach-vowel ἔφερον, see Sec. 52. Contracted verbs ἐτίμων, etc., from ἐτίμαον, *j* being dropped between the verbal stem and the personal ending. Forms of inflexion without tach-vowel, as ἐτίθεις, ἐδίδουν, ἴεις, follow the example of the contracted verbs. 3rd plural σαν Sec. 52. Middle forms Sec. 53.

(2) COMPOUND TENSE-STEMS.

A. GREEK COMPOUND TENSES.

LXIII. COMPOUND AORIST. WEAK OR SIGMATIC (SO-CALLED 'FIRST') AORIST.

1. Relation to the strong aorist. Its function is the same as that of the simple aorist, to express momentary action in past time. But as the latter can only be formed from such (mostly root) verbs as have a present stem different from the bare stem or the root, whether this stem be vocalic, as πείθω, or consonantal as τύπτω, βάλλω, μανθάνω, πάσχω, the compound aorist, originally a supplementary one, is annexed to pure verbs, denominative verbs, and all verbs whose present stem is

the root itself, as in ἄρχω, λέγω, γράφω, or a mere nominal stem, lengthened by *j*, as in ἐλπίζω, φυλάσσω, τελέω, Sec. 39, 2. Only a comparatively small number of verbs, *e.g.* those with vowel lengthening or a dental suffix in the present, as πείθω, λείπω, τύπτω, and verbs in μι, have both aorist forms, in some cases with the difference of an intransitive, or neutral, and a transitive, or active signification, as for example ἴστημι, βαίνω. On the other hand the same verb very frequently has, besides the weak aorist active, the so-called second or strong aorist passive formed from the bare root, that is, from the stem of the strong aorist active with ε, η annexed, as ζεύγνυμι, ἔζευξα, ἐζύγην; βλάπτω, ἔβλαψα, ἐβλάβην. The formation of the compound aorist has, in the later period of the language, even where the strong aorist might have existed, displaced and overgrown the latter.

2. Formation of the compound aorist. The past tense of the root *as*, ἔς (*asam*) '*to be*' is annexed to the verbal stem as auxiliary verb, with a long vowel in vowel stems, together with the augment. The vowel which begins the auxiliary verb is dropped. μ or ν falls away in the 1st sing. The stem-ending is α, only in 3rd sing. ε, ἔδειξε *adik-s-a(t)*. Second sing. imperative—ον. Original form from root *dik* was *adiksa(m)*, conjunctive *diksāmi*, optative *dik-saimi*. So ἔλυσα, λύσω, λύσαιμι. Middle ἐλυσάμην, λύσωμαι, λυσαίμην. 2nd sing. ἐλύσω from ἐλύσασο. Imperative active λῦσον, with fixed ν and ο instead of α; middle λῦσαι instead of, as would

Greek Future. 137

be expected, λυσασο, λυσω, compare the present form λύον from λυεο, λυεσο. σ is doubled in ἔσσα, root ϝες, ἐτέλεσσα, connected with ἐτέλεσα, stem τελες, τελέω, τελείω = τελεσjω. σ is dropped after ϝ in ἔκηα = ἐκηϝa, ἔχεα Homeric ἔχευα = ἐχεϝa, root χυ; after stems ending in λ, μ, ν, ρ, with compensatory lengthening, as ἔστειλα, ἔνειμα, ἔφηνα—for ἔστελσα, εμσα, ανσα,—ἤμῡνα, ἔκρινα, ἔκειρα by the side of Homeric ἔκελσα, ὦρσα, ἔκερσα, κύρσας. The σ is assimilated in the Æolic ἔνεμμα, ἔστελλαν, ἐγέννατο. Denominatives with *ja*, and contracted verbs, have, as in the future, a long vowel before the auxiliary verb, and α at the end of a stem is generally lengthened to η; ἐφίλησα, ἐτίμησα, ἐδήλωσα, except ἤροσα, ἐκάλεσα, ἤνεσα, and also, in analogy to verbs with the nominal stem ες, ἐτέλεσα. Æolic optative forms are λύσεια, λύσειας, λύσειε, 3rd plural λύσειαν, instead of, as would be expected, λυσειην, λυσειης, λυσειη, λυσειεν in analogy to ἱείην, τιθείην.

3. The earlier sigmatic aorist formation had a tach-vowel instead of the stem-ending α as in the imperfect and strong aorist of the O-conjugation; Homeric ἷξον, ἷξες = ἱκσ., ἐβήσετο, δύσετο, more frequent in the imperative λέξεο, ἄξετε, ὄρσεο, ὄρσεν; ὄρσο, δέξο, λέξο with ε elided from ὄρσεσο, etc.; οἷσε, οἴσετε, βήσεο, δύσεο.

LXIV. The Greek Future.

This is formed like the compound aorist by means of an auxiliary verb from the root ἐς, but in the form of a present lengthened by the suffix *ja*, which as in many present stems, Sec. 61, gives it a future signification. Original form *asjami*, in the Greek ἐσjω, weakened to ἐσω, σω compare Latin *ero* from *esio*. This form is preserved as an independent word in the middle voice, ἔσσομαι = ἐσj., whence ἔσομαι. Original form of the compound tense-stem *dasjami* = δώσω. Primary personal-endings as in the present. The various forms of the future are determined by the fuller or weaker form of the auxiliary verb, which is always added to the verbal stem after the final letter (α) by retaining or dropping the σ of the root of the auxiliary verb, (β) by vocalising *j* into ι, (γ) by changing ι into ε, or (δ) by dropping the original *j*.

1. The original Doric future in σιω = σjω, as πραξίομες from πραγσj, φυλαξίομες, δωσίω; compare desideratives in σειω.

2. The so-called Doric future, with ι changed to ε in the Attic middle forms, as φευξοῦμαι from φευγσεομαι, πλευσοῦμαι, so also ἐσσεῖται, by the side of ἔσσεται.

3. The ordinary form in which *j* is dropped, and the ending shortened to σω in stems which end in a mute or a vowel, as λύ'σω, στήσω, δώσω, ἐάσω, τιμήσω; τύψω, λείψω, πράξω. The stem-vowel is lengthened as in the present in φεύξομαι, independently of the present in πλεύσομαι, τεύξομαι, πεύσομαι, ἐλεύσομαι, φθήσομαι, λήψομαι etc. The present reduplication is sometimes retained in

the future; Homeric διδώσω Sec. 61, 3. Futures with a short vowel-stem-ending ἀρόσω, καλέσω; see also Compound Aorist.

4. The asigmatic future results from dropping the σ between vowels, and the insertion of a tach-vowel ε between the stem and the ending, which can also be considered as a retention of the first sound of the auxiliary verb εσω. In liquid stems, uncontracted Epic and Ionic τενέω from τενεσω, κτενέω, μενέω, or contracted βαλῶ, φανῶ, ἀμυνῶ Attic, by the side of isolated Epic forms where σ is retained without a tach-vowel, θέρσομαι, κύρσω, κέλσω, κέρσω, φύρσω in stems in ρ and λ; in other stems, as ἐδοῦμαι from ἐδεσομαι, μαχοῦμαι, Epic and Ionic μαχέσομαι, πεσοῦμαι Epic πεσέομαι, τελέω Epic, τελῶ Attic, so too τελέσσω, τελέσω, like the present, which itself indeed = τελεσjω, Sec. 39, 2; κομιῶ, κομιέω, κομιέομεν from κομισεω,* without subsidiary vowel βιβῶ from βιβάσω, ἐλῶ, ἐλᾷς, δαμῶ from δαμάσω, δαμᾷς. This is the so-called Attic future in which σ is rejected and the word contracted. Future form without σ and contraction in verbal stems in υ, as ἀνύω for ἀνύσω Il. IV. 56; ἐρύω XI. 454 *et passim;* τανύω Od. XXI. 174. The latter by dropping the original σ pass into future forms which resemble the present.

* So Curtius, Gramm. Sec. 263. Perhaps more correctly from κομι-εσω; stem κομι, connected with κομιδή, whence κομίζω = κομιjω, by the side of κομέω in κομέειν Od. VI. 207; so there lies at the root of the future forms ἐλπιῶ, φροντιῶ, by the side of ἐλπίσω, φροντίσω, ἐρίσω, from δσω, the weaker nominal stem ἐλπι, for ἐλπιδ, thence the future ἐλπιεσω, ἐλπιῶ.

5. The future without tense-characteristic. As such εἶμι Epic, Ionic, and Attic is especially used; the Epic verbal forms βέομαι, βείομαι, 2nd singular βέῃ, root βι Sec. 22, δήω, ἔδομαι, πίομαι, νέομαι, by the side of the future form νίσομαι Il. XXIII. 76, χέομαι compare aor. ἔχεα with loss of both σ and ϝ, as τελέω, τελῶ from τελέσω.

LXV. THE COMPOUND OR WEAK GREEK PERFECT AND PLUPERFECT, TOGETHER WITH THE FUTURUM EXACTUM.

1. The perfect in κα is found in Homer only when the root ends in a vowel, and then not in all forms. βέβηκα coexists with 1st plural βέβᾰμεν, 3rd plural βεβάασι, βεβαώς; ἕστηκα, ἕσταμεν, 2nd plural also ἕστητε; τέτληκα root τλα, τέτλαμεν, τετληώς; τέθνηκα root θνα, Homeric infinitive τεθνάμεν; κέκμηκα root κμα κεκμηώς; πέφυκα 3rd plural πεφύασι, δέδοικα plural δέδιμεν. In the later language κα is found after vowel, dental, and liquid stems, as πέπεικα, ἔσταλκα, ἔφθαρκα, κέκρῐκα, τέτακα, moreover ἐδήδοκα from the lengthened original stem ἐδ side by side with ἐδηδώς. Akin to this form of the perfect are the aorist forms ἔθηκα, ἔδωκα, ἧκα from the vowel roots θε, δο, ἑ, confined however to the indicative. In regard to κ lengthening the stem in ὀλεκ ὀλέκω, compare the perfect ὀλώλεκα, and in ἥκω from root ἑ in ἵημι with a fixed perfect signification compare ἱλήκω in ἱλήκῃσι Od. XXI. 365. As regards the root-form πτακ in πτήσσω by the side of πτα in πτήτην, δακ, δαχ in διδάσκω by the side

Aorist and Future Passive. 141

of δα in δαῆναι, ἐρύκω by the side of ἐρύω, the κ of the perfect comes to be considered as an original root determinative applied to form the tense.

2. The compound pluperfect in the earlier language is found chiefly in intransitive verbs, the perfect of which has the signification of the present. It is formed by the addition of a past tense from the root ἐς to the perfect stem; 1st sing. originally εσα(μ), compare ἦν ἔα *eram* Sec. 62, thence εα, η, ειν: ἐπεποίθεα Ionic and Epic, thence η, ειν Attic, compare πόλεις from πολεας. 2nd sing. originally εσας, thence εας Ionic and Epic, ης, εις Attic. 3rd sing. originally εσε(τ), thence εε(ν) Ionic, ει, η, ειν Attic. 3rd plural εσαν in which σ is retained.

3. The middle-passive futurum exactum, which expresses completion in futurity, is formed by the addition of the future ending in the middle form to the perfect stem, which implies the idea of completion. λελύσομαι perfect stem λελυ from λέλυμαι, πεπράξεται stem πεπραγ, γεγράψεται, δεδήσεται. Isolated forms of the futurum exactum active from the perfect in κα: τεθνήξω, ἑστήξω.

LXVI. THE GREEK AORIST AND FUTURE PASSIVE.

1. The simpler form of the passive aorist, and the form more closely allied to the strong aorist active— whence it also is called 'strong,'—or the so-called 2nd aorist, is formed by the addition to the root of the auxiliary

vowel ε (or perhaps the auxiliary verb ἐ, *to go*, in ἵημι with causative signification?), which is lengthened to η in the indicative and imperative; it takes the augment, and the active personal endings without tach-vowel; it is almost confined to verbs which have no strong aorist active: e.g. root φαν ἐφάνην etc., conjunctive φανέω, φανῶ, optative φανε-ιη-ν φανείην. Imperative φάνηθι.

2. The weaker aorist passive, the so-called 1st aorist passive, only differs from the former in taking θ before ε, η, or in annexing, conformably to the laws of sound, the syllable θε to the verbal stem partially lengthened as in the present; ἐπράχθην, ἐλείφθην, ἐψεύσθην, ἐκρίθην. This θε, perhaps the root θε, *to set, to do*, is here used in a passive signification,—compare *veneo, venum ire*. Cognate to this may be the formation of the German preterite of the weak conjugation by compounding the stem with the root of *tuon, to do*, answering to the Greek θε Gothic *do*, O. H. G. *to*: thus Gothic *salbôda*, O. H. G., *salbôta*, H. G. *salbte*, though here certainly only with an active signification. Compare in Greek, the lengthening of the stem or formation of the present with θ in πρήθω, root πρα, φθινύθω, aorist form ἔσχεθον, imperfect ἔφθιθον Od. V. 110 (?).

3. The passive future forms are formed by annexing the future ending of the middle to the stems of the two passive aorists, or the middle form of the future from the root θε θήσομαι to the verbal stem; as φανήσομαι,

Latin Compound Tenses. 143

λυθήσομαι. The Homeric dialect knows no future form in θήσομαι, a passive future in ησομαι occurs clearly only once, μιγήσεσθαι Il. X. 365—on δαήσομαι compare perfect δεδάηκα—everywhere else in Homer the passive future is expressed by the middle forms.

B. LATIN COMPOUND TENSES.

LXVII. SUMMARY.

On account of the poverty of the Latin language in forms of original verbal inflexion compound tense-stems and new formations are more numerous in it than in Greek. They are the following: (α) the two forms of the weak perfect in *si* and *ui, vi ;* (β) the tense and modal forms derived from the perfect stem, that is to say, the futurum exactum, optative-conjunctive perfect, infinitive perfect, indicative and conjunctive pluperfect. These are compounds of the perfect stem with the future—properly the present with future signification, Sec. 64,—the optative-conjunctive present, the infinitive present, and the indicative and conjunctive-optative imperfect of the auxiliary verb *esse*. (γ) The indicative and conjunctive imperfect. (δ) The future in *bo*. With respect to the auxiliary verbs employed in these formations these verbal forms divide themselves into those with root or auxiliary verb *esse* and the endings *si, so, ro, sim, rim, sem, rem*, and those with root or auxiliary verb *fu*, Greek φυ, and the endings *·ui, vi, bam, bo ;* both roots are amalgamated in the endings *sso*,—from *viso*,—*uero, vero, uissem, vissem.*

LXVIII. WEAK LATIN PERFECT.

1. The perfect in *si* = *esi*, which is a remnant of a perfect form from root *es*, original *âsa ?*—appears in primitive or stem verbs with consonantal root endings whether these be gutturals, dentals, or labials: *lexi* = *legsi* in *intellexi*, or *lēgi*, *panxi* from present stem *pang*, by the side of the earlier *pepigi*, *punxi* by the side of *pupugi*, *fluxi* from stem *flug*, *vixi* from *vig*, *traxi*, *vexi*, *rexi*; after *l* only in *vulsi*, after *n* in *mansi*, after *m* in *sumpsi*; *lusi*, *clausi*, *misi* from *lud-si* etc.; the guttural is dropped between *r* or *l* and *s* in *alsi*, stem *alg*, *fulsi fulg*, *indulsi*, *fulsi fulc*, *sparsi*, *mersi*, *torsi*. Regressive assimilation in *jussi* from *jubsi*, *cessi*, *pressi*; *ussi* from *us* in *uro* Sec. 33, *gessi*; *hausi*, *haesi* from *haus-si*. Syncopated forms *dixti*, *scripsti* with which compare the archaic infinitives *dixe*, *detraxe*, *despexe*, *surrexe*.

2. The perfect in *ui, vi*, from the perfect of the auxiliary verb *fui* with initial *f* dropped; *u* remains after a consonantal ending of the root or stem, after vowels it is hardened into the semi-vowel *v* in *vi*. (a) This form of the perfect is chiefly found in derived verbs—analogous to the contracted verbs in Greek—in *are, ēre, ire*, as *amavi* from *ama-fui*, *delevi*, *audivi*; verbs with infinitive in *are* and perfect in *ui* instead of *avi*, as the archaic form *necui* instead of *necavi*, *sonui* from *sonare*, form the

Weak Latin Perfect. 145

perfect from the present stem which is identical with the simple root *nec, son*, hence the ending is *ui* instead of *ai;* *avi* is from the present stem of derived verbs *ama, amo* from *amao;* verbs of the so-called 2nd conjugation in *eo* with perfect *ui* instead of *evi* form the perfect by dropping the stem-ending *e* as if from a consonantal stem: thus *monui* instead of *monevi*, so the participle passive with short tach-vowel *monitus, habitus; ferveo* hardens *v* to *b* in the perfect *ferbui;* *e* is retained in *abolevi, delevi*, and in verbs with an inchoative present form *suesco, quiesco*. The formation of the perfect of verbs in *io*, infinitive *īre*, by apocope of the *i* of the present stem is analogous; thus *salui, aperui* instead of *aperi-vi;* with syncope throughout in *rapio*, perfect *rapui*, infinitive *rapere*. On the other hand the perfect *ivi* of present stems in *esso*, as if from *essio*, in *arcessivi, capessivi, lacessivi*, coexists with the simple perfect *facessi*, participle *ītus*, infinitive *ĕre*, by the side of *arcessire*. Perfects analogous to the *j*-stems where the present stem = the root: *petivi, quaesivi*. (β) The perfect form in *vi, ui*, is however found also in a number of root or stem verbs with a partially lengthened present stem in *no, sco;* to these belongs *eo, ivi*, which except in the supine *ītum* and in the changing of *i* to *e* before the vowels *a, o, u* passes over into the J-conjugation, Sec. 61, 1. 2; also *sero = siso*, perfect *sevi*, Sec. 61, 3, *lino livi levi, cresco crevi, sino sivi, gnosco gnovi;* certain verbs whose root ends in a consonant make by metathesis in the perfect *sterno stravi, sperno sprevi, tero trivi;* the perfect *uı* after roots ending in *l m n r: calui, colui, volui, con-*

10

sului, excellui, fremui, vomui, genui, tenui, supine *tentum,* compare *tetini* Sec. 59, *serui; strepui;* in *posui* from *pono* from *posino, posno,* where the root consonant *s* has been dropped, *s* reappears, hence the archaic form *posivi,* and *i* is then dropped, and we get the ending *ui* in *posui ; ui* follows double consonants *texui, stertui.* (γ) Lastly, denominatives in *uo* from a noun-stem in *u* form the perfect in *ui* instead of *uvi* by syncope of *v* and shortening the *u*, like the derived verbs in *io ;* as *acuo, arguo, statuo, tribuo ; argui* from *arguvi, statui* from *statuvi—* stem *statu, tribu—*compare *audivi.*

3. A combination of the two forms of the compound perfect, the sigmatic in *si* and that in *ui*, takes place in perfect forms in *sui*, as *messui*, root *met*, compare *messum*, from *metsui, nexui* co-existing with *nexi* from *necto* stem *nec, pexui* a rare form for *pexi* from *pec-to.*

The *v* of the perfect ending *vi* disappears between vowels and *ii* is contracted to *ī* in *isti, īt, isse, peristis, redissem, nossem, audīt, audissem* compare *dis* from *dives, ditior, sīs,* from *si vis; v* is also dropped in the pluperfect and futurum exactum.

LXIX. Tenses and Moods formed from the Perfect.

1. Second future or futurum exactum. (*a*) The shorter and earlier form. To the bare verbal stem is annexed he future *so, sis, sit* from root *es* (compare *ero* from *esio,* εσjω, σω Sec. 64) with the signification of the future—

or more properly futurum exactum, as *axo, capso, faxo, rapso*. (β) The longer and more recent formation: *so* is annexed to the perfect stem in *i* or *si*, *s* between vowels becoming *r: dedero* from *dediso, dederunt* from *dedisonti, stetero, scripsero;* syncopated forms of the perfect in *si, dixis = dicsi-sis, jussit = jub-si-sit;* so in the perfect stem of derived verbs in *vi, amasso* from *amaviso,* where *s* is doubled to compensate for dropping the perfect suffix *vi*, or by syncope and assimilation, *peccassit, habessit* from *habevisit* from the original perfect of the 2nd conjugation in *evi*. Instead of these archaic forms in which *s* is retained and *v* is assimilated to *ss*, the more developed language constructs forms with *r* as *amavero, habuero;* the last being produced by syncope of *e* at the end of the root and by vocalisation of *v*. (γ) In consideration of the clear and thorough-going signification of even the shorter forms, etc., as futura exacta, these also are to be regarded as early future forms of the futurum exactum constructed from the perfect stem with *i* syncopated, as *faxo = fac-si-so, faxim = fac-si-sim*. There lies at the root of these forms a hypothetical perfect form in *si faxi, axi, capsi,* by the side of the perfect forms proceeding from the original reduplication *fēci, ēgi, cēpi,* Sec. 59, 3.

2. Conjunctive-optative perfect. The optative from root *es, sim* from *siem, esiem,* is annexed to the perfect stem: *fecerim* from *feci-siem* (or *fec-esim ?*), *legerim* from *legisim, dederim = dedisiem, tutuderim = tutudisim*. Archaic syncopated forms are *faxim = fac-si-sim* (see above,

faxo), *dixim, taxim* (indicative *tetigi*), *axim, comessim, conjexim, ausim* = *audsi-sim,* compare indicative *ausi* by the side of *ausus sum ; negassim* from *negavi-sim,* as *negaverim* with *r* instead of *s* and *e* instead of *i* before *r*, *habessim* from *habevi-sim ; habuerim.*

3. For the infinitive perfect see above Secs. 40. 68, 1. Syncopated form *dixe*, archaic from *dic-si-sse, dixim, dixis, dixti.*

4. The pluperfect indicative ends in *ram* from *eram* = *esam,* compare ἦν, ἦα, ἔα Sec. 62, annexed to the perfect stem in *i: feceram, dederam, steteram* = *dedi-sam.* Compare the passive *amatus eram.* Conjunctive *sem*— optative of the imperfect (*e*)*sam, esaim* compare *amem* from *amaim,* Sec. 56, 3—is annexed to the perfect stem in *i*, with the *s* doubled as in *essem, legissem* = *legi-sem, fecissem, fuissem* indicative *fueram.* Earlier syncopated forms are *faxem* from *fac-si-sem* (see above, *faxo, faxim*), *intellexem, dixem.*

LXX. Future in *b.*

Besides the originally optative form in *e* of the stem-verbs of the 3rd conjugation, and the originally optative form of the derived verbs in *io* of the 4th conjugation which have *a* in the 1st sing., both of them optative forms which came to be used as futures,—besides also the termination *so* from the root *es* applied to the perfect stem to form the futurum exactum; the Latin language forms another

Imperfect Indicative.

special future, simple and precise in its signification, from derived verbs in *a, e* of the 1st and 2nd conjugations, by annexing *fuo* of the present *fore*, root *fu* (φυ), *to become*, to the present stem as the Greek future suffix in σω comes from the root ες. From *fuo* comes by aphæresis *uo*, after vowels *vo*, which is hardened to *bo, bis, bit* (compare *bis* = *dvis*), compare also the imperfect *bam* from *fuam* Sec. 71; *amabo, docebo*. This form of the future is rare in stem-verbs, as *ībo, dăbo, stābo*; archaic also *dicēbo, audibo, scibo*; everywhere else, in conjugations 3 and 4, in consonantal, J and U stems, the optative form, with 1st sing. in *a* instead of *e*, elsewhere *ē*, which has passed into a future signification, is used as *legam leges, audiam, statuam*.

LXXI. Imperfect Indicative.

The imperfect from root *fu, fuam*,—compare *eram* from *esam*—is annexed to the root or present stem like the future in *bo* by dropping the first letters and hardening the *u* by transition from *v* to *b, ībam, dăbam, stābam*; stem verbs with a mere tach-vowel lengthen it anomalously to *ē* as *legēbam*, as also do derived verbs of the J conjugation *audiebam*, compare *dedērunt* from original *dedērunt*; derived verbs in *a* and *e* join *bam* without a tach-vowel to the vowel-ending of the stem: *amābam, docēbam*, and so do derived verbs in *i* in the earlier and later poetical language, *scibam, audibam*.

LXXII. Imperfect Conjunctive.

As the optative form *sem*, see Sec. 69, 4, is annexed to the perfect stem in the conjunctive pluperfect, to express the subjective idea of completion in past time, or in other words to denote the conditional preterite, so in the conjunctive imperfect it expresses subjectively duration in past time, that is the conditional present, by being annexed to the present stem. The conjunctive imperfect of the auxiliary verb as an independent verb is *essem* from *esaim* with *ss* instead of *esem*, *erem*, as might have been expected. (α) *sem* with *s* changed into *r* is annexed to a root ending in a vowel, as *forem* from *fosem*, *irem*, *darem*, *starem* = *stasem*. (β) *s* is retained without tach-vowel when the root ends in a consonant, as *essem* from *ed*, *to eat* = *edsem*, *possem* from *potsem* with regressive assimilation; with assimilated *s* (progressive assimilation) in *ferrem*, *vellem*, from *fersem*, *velsem*, compare *fert*, *vult*. (γ) In stem-verbs ending in a consonant, in those in *io* of the 3rd conjugation with syncopated inflexion, in those in *uo*, as well as those with a tach-vowel *ĕ*, and in derived verbs in *ā*, *ē*, *ī*, *sem* is changed into *rem* after a vowel, as *dicerem* from *dicesem*, *caperem*, *acuerem*, *amarem*, *docerem*, *audirem*.

INDEX.

	Page		Page
Adverbs	99	Formal Elements	11
Affixes	7		
Analysis, linguistic	71	Gender	89
Aorist, Compound (or First)	16	Glottology, "the Science of Sound"	7, 11
Aspirates	18, 42		
,, phonetic law of	66	Grammar, "the Science of Lingual Form"	7
Assimilation of sound, progressive	64	Grimm's law (or "law of Sound-shifting")	21, 23
,, regressive	63		
		Imagination vigorous in the early periods of language	3
Case	91		
Conjugations	101		
Consonants	17	Infinitive, the	81, 83
,, as root consonants	27	Inflexion, the (Word-formation)	6, 87
,, classes of	17		
,, Greek system of	17	Inflexional suffixes	87
, resistance of, to phonetic changes	21	Interjections	2, 88
		Iota "a double power of j"	15
,, significance of, to philology	20	,, epenthetic	15
		,, subscript	12
Consonantal relation between Greek and Latin	25	Language and reason inseparable	1
Cuneiform Inscriptions	9		
		,, classes and stages of	7
Declension	88, 90	,, elements of	4
Denominative stems (in which the verbal suffixes are attached to a noun stem ending in a vowel)	79	,, Inflexional	8
		,, ,, tokens of	8
		,, Interjectional,"Sounds arising from Sensation"	1
Digamma, the	18	,, nature and origin of	4
Diphthongs, Old Latin	12	,, onomatopœic, "the mere imitation of sounds"	1
Ending, the laws of	68		
Ephelkystic ν, or ν suffixed	69	Languages, agglutinative. "In these two or more roots grow together in a single word"	7
Etymology, "the Science of what is true and genuine in Language"	21		

	Page		Page
Letters	4	Root, the, "the expression of a general idea"	5
Liquids	49	Roots, "always and unconditionally monosyllables"	75
Medials	37	,, classes of	75
Metaphor, its importance in the formation of language	3	,, formation of	70
		,, Greek pure vowel	63
Metathesis, "a change in the position of sounds"	75	,, marks and peculiarities of	74
Mood, Conjunctive and Optative (Greek)	113	,, or phonetic Types	2
		,, primary and secondary	73
,, Conjunctive and Optative (Latin)	115	,, pronominal	78
,, Subjunctive (Latin)	113	,, "The indivisible atoms of language, the primitive elements of words which cannot be further analysed"	5
Nominal stems (those in which the verbal suffixes are attached to a noun stem which ends with a consonant)	79	Sound, Consonantal laws of	63
Noun, the	5	,, Complex	4
Numerals, Cardinal	85	,, Lingual	4
,, Ordinal	86	,, ,, formal elements of	4
Participle, the	81	,, ,, material elements of	4
Philology, divisions of	6	,, ,, radical elements of	4
Phonetic decay, "Degradation and mutilation of an older and fuller form"	10	,, -shifting, law of (Grimm's law)	21, 23
,, Types or Roots, "the fundamental elements of language"		,, the material basis of	6
		,, the science of (Glottology)	7
, Types or Roots, "the irreducible residuum of linguistic analysis"	3	Sounds, analysis of	11
		Spirants	18
		,, original	56
Prepositions	100	Stem, the	6
Pronouns	97	Stems, Comparative	83
		,, formation of	76
		,, Nominal	81
Reason and Language Inseparable	1	,, Superlative	85
Reduplication, law of	67	,, Verbal	78
,, "An amplification of the root in order to express relation"	72	,, Nominal verbal	79
		,, a-stem	91
		,, o ,,	91
		,, uj ,,	91

Index.

	Page
Tense, Aorist passive Greek	141
,, Compound Greek	135
,, ,, Latin	143
,, ,, Perfect and Pluperfect (Greek)	140
,, Future Greek	137
,, ,, passive Greek	142
,, ,, in *bo* Latin	148
,, Futurum Exactum Greek	141
., Imperfect conjunctive	150
,, ,, Greek	134
,, ,, indicative Latin	149
,, Perfect, the, tenses and moods formed from	146
,, Present Greek and Latin	127
,, simple or strong Aorist (Greek)	125
,, simple or strong Aorist (Latin)	122
,, simple Perfect and Pluperfect (Greek)	119
,, weak Perfect (Latin)	144
Tenses, compound	118
,, of verbs	101, 117
Tenues	27
Verb, the	5
,, Contracted	80
,, Denominative	79
,, Desiderative	80
Verbs, moods of	101

	Page
Verbs, personal endings of	103
,, persons of	101
,, tenses of	101, 117
,, voices of	102
Vis Inertiæ (Laziness), effect of	10
Voice, Middle-passive (Greek)	111
,, ,, (Latin)	112
Vowels	11
,, changes of	12
,, ,, under consonantal influence	14
,, exposed to greater changes than consonants	21
,, fundamental (Indo-Germanic)	11
Word, the	5, 87
,, "the complete form of language"	5
,, "The complete combination of sounds which express meaning and relation"	6
,, "the single phonetic expression of a complete and independent perception"	5
,, -formation or inflexion	87
Words "The phonetic embodiments and the only exponents of conceptions"	2

A LIST OF

*KEGAN PAUL, TRENCH & CO.'S
PUBLICATIONS.*

3. 86

1, *Paternoster Square,*
London.

A LIST OF

KEGAN PAUL, TRENCH & CO.'S PUBLICATIONS.

—◆—

CONTENTS.

	PAGE		PAGE
GENERAL LITERATURE.	2	MILITARY WORKS.	34
PARCHMENT LIBRARY.	21	POETRY.	35
PULPIT COMMENTARY.	23	WORKS OF FICTION	42
INTERNATIONAL SCIENTIFIC SERIES.	31	BOOKS FOR THE YOUNG	43

GENERAL LITERATURE.

A. K. H. B.—From a Quiet Place. A Volume of Sermons. Crown 8vo, 5s.

ALEXANDER, William, D.D., Bishop of Derry.—The Great Question, and other Sermons. Crown 8vo, 6s.

ALLEN, Rev. R., M.A.—Abraham: his Life, Times, and Travels, 3800 years ago. With Map. Second Edition. Post 8vo, 6s.

ALLIES, T. W., M.A.—Per Crucem ad Lucem. The Result of a Life. 2 vols. Demy 8vo, 25s.

A Life's Decision. Crown 8vo, 7s. 6d.

ALLNATT, F. J. B., B.D.—The Witness of St. Matthew. An Inquiry into the Sequence of Inspired Thought pervading the First Gospel, and into its Result of Unity, Symmetry, and Completeness, as a Perfect Portrait of the Perfect Man. Crown 8vo, 5s.

AMHERST, Rev. W. J.—The History of Catholic Emancipation and the Progress of the Catholic Church in the British Isles (chiefly in England) from 1771-1820. 2 vols. Demy 8vo, 24s.

AMOS, Professor Sheldon.—The History and Principles of the Civil Law of Rome. An aid to the Study of Scientific and Comparative Jurisprudence. Demy 8vo. 16s.

Ancient and Modern Britons. A Retrospect. 2 vols. Demy 8vo, 24*s*.

ANDERDON, Rev. W. H.—**Fasti Apostolici**; a Chronology of the Years between the Ascension of our Lord and the Martyrdom of SS. Peter and Paul. Second Edition. Enlarged. Square 8vo, 5*s*.

Evenings with the Saints. Crown 8vo, 5*s*.

ANDERSON, David.—**"Scenes" in the Commons.** Crown 8vo, 5*s*.

ARISTOTLE.—**The Nicomachean Ethics of Aristotle.** Translated by F. H. Peters, M.A. Second Edition. Crown 8vo, 6*s*.

ARMSTRONG, Richard A., B.A.—**Latter-Day Teachers.** Six Lectures. Small crown 8vo, 2*s*. 6*d*.

AUBERTIN, J. J.—**A Flight to Mexico.** With Seven full-page Illustrations and a Railway Map of Mexico. Crown 8vo, 7*s*. 6*d*.

Six Months in Cape Colony and Natal. With Illustrations and Map. Crown 8vo, 7*s*. 6*d*.

BADGER, George Percy, D.C.L.—**An English-Arabic Lexicon.** In which the equivalent for English Words and Idiomatic Sentences are rendered into literary and colloquial Arabic. Royal 4to, 80*s*.

BAGEHOT, Walter.—**The English Constitution.** New and Revised Edition. Crown 8vo, 7*s*. 6*d*.

Lombard Street. A Description of the Money Market. Eighth Edition. Crown 8vo, 7*s*. 6*d*.

Essays on Parliamentary Reform. Crown 8vo, 5*s*.

Some Articles on the Depreciation of Silver, and Topics connected with it. Demy 8vo, 5*s*.

BAGENAL, Philip H.—**The American-Irish and their Influence on Irish Politics.** Crown 8vo, 5*s*.

BAGOT, Alan, C.E.—**Accidents in Mines:** their Causes and Prevention. Crown 8vo, 6*s*.

The Principles of Colliery Ventilation. Second Edition, greatly enlarged. Crown 8vo, 5*s*.

The Principles of Civil Engineering as applied to Agriculture and Estate Management. Crown 8vo, 7*s*. 6*d*.

BAKER, Sir Sherston, Bart.—**The Laws relating to Quarantine.** Crown 8vo, 12*s*. 6*d*.

BAKER, Thomas.—**A Battling Life;** chiefly in the Civil Service. An Autobiography, with Fugitive Papers on Subjects of Public Importance. Crown 8vo, 7*s*. 6*d*.

BALDWIN, Capt. J. H.—**The Large and Small Game of Bengal and the North-Western Provinces of India.** With 20 Illustrations. New and Cheaper Edition. Small 4to, 10*s*. 6*d*.

BALLIN, Ada S. and F. L.—**A Hebrew Grammar.** With Exercises selected from the Bible. Crown 8vo, 7s. 6d.

BARCLAY, Edgar.—**Mountain Life in Algeria.** With numerous Illustrations by Photogravure. Crown 4to, 16s.

BARLOW, James W.—**The Ultimatum of Pessimism.** An Ethical Study. Demy 8vo, 6s.

The Normans in South Europe. Demy 8vo, 7s. 6d.

BARNES, William.—**Outlines of Redecraft (Logic).** With English Wording. Crown 8vo, 3s.

BAUR, Ferdinand, Dr. Ph.—**A Philological Introduction to Greek and Latin for Students.** Translated and adapted from the German, by C. KEGAN PAUL, M.A., and E. D. STONE, M.A. Third Edition. Crown 8vo, 6s.

BAYLY, Capt. George.—**Sea Life Sixty Years Ago.** A Record of Adventures which led up to the Discovery of the Relics of the long-missing Expedition commanded by the Comte de la Perouse. Crown 8vo, 3s. 6d.

BELLARS, Rev. W.—**The Testimony of Conscience to the Truth and Divine Origin of the Christian Revelation.** Burney Prize Essay. Small crown 8vo, 3s. 6d.

BELLASIS, Edward.—**The Money Jar of Plautus at the Oratory School.** An Account of the Recent Representation. With Appendix and 16 Illustrations. Small 4to, sewed, 2s.

The New Terence at Edgbaston. Being Notices of the Performances in 1880 and 1881. With Preface, Notes, and Appendix. Third Issue. Small 4to, 1s. 6d.

BENN, Alfred W.—**The Greek Philosophers.** 2 vols. Demy 8vo, 28s.

Bible Folk-Lore. A Study in Comparative Mythology. Crown 8vo, 10s. 6d.

BIRD, Charles, F.G.S.—**Higher Education in Germany and England.** Being a brief Practical Account of the Organization and Curriculum of the German Higher Schools. With critical Remarks and Suggestions with reference to those of England. Small crown 8vo, 2s. 6d.

BLECKLY, Henry.—**Socrates and the Athenians:** An Apology. Crown 8vo, 2s. 6d.

BLOOMFIELD, The Lady.—**Reminiscences of Court and Diplomatic Life.** New and Cheaper Edition. With Frontispiece. Crown 8vo, 6s.

BLUNT, The Ven. Archdeacon.—**The Divine Patriot, and other Sermons.** Preached in Scarborough and in Cannes. New and Cheaper Edition. Crown 8vo, 4s. 6d.

BLUNT, Wilfrid S.—**The Future of Islam.** Crown 8vo, 6s.

Ideas about India. Crown 8vo. Cloth, 6s.

Kegan Paul, Trench & Co.'s Publications. 5

BODDY, Alexander A.—To Kairwân the Holy. Scenes in Muhammedan Africa. With Route Map, and Eight Illustrations by A. F. JACASSEY. Crown 8vo, 6s.

BOSANQUET, Bernard.—Knowledge and Reality. A Criticism of Mr. F. H. Bradley's "Principles of Logic." Crown 8vo, 9s.

BOUVERIE-PUSEY, S. E. B.—Permanence and Evolution. An Inquiry into the Supposed Mutability of Animal Types. Crown 8vo, 5s.

BOWEN, H. C., M.A.—Studies in English. For the use of Modern Schools. Eighth Thousand. Small crown 8vo, 1s. 6d.

English Grammar for Beginners. Fcap. 8vo, 1s.

Simple English Poems. English Literature for Junior Classes. In four parts. Parts I., II., and III., 6d. each. Part IV., 1s. Complete, 3s.

BRADLEY, F. H.—The Principles of Logic. Demy 8vo, 16s.

BRIDGETT, Rev. T. E.—History of the Holy Eucharist in Great Britain. 2 vols. Demy 8vo, 18s.

BROOKE, Rev. S. A.—Life and Letters of the Late Rev. F. W. Robertson, M.A. Edited by.

I. Uniform with Robertson's Sermons. 2 vols. With Steel Portrait. 7s. 6d.
II. Library Edition. With Portrait. 8vo, 12s.
III. A Popular Edition. In 1 vol., 8vo, 6s.

The Fight of Faith. Sermons preached on various occasions. Fifth Edition. Crown 8vo, 7s. 6d.

The Spirit of the Christian Life. Third Edition. Crown 8vo, 5s.

Theology in the English Poets.—Cowper, Coleridge, Wordsworth, and Burns. Fifth Edition. Post 8vo, 5s.

Christ in Modern Life. Sixteenth Edition. Crown 8vo, 5s.

Sermons. First Series. Thirteenth Edition. Crown 8vo, 5s.

Sermons. Second Series. Sixth Edition. Crown 8vo, 5s.

BROWN, Rev. J. Baldwin, B.A.—The Higher Life. Its Reality, Experience, and Destiny. Sixth Edition. Crown 8vo, 5s.

Doctrine of Annihilation in the Light of the Gospel of Love. Five Discourses. Fourth Edition. Crown 8vo, 2s. 6d.

The Christian Policy of Life. A Book for Young Men of Business. Third Edition. Crown 8vo, 3s. 6d.

BROWN, Horatio F.—Life on the Lagoons. With two Illustrations and Map. Crown 8vo, 6s.

BROWNE, H. L.—Reason and Religious Belief. Crown 8vo, 3s. 6d.

BROWNBILL, *John.*—**Principles of English Canon Law.** Part I. General Introduction. Crown 8vo, 6s.

BUMPUS, A. A.—**New Social Teachings.** Small crown, 8vo, 5s.

BURDETT, *Henry C.*—**Help in Sickness—Where to Go and What to Do.** Crown 8vo, 1s. 6d.

    Helps to Health. The Habitation—The Nursery—The Schoolroom and—The Person. With a Chapter on Pleasure and Health Resorts. Crown 8vo, 1s. 6d.

BURKE, *The Late Very Rev. T. N.*—**His Life.** By W. J. FITZPATRICK. 2 vols. With Portrait. Demy 8vo, 30s.

BURTON, *Mrs. Richard.*—**The Inner Life of Syria, Palestine, and the Holy Land.** Post 8vo, 6s.

CAPES, *J. M.*—**The Church of the Apostles**: an Historical Inquiry. Demy 8vo, 9s.

CARPENTER, *W. B., LL.D., M.D., F.R.S., etc.*—**The Principles of Mental Physiology.** With their Applications to the Training and Discipline of the Mind, and the Study of its Morbid Conditions. Illustrated. Sixth Edition. 8vo, 12s.

Catholic Dictionary. Containing some Account of the Doctrine, Discipline, Rites, Ceremonies, Councils, and Religious Orders of the Catholic Church. By WILLIAM E. ADDIS and THOMAS ARNOLD, M.A. Third Edition. Demy 8vo, 21s.

CHEYNE, *Rev. T. K.*—**The Prophecies of Isaiah.** Translated with Critical Notes and Dissertations. 2 vols. Third Edition. Demy 8vo, 25s.

CHICHELE, *Mary.*—**Doing and Undoing.** A Story. 1 vol. Crown 8vo, 4s. 6d.

Circulating Capital. Being an Inquiry into the Fundamental Laws of Money. An Essay by an East India Merchant. Small crown 8vo, 6s.

CLAIRAUT.—**Elements of Geometry.** Translated by Dr. KAINES. With 145 Figures. Crown 8vo, 4s. 6d.

CLAPPERTON, *Jane Hume.*—**Scientific Meliorism and the Evolution of Happiness.** Large crown 8vo, 8s. 6d.

CLARKE, *Rev. Henry James, A.K.C.*—**The Fundamental Science.** Demy 8vo, 10s. 6d.

CLAYDEN, *P. W.*—**Samuel Sharpe.** Egyptologist and Translator of the Bible. Crown 8vo, 6s.

CLIFFORD, *Samuel.*—**What Think Ye of the Christ?** Crown 8vo, 6s.

CLODD, *Edward, F.R.A.S.*—**The Childhood of the World**: a Simple Account of Man in Early Times. Seventh Edition. Crown 8vo, 3s.

    A Special Edition for Schools. 1s.

CLODD, Edward, F.R.A.S.—continued.

The Childhood of Religions. Including a Simple Account of the Birth and Growth of Myths and Legends. Eighth Thousand. Crown 8vo, 5s.
A Special Edition for Schools. 1s. 6d.

Jesus of Nazareth. With a brief sketch of Jewish History to the Time of His Birth. Small crown 8vo, 6s.

COGHLAN, J. Cole, D.D.—**The Modern Pharisee and other Sermons.** Edited by the Very Rev. H. H. DICKINSON, D.D., Dean of Chapel Royal, Dublin. New and Cheaper Edition. Crown 8vo, 7s. 6d.

COLE, George R. Fitz-Roy.—**The Peruvians at Home.** Crown 8vo, 6s.

COLERIDGE, Sara.—Memoir and Letters of Sara Coleridge. Edited by her Daughter. With Index. Cheap Edition. With Portrait. 7s. 6d.

Collects Exemplified. Being Illustrations from the Old and New Testaments of the Collects for the Sundays after Trinity. By the Author of "A Commentary on the Epistles and Gospels." Edited by the Rev. JOSEPH JACKSON. Crown 8vo, 5s.

CONNELL, A. K.—**Discontent and Danger in India.** Small crown 8vo, 3s. 6d.

The Economic Revolution of India. Crown 8vo, 4s. 6d.

COOK, Keningale.—**Fathers of Jesus.** 2 vols. Demy 8vo, 28s.

CORY, William.—**A Guide to Modern English History.** Part I.—MDCCCXV.-MDCCCXXX. Demy 8vo, 9s. Part II.—MDCCCXXX.-MDCCCXXXV., 15s.

COTTERILL, H. B.—**An Introduction to the Study of Poetry.** Crown 8vo, 7s. 6d.

COTTON, H. J. S.—**New India, or India in Transition.** Crown 8vo, 4s. 6d.

COUTTS, Francis Burdett Money.—**The Training of the Instinct of Love.** With a Preface by the Rev. EDWARD THRING, M.A. Small crown 8vo, 2s. 6d.

COX, Rev. Sir George W., M.A., Bart.—**The Mythology of the Aryan Nations.** New Edition. Demy 8vo, 16s.

Tales of Ancient Greece. New Edition. Small crown 8vo, 6s.

A Manual of Mythology in the form of Question and Answer. New Edition. Fcap. 8vo, 3s.

An Introduction to the Science of Comparative Mythology and Folk-Lore. Second Edition. Crown 8vo. 7s. 6d.

COX, Rev. Sir G. W., M.A., Bart., and JONES, Eustace Hinton.—
Popular Romances of the Middle Ages. Third
Edition, in 1 vol. Crown 8vo, 6s.

COX, Rev. Samuel, D.D.—A Commentary on the Book of Job.
With a Translation. Second Edition. Demy 8vo, 15s.

Salvator Mundi; or, Is Christ the Saviour of all Men? Tenth
Edition. Crown 8vo, 5s.

The Larger Hope. A Sequel to "Salvator Mundi." Second
Edition. 16mo, 1s.

The Genesis of Evil, and other Sermons, mainly expository.
Third Edition. Crown 8vo, 6s.

Balaam. An Exposition and a Study. Crown 8vo, 5s.

Miracles. An Argument and a Challenge. Crown 8vo, 2s. 6d.

CRAVEN, Mrs.—A Year's Meditations. Crown 8vo, 6s.

CRAWFURD, Oswald.—Portugal, Old and New. With Illustrations and Maps. New and Cheaper Edition. Crown 8vo, 6s.

CROZIER, John Beattie, M.B.—The Religion of the Future.
Crown 8vo, 6s.

CUNNINGHAM, W., B.D.—Politics and Economics: An Essay
on the Nature of the Principles of Political Economy, together
with a survey of Recent Legislation. Crown 8vo, 5s.

DANIELL, Clarmont.—The Gold Treasure of India. An Inquiry
into its Amount, the Cause of its Accumulation, and the Proper
Means of using it as Money. Crown 8vo, 5s.

Discarded Silver: a Plan for its Use as Money. Small crown,
8vo, 2s.

Darkness and Dawn: the Peaceful Birth of a New Age. Small
crown 8vo, 2s. 6d.

DAVIDSON, Rev. Samuel, D.D., LL.D.—Canon of the Bible:
Its Formation, History, and Fluctuations. Third and Revised
Edition. Small crown 8vo, 5s.

The Doctrine of Last Things contained in the New Testament compared with the Notions of the Jews and the Statements
of Church Creeds. Small crown 8vo, 3s. 6d.

DAWSON, Geo., M.A. Prayers, with a Discourse on Prayer.
Edited by his Wife. First Series. Ninth Edition. Crown
8vo, 3s. 6d.

Prayers, with a Discourse on Prayer. Edited by GEORGE
ST. CLAIR. Second Series. Crown 8vo, 6s.

Sermons on Disputed Points and Special Occasions.
Edited by his Wife. Fourth Edition. Crown 8vo, 6s.

Sermons on Daily Life and Duty. Edited by his Wife.
Fourth Edition. Crown 8vo, 6s.

DAWSON, Geo., M.A.—continued.

The Authentic Gospel, and other Sermons. Edited by GEORGE ST. CLAIR, F.G.S. Third Edition. Crown 8vo, 6s.

Three Books of God: Nature, History, and Scripture. Sermons edited by GEORGE ST. CLAIR, F.G.S. Crown 8vo, 6s.

Biographical Lectures. Edited by GEORGE ST. CLAIR, F.G.S. Large crown, 8vo, 7s. 6d.

DE JONCOURT, Madame Marie.—Wholesome Cookery. Third Edition. Crown 8vo, 3s. 6d.

Democracy in the Old World and the New. By the Author of "The Suez Canal, the Eastern Question, and Abyssinia," etc. Small crown 8vo, 2s. 6d.

DENT, Hastings C.—A Year in Brazil. With Illustrations. Demy 8vo, 18s.

Discourse on the Shedding of Blood, and The Laws of War. Demy 8vo, 2s. 6d.

DOUGLAS, Rev. Herman.—Into the Deep; or, The Wonders of the Lord's Person. Crown 8vo, 2s. 6d.

DOWDEN, Edward, LL.D.—Shakspere: a Critical Study of his Mind and Art. Seventh Edition. Post 8vo, 12s.

Studies in Literature, 1789-1877. Third Edition. Large post 8vo, 6s.

DU MONCEL, Count.—The Telephone, the Microphone, and the Phonograph. With 74 Illustrations. Third Edition. Small crown 8vo, 5s.

DURUY, Victor.—History of Rome and the Roman People. Edited by Prof. MAHAFFY. With nearly 3000 Illustrations. 4to. Vols. I.–V. in 10 parts, 30s. each vol.

EDGEWORTH, F. Y.—Mathematical Psychics. An Essay on the Application of Mathematics to Social Science. Demy 8vo, 7s. 6d.

Educational Code of the Prussian Nation, in its Present Form. In accordance with the Decisions of the Common Provincial Law, and with those of Recent Legislation. Crown 8vo, 2s. 6d.

Education Library. Edited by PHILIP MAGNUS:—

An Introduction to the History of Educational Theories. By OSCAR BROWNING, M.A. Second Edition. 3s. 6d.

Old Greek Education. By the Rev. Prof. MAHAFFY, M.A. Second Edition. 3s. 6d.

School Management. Including a general view of the work of Education, Organization and Discipline. By JOSEPH LANDON. Fourth Edition. 6s.

EDWARDES, The Late Major-General Sir Herbert B., K.C.B., &c.— **Memorials of the Life and Letters of.** By his Wife. 2 vols. With Illustrations. Demy 8vo. Cloth.

ELSDALE, Henry.—**Studies in Tennyson's Idylls.** Crown 8vo, 5s.

ELYOT, Sir Thomas.—**The Boke named the Gouernour.** Edited from the First Edition of 1531 by HENRY HERBERT STEPHEN CROFT, M.A., Barrister-at-Law. 2 vols. Fcap. 4to, 50s.

Emerson's (Ralph Waldo) Life. By OLIVER WENDELL HOLMES. English Copyright Edition. With Portrait. Crown 8vo, 6s.

Enoch the Prophet. The Book of. Archbishop LAURENCE's Translation, with an Introduction by the Author of "The Evolution of Christianity." Crown 8vo, 5s.

Eranus. A Collection of Exercises in the Alcaic and Sapphic Metres. Edited by F. W. CORNISH, Assistant Master at Eton. Second Edition. Crown 8vo, 2s.

EVANS, Mark.—**The Story of Our Father's Love,** told to Children. Sixth and Cheaper Edition. With Four Illustrations. Fcap. 8vo, 1s. 6d.

"Fan Kwae" at Canton before Treaty Days 1825-1844. By an old Resident. With Frontispiece. Crown 8vo, 5s.

Faith of the Unlearned, The. Authority, apart from the Sanction of Reason, an Insufficient Basis for It. By "One Unlearned." Crown 8vo, 6s.

FEIS, Jacob.—**Shakspere and Montaigne.** An Endeavour to Explain the Tendency of Hamlet from Allusions in Contemporary Works. Crown 8vo, 5s.

FLECKER, Rev. Eliezer.—**Scripture Onomatology.** Being Critical Notes on the Septuagint and other Versions. Second Edition. Crown 8vo, 3s. 6d.

FLOREDICE, W. H.—**A Month among the Mere Irish.** Small crown 8vo, 5s.

Frank Leward. Edited by CHARLES BAMPTON. Crown 8vo, 7s. 6d.

FULLER, Rev. Morris.—**The Lord's Day; or, Christian Sunday.** Its Unity, History, Philosophy, and Perpetual Obligation. Sermons. Demy 8vo, 10s. 6d.

GARDINER, Samuel R., and J. BASS MULLINGER, M.A.— **Introduction to the Study of English History.** Second Edition. Large crown 8vo, 9s.

GARDNER, Dorsey.—**Quatre Bras, Ligny, and Waterloo.** A Narrative of the Campaign in Belgium, 1815. With Maps and Plans. Demy 8vo, 16s.

Genesis in Advance of Present Science. A Critical Investigation of Chapters I.-IX. By a Septuagenarian Beneficed Presbyter. Demy 8vo. 10s. 6d.

GEORGE, Henry.—**Progress and Poverty:** An Inquiry into the Causes of Industrial Depressions, and of Increase of Want with Increase of Wealth. The Remedy. Fifth Library Edition. Post 8vo, 7s. 6d. Cabinet Edition. Crown 8vo, 2s. 6d. Also a Cheap Edition. Limp cloth, 1s. 6d. Paper covers, 1s.

Social Problems. Fourth Thousand. Crown 8vo, 5s. Cheap Edition. Paper covers, 1s.

GLANVILL, Joseph.—**Scepsis Scientifica;** or, Confest Ignorance, the Way to Science; in an Essay of the Vanity of Dogmatizing and Confident Opinion. Edited, with Introductory Essay, by JOHN OWEN. Elzevir 8vo, printed on hand-made paper, 6s.

Glossary of Terms and Phrases. Edited by the Rev. H. PERCY SMITH and others. Second and Cheaper Edition. Medium 8vo, 7s. 6d.

GLOVER, F., M.A.—**Exempla Latina.** A First Construing Book, with Short Notes, Lexicon, and an Introduction to the Analysis of Sentences. Second Edition. Fcap. 8vo, 2s.

GOLDSMID, Sir Francis Henry, Bart., Q.C., M.P.—**Memoir of.** With Portrait. Second Edition, Revised. Crown 8vo, 6s.

GOODENOUGH, Commodore J. G.—**Memoir of,** with Extracts from his Letters and Journals. Edited by his Widow. With Steel Engraved Portrait. Third Edition. Crown 8vo, 5s.

GORDON, Major-Genl. C. G.—**His Journals at Kartoum.** Printed from the original MS. With Introduction and Notes by A. EGMONT HAKE. Portrait, 2 Maps, and 30 Illustrations. Two vols., demy 8vo, 21s. Also a Cheap Edition in 1 vol., 6s.

Gordon's (General) Last Journal. A Facsimile of the last Journal received in England from GENERAL GORDON. Reproduced by Photo-lithography. Imperial 4to, £3 3s.

Events in the Life of. Crown 8vo, 5s.

GOSSE, Edmund.—**Studies in the Literature of Northern Europe.** New Edition. Large crown 8vo, 6s.

Seventeenth Century Studies. A Contribution to the History of English Poetry. Demy 8vo, 10s. 6d.

GOULD, Rev. S. Baring, M.A.—**Germany, Present and Past.** New and Cheaper Edition. Large crown 8vo, 7s. 6d.

GOWAN, Major Walter E.—**A. Ivanoff's Russian Grammar.** (16th Edition.) Translated, enlarged, and arranged for use of Students of the Russian Language. Demy 8vo, 6s.

GOWER, Lord Ronald. **My Reminiscences.** MINIATURE EDITION, printed on hand-made paper, limp parchment antique, 10s. 6d.

Last Days of Mary Antoinette. An Historical Sketch. With Portrait and Facsimiles. Fcap. 4to, 10s. 6d.

GOWER, Lord Ronald.—continued.

Notes of a Tour from Brindisi to Yokohama, 1883-1884. Fcap. 8vo, 2s. 6d.

GRAHAM, William, M.A.—The Creed of Science, Religious, Moral, and Social. Second Edition, Revised. Crown 8vo, 6s.

The Social Problem in its Economic, Moral, and Political Aspects. Demy 8vo.

GREY, Rowland.—In Sunny Switzerland. A Tale of Six Weeks. Second Edition. Small crown 8vo, 5s.

Lindenblumen and other Stories. Small crown 8vo, 5s.

GRIMLEY, Rev. H. N., M.A.—Tremadoc Sermons, chiefly on the Spiritual Body, the Unseen World, and the Divine Humanity. Fourth Edition. Crown 8vo, 6s.

GUSTAFSON, Alex.—The Foundation of Death. Third Edition. Crown 8vo, 5s.

Some Thoughts on Moderation. Reprinted from a Paper read at the Reeve Mission Room, Manchester Square, June 8, 1885. Crown 8vo, 1s.

HADDON, Caroline.—The Larger Life, Studies in Hinton's Ethics. Crown 8vo, 5s.

HAECKEL, Prof. Ernst.—The History of Creation. Translation revised by Professor E. RAY LANKESTER, M.A., F.R.S. With Coloured Plates and Genealogical Trees of the various groups of both Plants and Animals. 2 vols. Third Edition. Post 8vo, 32s.

The History of the Evolution of Man. With numerous Illustrations. 2 vols. Post 8vo, 32s.

A Visit to Ceylon. Post 8vo, 7s. 6d.

Freedom in Science and Teaching. With a Prefatory Note by T. H. HUXLEY, F.R.S. Crown 8vo, 5s.

HALF-CROWN SERIES :—

A Lost Love. By ANNA C. OGLE [Ashford Owen].

Sister Dora : a Biography. By MARGARET LONSDALE.

True Words for Brave Men : a Book for Soldiers and Sailors. By the late CHARLES KINGSLEY.

Notes of Travel : being Extracts from the Journals of Count VON MOLTKE.

English Sonnets. Collected and Arranged by J. DENNIS.

Home Songs for Quiet Hours. By the Rev. Canon R. H. BAYNES.

Hamilton, Memoirs of Arthur, B.A., of Trinity College, Cambridge. Crown 8vo, 6s.

Kegan Paul, Trench & Co.'s Publications. 13

HARRIS, William.—The History of the Radical Party in Parliament. Demy 8vo, 15*s.*

HARROP, Robert.—Bolingbroke. A Political Study and Criticism. Demy 8vo, 14*s.*

HART, Rev. J. W. T.—The Autobiography of Judas Iscariot. A Character Study. Crown 8vo, 3*s.* 6*d.*

HAWEIS, Rev. H. R., M.A.—Current Coin. Materialism—The Devil—Crime—Drunkenness—Pauperism—Emotion—Recreation —The Sabbath. Fifth Edition. Crown 8vo, 5*s.*

Arrows in the Air. Fifth Edition. Crown 8vo, 5*s.*

Speech in Season. Fifth Edition. Crown 8vo, 5*s.*

Thoughts for the Times. Thirteenth Edition. Crown 8vo, 5*s.*

Unsectarian Family Prayers. New Edition. Fcap. 8vo, 1*s.* 6*d.*

HAWKINS, Edwards Comerford.—Spirit and Form. Sermons preached in the Parish Church of Leatherhead. Crown 8vo, 6*s.*

HAWTHORNE, Nathaniel.—Works. Complete in Twelve Volumes. Large post 8vo, 7*s.* 6*d.* each volume.

VOL. I. TWICE-TOLD TALES.
II. MOSSES FROM AN OLD MANSE.
III. THE HOUSE OF THE SEVEN GABLES, AND THE SNOW IMAGE.
IV. THE WONDERBOOK, TANGLEWOOD TALES, AND GRANDFATHER'S CHAIR.
V. THE SCARLET LETTER, AND THE BLITHEDALE ROMANCE.
VI. THE MARBLE FAUN. [Transformation.]
VII. } OUR OLD HOME, AND ENGLISH NOTE-BOOKS.
VIII. }
IX. AMERICAN NOTE-BOOKS.
X. FRENCH AND ITALIAN NOTE-BOOKS.
XI. SEPTIMIUS FELTON, THE DOLLIVER ROMANCE, FANSHAWE, AND, IN AN APPENDIX, THE ANCESTRAL FOOTSTEP.
XII. TALES AND ESSAYS, AND OTHER PAPERS, WITH A BIOGRAPHICAL SKETCH OF HAWTHORNE.

HEATH, Francis George.—Autumnal Leaves. Third and cheaper Edition. Large crown 8vo, 6*s.*

Sylvan Winter. With 70 Illustrations. Large crown 8vo, 14*s.*

HENNESSY, Sir John Pope.—Ralegh in Ireland. With his Letters on Irish Affairs and some Contemporary Documents. Large crown 8vo, printed on hand-made paper, parchment, 10*s.* 6*d.*

HENRY, Philip.—Diaries and Letters of. Edited by MATTHEW HENRY LEE, M.A. Large crown 8vo, 7*s.* 6*d.*

HIDE, Albert.—The Age to Come. Small crown 8vo, 2*s.* 6*d.*

HINTON, J.—**Life and Letters.** With an Introduction by Sir W. W. GULL, Bart., and Portrait engraved on Steel by C. H. Jeens. Fifth Edition. Crown 8vo, 8s. 6d.

Philosophy and Religion. Selections from the Manuscripts of the late James Hinton. Edited by CAROLINE HADDON. Second Edition. Crown 8vo, 5s.

The Law Breaker, and The Coming of the Law. Edited by MARGARET HINTON. Crown 8vo, 6s.

The Mystery of Pain. New Edition. Fcap. 8vo, 1s.

Hodson of Hodson's Horse; or, Twelve Years of a Soldier's Life in India. Being extracts from the Letters of the late Major W. S. R. Hodson. With a Vindication from the Attack of Mr. Bosworth Smith. Edited by his brother, G. H. HODSON, M.A. Fourth Edition. Large crown 8vo, 5s.

HOLTHAM, E. G.—**Eight Years in Japan, 1873-1881.** Work, Travel, and Recreation. With three Maps. Large crown 8vo, 9s.

Homology of Economic Justice. An Essay by an East India Merchant. Small crown 8vo, 5s.

HOOPER, Mary.—**Little Dinners: How to Serve them with Elegance and Economy.** Nineteenth Edition. Crown 8vo, 2s. 6d.

Cookery for Invalids, Persons of Delicate Digestion, and Children. Fourth Edition. Crown 8vo, 2s. 6d.

Every-Day Meals. Being Economical and Wholesome Recipes for Breakfast, Luncheon, and Supper. Sixth Edition. Crown 8vo, 2s. 6d.

HOPKINS, Ellice.—**Work amongst Working Men.** Fifth Edition. Crown 8vo, 3s. 6d.

HORNADAY, W. T.—**Two Years in a Jungle.** With Illustrations. Demy 8vo, 21s.

HOSPITALIER, E.—**The Modern Applications of Electricity.** Translated and Enlarged by JULIUS MAIER, Ph.D. 2 vols. Second Edition, Revised, with many additions and numerous Illustrations. Demy 8vo, 12s. 6d. each volume.

VOL. I.—Electric Generators, Electric Light.
VOL. II.—Telephone : Various Applications : Electrical Transmission of Energy.

Household Readings on Prophecy. By a Layman. Small crown 8vo, 3s. 6d.

HOWARD, Robert, M.A.—**The Church of England and other Religious Communions.** A course of Lectures delivered in the Parish Church of Clapham. Crown 8vo, 7s. 6d.

HUGHES, Henry.—**The Redemption of the World.** Crown 8vo, 3s. 6d.

HUNTER, *Hay.*—The Crime of Christmas Day. A Tale of the Latin Quarter. 1*s.*

HUNTER, *William C.*—Bits of Old China. Small crown 8vo, 6*s.*

HUNTINGFORD, *Rev. E., D.C.L.*—The Apocalypse. With a Commentary and Introductory Essay. Demy 8vo, 5*s.*

HUTCHINSON, *H.*—Thought Symbolism, and Grammatic Illusions. Being a Treatise on the Nature, Purpose, and Material of Speech. Crown 8vo, 5*s.*

HUTTON, *Rev. C. F.*—Unconscious Testimony; or, The Silent Witness of the Hebrew to the Truth of the Historical Scriptures. Crown 8vo, 2*s.* 6*d.*

HYNDMAN, *H. M.*—The Historical Basis of Socialism in England. Large crown 8vo, 8*s.* 6*d.*

IDDESLEIGH, *Earl of.*—The Pleasures, Dangers, and Uses of Desultory Reading. Fcap. 8vo, in Whatman paper cover, 1*s.*

IM THURN, *Everard F.*—Among the Indians of Guiana. Being Sketches, chiefly anthropologic, from the Interior of British Guiana. With 53 Illustrations and a Map. Demy 8vo, 18*s.*

JACCOUD, *Prof. S.*—The Curability and Treatment of Pulmonary Phthisis. Translated and edited by MONTAGU LUBBOCK, M.D. Demy 8vo, 15*s.*

Jaunt in a Junk: A Ten Days' Cruise in Indian Seas. Large crown 8vo, 7*s.* 6*d.*

JENKINS, *E., and* RAYMOND, *J.*—The Architect's Legal Handbook. Third Edition, revised. Crown 8vo, 6*s.*

JENKINS, *Rev. Canon R. C.*—Heraldry: English and Foreign. With a Dictionary of Heraldic Terms and 156 Illustrations. Small crown 8vo, 3*s.* 6*d.*

JERVIS, *Rev. W. Henley.*—The Gallican Church and the Revolution. A Sequel to the History of the Church of France, from the Concordat of Bologna to, the Revolution. Demy 8vo, 18*s.*

JOEL, *L.*—A Consul's Manual and Shipowner's and Shipmaster's Practical Guide in their Transactions Abroad. With Definitions of Nautical, Mercantile, and Legal Terms; a Glossary of Mercantile Terms in English, French, German, Italian, and Spanish; Tables of the Money, Weights, and Measures of the Principal Commercial Nations and their Equivalents in British Standards; and Forms of Consular and Notarial Acts. Demy 8vo, 12*s.*

JOHNSTON, *H. H., F.Z.S.*—The Kilima-njaro Expedition. A Record of Scientific Exploration in Eastern Equatorial Africa, and a General Description of the Natural History, Languages, and Commerce of the Kilima-njaro District. With 6 Maps, and over 80 Illustrations by the Author. Demy 8vo, 21*s.*

JOYCE, P. W., LL.D., *etc.*—**Old Celtic Romances.** Translated from the Gaelic. Crown 8vo, 7s. 6d.

KAUFMANN, Rev. M., B.A.—**Socialism** : its Nature, its Dangers, and its Remedies considered. Crown 8vo, 7s. 6d.

 Utopias ; or, Schemes of Social Improvement, from Sir Thomas More to Karl Marx. Crown 8vo, 5s.

KAY, David, F.R.G.S.—**Education and Educators.** Crown 8vo, 7s. 6d.

KAY, Joseph.—**Free Trade in Land.** Edited by his Widow. With Preface by the Right Hon. JOHN BRIGHT, M.P. Seventh Edition. Crown 8vo, 5s.

 *** Also a cheaper edition, without the Appendix, but with a Revise of Recent Changes in the Land Laws of England, by the RIGHT HON. G. OSBORNE MORGAN, Q.C., M.P. Cloth, 1s. 6d. Paper covers, 1s.

KELKE, W. H. H.—**An Epitome of English Grammar for the Use of Students.** Adapted to the London Matriculation Course and Similar Examinations. Crown 8vo, 4s. 6d.

KEMPIS, Thomas à.—**Of the Imitation of Christ.** Parchment Library Edition.—Parchment or cloth, 6s. ; vellum, 7s. 6d. The Red Line Edition, fcap. 8vo, red edges, 2s. 6d. The Cabinet Edition, small 8vo, cloth limp, 1s. ; cloth boards, red edges, 1s. 6d. The Miniature Edition, red edges, 32mo, 1s.

 *** All the above Editions may be had in various extra bindings.

KENT, C.—**Corona Catholica ad Petri successoris Pedes Oblata; De Summi Pontificis Leonis XIII. Assumptione Epigramma.** In Quinquaginta Linguis. Fcap. 4to, 15s.

KETTLEWELL, Rev. S.—**Thomas à Kempis and the Brothers of Common Life.** 2 vols. With Frontispieces. Demy 8vo, 30s.

 *** Also an Abridged Edition, in one volume. With Portrait. Crown 8vo, 7s. 6d.

KIDD, Joseph, M.D.—**The Laws of Therapeutics** ; or, the Science and Art of Medicine. Second Edition. Crown 8vo, 6s.

KINGSFORD, Anna, M.D.—**The Perfect Way in Diet.** A Treatise advocating a Return to the Natural and Ancient Food of our Race. Second Edition. Small crown 8vo, 2s.

KINGSLEY, Charles, M.A.—**Letters and Memories of his Life.** Edited by his Wife. With two. Steel Engraved Portraits, and Vignettes on Wood. Fifteenth Cabinet Edition. 2 vols. Crown 8vo, 12s.

 *** Also a People's Edition, in one volume. With Portrait. Crown 8vo, 6s.

 All Saints' Day, and other Sermons. Edited by the Rev. W. HARRISON. Third Edition. Crown 8vo, 7s. 6d.

KINGSLEY, Charles, M.A.—continued.
True Words for Brave Men. A Book for Soldiers' and Sailors' Libraries. Eleventh Edition. Crown 8vo, 2s. 6d.

KNOX, Alexander A.—**The New Playground**; or, Wanderings in Algeria. New and Cheaper Edition. Large crown 8vo, 6s.

LANDON, Joseph.—**School Management**; Including a General View of the Work of Education, Organization, and Discipline. Fourth Edition. Crown 8vo, 6s.

LAURIE, S. S.—**The Training of Teachers**, and other Educational Papers. Crown 8vo, 7s. 6d.

LEE, Rev. F. G., D.C.L.—**The Other World**; or, Glimpses of the Supernatural. 2 vols. A New Edition. Crown 8vo, 15s.

Letters from an Unknown Friend. By the Author of "Charles Lowder." With a Preface by the Rev. W. H. CLEAVER. Fcap. 8vo, 1s.

Letters from a Young Emigrant in Manitoba. Second Edition. Small crown 8vo, 3s. 6d.

Leward, Frank. Edited by CHARLES BAMPTON. Crown 8vo, 7s. 6d.

LEWIS, Edward Dillon.—**A Draft Code of Criminal Law and Procedure.** Demy 8vo, 21s.

Life of a Prig. By ONE. Second Edition. Fcap. 8vo, 3s. 6d.

LILLIE, Arthur, M.R.A.S.—**The Popular Life of Buddha.** Containing an Answer to the Hibbert Lectures of 1881. With Illustrations. Crown 8vo, 6s.

LLOYD, Walter.—**The Hope of the World**: An Essay on Universal Redemption. Crown 8vo, 5s.

LONSDALE, Margaret.—**Sister Dora**: a Biography. With Portrait. Cheap Edition. Crown 8vo, 2s. 6d.

George Eliot: Thoughts upon her Life, her Books, and Herself. Second Edition. Crown 8vo, 1s. 6d.

LOUNSBURY, Thomas R.—**James Fenimore Cooper.** With Portrait. Crown 8vo, 5s.

LOWDER, Charles.—**A Biography.** By the Author of "St. Teresa." New and Cheaper Edition. Crown 8vo. With Portrait. 3s. 6d.

LÜCKES, Eva C. E.—**Lectures on General Nursing,** delivered to the Probationers of the London Hospital Training School for Nurses. Crown 8vo, 2s. 6d.

LYALL, William Rowe, D.D.—**Propædeia Prophetica**; or, The Use and Design of the Old Testament Examined. New Edition. With Notices by GEORGE C. PEARSON, M.A., Hon. Canon of Canterbury. Demy 8vo, 10s. 6d.

LYTTON, Edward Bulwer, Lord.—**Life, Letters and Literary Remains.** By his Son, the EARL OF LYTTON. With Portraits, Illustrations and Facsimiles. Demy 8vo. Vols. I. and II., 32s.

MACAULAY, G. C.—**Francis Beaumont :** A Critical Study. Crown 8vo, 5s.

MAC CALLUM, M. W.—**Studies in Low German and High German Literature.** Crown 8vo, 6s.

MACHIAVELLI, Niccolò. — **Life and Times.** By Prof. VILLARI. Translated by LINDA VILLARI. 4 vols. Large post 8vo, 48s.

MACHIAVELLI, Niccolò.—**Discourses on the First Decade of Titus Livius.** Translated from the Italian by NINIAN HILL THOMSON, M.A. Large crown 8vo, 12s.

The Prince. Translated from the Italian by N. H. T. Small crown 8vo, printed on hand-made paper, bevelled boards, 6s.

MACKENZIE, Alexander.—**How India is Governed.** Being an Account of England's Work in India. Small crown 8vo, 2s.

MAGNUS, Mrs.—**About the Jews since Bible Times.** From the Babylonian Exile till the English Exodus. Small crown 8vo, 6s.

MAGUIRE, Thomas.—**Lectures on Philosophy.** Demy 8vo, 9s.

MAIR, R. S., M.D., F.R.C.S.E.—**The Medical Guide for Anglo-Indians.** Being a Compendium of Advice to Europeans in India, relating to the Preservation and Regulation of Health. With a Supplement on the Management of Children in India. Second Edition. Crown 8vo, limp cloth, 3s. 6d.

MALDEN, Henry Elliot.—**Vienna, 1683.** The History and Consequences of the Defeat of the Turks before Vienna, September 12th, 1683, by John Sobieski, King of Poland, and Charles Leopold, Duke of Lorraine. Crown 8vo, 4s. 6d.

Many Voices. A volume of Extracts from the Religious Writers of Christendom from the First to the Sixteenth Century. With Biographical Sketches. Crown 8vo, cloth extra, red edges, 6s.

MARKHAM, Capt. Albert Hastings, R.N.—**The Great Frozen Sea :** A Personal Narrative of the Voyage of the *Alert* during the Arctic Expedition of 1875-6. With 6 Full-page Illustrations, 2 Maps, and 27 Woodcuts. Sixth and Cheaper Edition. Crown 8vo, 6s.

MARTINEAU, Gertrude.—**Outline Lessons on Morals.** Small crown 8vo, 3s. 6d.

MAUDSLEY, H., M.D.—**Body and Will.** Being an Essay concerning Will, in its Metaphysical, Physiological, and Pathological Aspects. 8vo, 12s.

Natural Causes and Supernatural Seemings. Crown 8vo.

McGRATH, Terence.—**Pictures from Ireland.** New and Cheaper Edition. Crown 8vo, 2s.

MEREDITH, M.A.—**Theotokos, the Example for Woman.** Dedicated, by permission, to Lady Agnes Wood. Revised by the Venerable Archdeacon DENISON. 32mo, limp cloth, 1s. 6d.

MILLER, Edward.—**The History and Doctrines of Irvingism ;** or, The so-called Catholic and Apostolic Church. 2 vols. Large post 8vo, 25s.

MILLER, Edward—continued.
   The Church in Relation to the State. Large crown 8vo, 7s. 6d.

MITCHELL, Lucy M.—A History of Ancient Sculpture. With numerous Illustrations, including 6 Plates in Phototype. Super royal 8vo, 42s.

MITFORD, Bertram.—Through the Zulu Country. Its Battlefields and its People. With Five Illustrations. Demy 8vo, 14s.

MOCKLER, E.—A Grammar of the Baloochee Language, as it is spoken in Makran (Ancient Gedrosia), in the Persia-Arabic and Roman characters. Fcap. 8vo, 5s.

MOLESWORTH, Rev. W. Nassau, M.A.—History of the Church of England from 1660. Large crown 8vo, 7s. 6d.

MORELL, J. R.—Euclid Simplified in Method and Language. Being a Manual of Geometry. Compiled from the most important French Works, approved by the University of Paris and the Minister of Public Instruction. Fcap. 8vo, 2s. 6d.

MORGAN, C. Lloyd.—The Springs of Conduct. An Essay in Evolution. Large crown 8vo, cloth, 7s. 6d.

MORRIS, George.—The Duality of all Divine Truth in our Lord Jesus Christ. For God's Self-manifestation in the Impartation of the Divine Nature to Man. Large crown 8vo, 7s. 6d.

MORSE, E. S., Ph.D.—First Book of Zoology. With numerous Illustrations. New and Cheaper Edition. Crown 8vo, 2s. 6d.

MULL, Matthias.—Paradise Lost. By JOHN MILTON. Books I.—VI. The Mutilations of the Text emended, the Punctuation revised, and all collectively presented, with Notes and Preface; also a short Essay on the Intellectual Value of Milton's Works, etc. Demy 8vo, 6s.

   Shakspere's Hamlet. The Text Revised. Lines pronounced Corrupt restored, and Mutilations before unsuspected emended. With Preface and Notes. Demy 8vo, 3s.

NELSON, J. H., M.A.—A Prospectus of the Scientific Study of the Hindû Law. Demy 8vo, 9s.

NEWMAN, Cardinal.—Characteristics from the Writings of. Being Selections from his various Works. Arranged with the Author's personal Approval. Sixth Edition. With Portrait. Crown 8vo, 6s.

   ⁎ A Portrait of Cardinal Newman, mounted for framing, can be had, 2s. 6d.

NEWMAN, Francis William.—Essays on Diet. Small crown 8vo, cloth limp, 2s.

New Truth and the Old Faith: Are they Incompatible? By a Scientific Layman. Demy 8vo, 10s. 6d.

NICOLS, Arthur, F.G.S., F.R.G.S.—**Chapters from the Physical History of the Earth:** an Introduction to Geology and Palæontology. With numerous Illustrations. Crown 8vo, 5s.

NOEL, The Hon. Roden.—**Essays on Poetry and Poets.** Demy 8vo, 12s.

NOPS, Marianne.—**Class Lessons on Euclid.** Part I. containing the First Two Books of the Elements. Crown 8vo, 2s. 6d.

Nuces: EXERCISES ON THE SYNTAX OF THE PUBLIC SCHOOL LATIN PRIMER. New Edition in Three Parts. Crown 8vo, each 1s.
*** The Three Parts can also be had bound together, 3s.

OATES, Frank, F.R.G.S.—**Matabele Land and the Victoria Falls.** A Naturalist's Wanderings in the Interior of South Africa. Edited by C. G. OATES, B.A. With numerous Illustrations and 4 Maps. Demy 8vo, 21s.

O'CONNOR, T. P., M.P.—**The Parnell Movement.** With a Sketch of Irish Parties from 1843. Demy 8vo, 18s.

OGLE, W., M.D., F.R.C.P.—**Aristotle on the Parts of Animals.** Translated, with Introduction and Notes. Royal 8vo, 12s. 6d.

O'HAGAN, Lord, K.P.—**Occasional Papers and Addresses.** Large crown 8vo, 7s. 6d.

O'MEARA, Kathleen.—**Frederic Ozanam,** Professor of the Sorbonne: His Life and Work. Second Edition. Crown 8vo, 7s. 6d.

Henri Perreyve and his Counsels to the Sick. Small crown 8vo, 5s.

One and a Half in Norway. A Chronicle of Small Beer. By Either and Both. Small crown 8vo, 3s. 6d.

O'NEIL, the late Rev. Lord.—**Sermons.** With Memoir and Portrait. Crown 8vo, 6s.

Essays and Addresses. Crown 8vo, 5s.

Only Passport to Heaven, The. By One who has it. Small crown 8vo, 1s. 6d.

OSBORNE, Rev. W. A.—**The Revised Version of the New Testament.** A Critical Commentary, with Notes upon the Text. Crown 8vo, 5s.

OTTLEY, H. Bickersteth.—**The Great Dilemma.** Christ His Own Witness or His Own Accuser. Six Lectures. Second Edition. Crown 8vo, 3s. 6d.

Our Public Schools—Eton, Harrow, Winchester, Rugby, Westminster, Marlborough, The Charterhouse. Crown 8vo, 6s.

OWEN, F. M.—**John Keats:** a Study. Crown 8vo, 6s.

Across the Hills. Small crown 8vo, 1s. 6d.

OWEN, Rev. Robert, B.D.—**Sanctorale Catholicum**; or, Book of Saints. With Notes, Critical, Exegetical, and Historical. Demy 8vo, 18s.

OXENHAM, Rev. F. Nutcombe.—**What is the Truth as to Everlasting Punishment.** Part II. Being an Historical Inquiry into the Witness and Weight of certain Anti-Origenist Councils. Crown 8vo, 2s. 6d.

OXONIENSIS. — **Romanism, Protestantism, Anglicanism.** Being a Layman's View of some questions of the Day. Together with Remarks on Dr. Littledale's "Plain Reasons against joining the Church of Rome." Crown 8vo, 3s. 6d.

PALMER, the late William.—**Notes of a Visit to Russia in 1840-1841.** Selected and arranged by JOHN H. CARDINAL NEWMAN, with Portrait. Crown 8vo, 8s. 6d.

Early Christian Symbolism. A Series of Compositions from Fresco Paintings, Glasses, and Sculptured Sarcophagi. Edited by the Rev. Provost NORTHCOTE, D.D., and the Rev. Canon BROWNLOW, M.A. With Coloured Plates, folio, 42s., or with Plain Plates, folio, 25s.

Parchment Library. Choicely Printed on hand-made paper, limp parchment antique or cloth, 6s.; vellum, 7s. 6d. each volume.

The Poetical Works of John Milton. 2 vols.

Letters and Journals of Jonathan Swift. Selected and edited, with a Commentary and Notes, by STANLEY LANE POOLE.

De Quincey's Confessions of an English Opium Eater. Reprinted from the First Edition. Edited by RICHARD GARNETT.

The Gospel according to **Matthew, Mark,** and **Luke.**

Selections from the Prose Writings of Jonathan Swift. With a Preface and Notes by STANLEY LANE-POOLE and Portrait.

English Sacred Lyrics.

Sir Joshua Reynolds's Discourses. Edited by EDMUND GOSSE.

Selections from Milton's Prose Writings. Edited by ERNEST MYERS.

The Book of Psalms. Translated by the Rev. T. K. CHEYNE, M.A.

The Vicar of Wakefield. With Preface and Notes by AUSTIN DOBSON.

English Comic Dramatists. Edited by OSWALD CRAWFURD.

English Lyrics.

The Sonnets of John Milton. Edited by MARK PATTISON. With Portrait after Vertue.

Parchment Library—*continued*.

French Lyrics. Selected and Annotated by GEORGE SAINTSBURY. With a Miniature Frontispiece designed and etched by H. G. Glindoni.

Fables by Mr. John Gay. With Memoir by AUSTIN DOBSON, and an Etched Portrait from an unfinished Oil Sketch by Sir Godfrey Kneller.

Select Letters of Percy Bysshe Shelley. Edited, with an Introduction, by RICHARD GARNETT.

The Christian Year. Thoughts in Verse for the Sundays and Holy Days throughout the Year. With Miniature Portrait of the Rev. J. Keble, after a Drawing by G. Richmond, R.A.

Shakspere's Works. Complete in Twelve Volumes.

Eighteenth Century Essays. Selected and Edited by AUSTIN DOBSON. With a Miniature Frontispiece by R. Caldecott.

Q. Horati Flacci Opera. Edited by F. A. CORNISH, Assistant Master at Eton. With a Frontispiece after a design by L. Alma Tadema, etched by Leopold Lowenstam.

Edgar Allan Poe's Poems. With an Essay on his Poetry by ANDREW LANG, and a Frontispiece by Linley Sambourne.

Shakspere's Sonnets. Edited by EDWARD DOWDEN. With a Frontispiece etched by Leopold Lowenstam, after the Death Mask.

English Odes. Selected by EDMUND GOSSE. With Frontispiece on India paper by Hamo Thornycroft, A.R.A.

Of the Imitation of Christ. By THOMAS À KEMPIS. A revised Translation. With Frontispiece on India paper, from a Design by W. B. Richmond.

Poems: Selected from PERCY BYSSHE SHELLEY. Dedicated to Lady Shelley. With a Preface by RICHARD GARNETT and a Miniature Frontispiece.

*** The above volumes may also be had in a variety of leather bindings.

PARSLOE, Joseph.—**Our Railways.** Sketches, Historical and Descriptive. With Practical Information as to Fares and Rates, etc., and a Chapter on Railway Reform. Crown 8vo, 6s.

PASCAL, Blaise.—**The Thoughts of.** Translated from the Text of Auguste Molinier, by C. KEGAN PAUL. Large crown 8vo, with Frontispiece, printed on hand-made paper, parchment antique, or cloth, 12s.; vellum, 15s.

PAUL, Alexander.—**Short Parliaments.** A History of the National Demand for frequent General Elections. Small crown 8vo, 3s. 6d.

PAUL, C. Kegan.—**Biographical Sketches.** Printed on hand-made paper, bound in buckram. Second Edition. Crown 8vo, 7s. 6d.

PEARSON, Rev. S.—**Week-day Living.** A Book for Young Men and Women. Second Edition. Crown 8vo, 5*s*.

PESCHEL, Dr. Oscar.—**The Races of Man and their Geographical Distribution.** Second Edition. Large crown 8vo, 9*s*.

PHIPSON, E.—**The Animal Lore of Shakspeare's Time.** Including Quadrupeds, Birds, Reptiles, Fish and Insects. Large post 8vo, 9*s*.

PIDGEON, D.—**An Engineer's Holiday**; or, Notes of a Round Trip from Long. 0° to 0°. New and Cheaper Edition. Large crown 8vo, 7*s*. 6*d*.

Old World Questions and New World Answers. Second Edition. Large crown 8vo, 7*s*. 6*d*.

Plain Thoughts for Men. Eight Lectures delivered at Forester's Hall, Clerkenwell, during the London Mission, 1884. Crown 8vo, cloth, 1*s*. 6*d*; paper covers, 1*s*.

POE, Edgar Allan.—**Works of.** With an Introduction and a Memoir by RICHARD HENRY STODDARD. In 6 vols. With Frontispieces and Vignettes. Large crown 8vo, 6*s*. each.

POPE, J. Buckingham. — **Railway Rates and Radical Rule.** Trade Questions as Election Tests. Crown 8vo, 2*s*. 6*d*.

PRICE, Prof. Bonamy. — **Chapters on Practical Political Economy.** Being the Substance of Lectures delivered before the University of Oxford. New and Cheaper Edition. Large post 8vo, 5*s*.

Pulpit Commentary, The. (Old Testament Series.) Edited by the Rev. J. S. EXELL, M.A., and the Rev. Canon H. D. M. SPENCE.

> **Genesis.** By the Rev. T. WHITELAW, M.A. With Homilies by the Very Rev. J. F. MONTGOMERY, D.D., Rev. Prof. R. A. REDFORD, M.A., LL.B., Rev. F. HASTINGS, Rev. W. ROBERTS, M.A. An Introduction to the Study of the Old Testament by the Venerable Archdeacon FARRAR, D.D., F.R.S.; and Introductions to the Pentateuch by the Right Rev. H. COTTERILL, D.D., and Rev. T. WHITELAW, M.A. Eighth Edition. 1 vol., 15*s*.
>
> **Exodus.** By the Rev. Canon RAWLINSON. With Homilies by Rev. J. ORR, Rev. D. YOUNG, B.A., Rev. C. A. GOODHART, Rev. J. URQUHART, and the Rev. H. T. ROBJOHNS. Fourth Edition. 2 vols., 18*s*.
>
> **Leviticus.** By the Rev. Prebendary MEYRICK, M.A. With Introductions by the Rev. R. COLLINS, Rev. Professor A. CAVE, and Homilies by Rev. Prof. REDFORD, LL.B., Rev. J. A. MACDONALD, Rev. W. CLARKSON, B.A., Rev. S. R. ALDRIDGE, LL.B., and Rev. McCHEYNE EDGAR. Fourth Edition. 15*s*.

Pulpit Commentary, The—*continued*.

Numbers. By the Rev. R. WINTERBOTHAM, LL.B. With Homilies by the Rev. Professor W. BINNIE, D.D., Rev. E. S. PROUT, M.A., Rev. D. YOUNG, Rev. J. WAITE, and an Introduction by the Rev. THOMAS WHITELAW, M.A. Fourth Edition. 15s.

Deuteronomy. By the Rev. W. L. ALEXANDER, D.D. With Homilies by Rev. C. CLEMANCE, D.D., Rev. J. ORR, B.D., Rev. R. M. EDGAR, M.A., Rev. D. DAVIES, M.A. Fourth edition. 15s.

Joshua. By Rev. J. J. LIAS, M.A. With Homilies by Rev. S. R. ALDRIDGE, LL.B., Rev. R. GLOVER, REV. E. DE PRESSENSÉ, D.D., Rev. J. WAITE, B.A., Rev. W. F. ADENEY, M.A.; and an Introduction by the Rev. A. PLUMMER, M.A. Fifth Edition. 12s. 6d.

Judges and Ruth. By the Bishop of Bath and Wells, and Rev. J. MORISON, D.D. With Homilies by Rev. A. F. MUIR, M.A., Rev. W. F. ADENEY, M.A., Rev. W. M. STATHAM, and Rev. Professor J. THOMSON, M.A. Fourth Edition. 10s. 6d.

1 Samuel. By the Very Rev. R. P. SMITH, D.D. With Homilies by Rev. DONALD FRASER, D.D., Rev. Prof. CHAPMAN, and Rev. B. DALE. Sixth Edition. 15s.

1 Kings. By the Rev. JOSEPH HAMMOND, LL.B. With Homilies by the Rev. E. DE PRESSENSÉ, D.D., Rev. J. WAITE, B.A., Rev. A. ROWLAND, LL.B., Rev. J. A. MACDONALD, and Rev. J. URQUHART. Fourth Edition. 15s.

1 Chronicles. By the Rev. Prof. P. C. BARKER, M.A., LL.B. With Homilies by Rev. Prof. J. R. THOMSON, M.A., Rev. R. TUCK, B.A., Rev. W. CLARKSON, B.A., Rev. F. WHITFIELD, M.A., and Rev. RICHARD GLOVER. 15s.

Ezra, Nehemiah, and Esther. By Rev. Canon G. RAWLINSON, M.A. With Homilies by Rev. Prof. J. R. THOMSON, M.A., Rev. Prof. R. A. REDFORD, LL.B., M.A., Rev. W. S. LEWIS, M.A., Rev. J. A. MACDONALD, Rev. A. MACKENNAL, B.A., Rev. W. CLARKSON, B.A., Rev. F. HASTINGS, Rev. W. DINWIDDIE, LL.B., Rev. Prof. ROWLANDS, B.A., Rev. G. WOOD, B.A., Rev. Prof. P. C. BARKER, M.A., LL.B., and the Rev. J. S. EXELL, M.A. Sixth Edition. 1 vol., 12s. 6d.

Jeremiah. (Vol. I.) By the Rev. T. K. CHEYNE, M.A. With Homilies by the Rev. W. F. ADENEY, M.A., Rev. A. F. MUIR, M.A., Rev. S. CONWAY, B.A., Rev. J. WAITE, B.A., and Rev. D. YOUNG, B.A. Second Edition. 15s.

Jeremiah (Vol. II.) and Lamentations. By Rev. T. K. CHEYNE, M.A. With Homilies by Rev. Prof. J. R. THOMSON, M.A., Rev. W. F. ADENEY, M.A., Rev. A. F. MUIR, M.A., Rev. S. CONWAY, B.A., Rev. D. YOUNG, B.A. 15s.

Pulpit Commentary, The. (New Testament Series.)

St. Mark. By Very Rev. E. BICKERSTETH, D.D., Dean of Lichfield. With Homilies by Rev. Prof. THOMSON, M.A., Rev. Prof. GIVEN, M.A., Rev. Prof. JOHNSON, M.A., Rev. A. ROWLAND, B.A., LL.B., Rev. A. MUIR, and Rev. R. GREEN. Fourth Edition. 2 vols., 21s.

The Acts of the Apostles. By the Bishop of Bath and Wells. With Homilies by Rev. Prof. P. C. BARKER, M.A., LL.B., Rev. Prof. E. JOHNSON, M.A., Rev. Prof. R. A. REDFORD, M.A., Rev. R. TUCK, B.A., Rev. W. CLARKSON, B.A. Second Edition. 2 vols., 21s.

I. Corinthians. By the Ven. Archdeacon FARRAR, D.D. With Homilies by Rev. Ex-Chancellor LIPSCOMB, LL.D., Rev. DAVID THOMAS, D.D., Rev. D. FRASER, D.D., Rev. Prof. J. R. THOMSON, M.A., Rev. J. WAITE, B.A., Rev. R. TUCK, B.A., Rev. E. HURNDALL, M.A., and Rev. H. BREMNER, B.D. Second Edition. Price 15s.

II. Corinthians and Galatians. By the Ven. Archdeacon FARRAR, D.D., and Rev. Preb. E. HUXTABLE. With Homilies by Rev. Ex-Chancellor LIPSCOMB, LL.D., Rev. DAVID THOMAS, D.D., Rev. DONALD FRASER, D.D., Rev. R. TUCK, B.A., Rev. E. HURNDALL, M.A., Rev. Prof. J. R. THOMSON, M.A., Rev. R. FINLAYSON, B.A., Rev. W. F. ADENEY, M.A., Rev. R. M. EDGAR, M.A., and Rev. T. CROSKERRY, D.D. Price 21s.

Ephesians, Phillipians, and Colossians. By the Rev. Prof. W. G. BLACKIE, D.D., Rev. B. C. CAFFIN, M.A., and Rev. G. G. FINDLAY, B.A. With Homilies by Rev. D. THOMAS, D.D., Rev. R. M. EDGAR, M.A., Rev. R. FINLAYSON, B.A., Rev. W. F. ADENEY, M.A., Rev. Prof. T. CROSKERRY, D.D., Rev. E. S. PROUT, M.A., Rev. Canon VERNON HUTTON, and Rev. U. R. THOMAS, D.D. Price 21s.

PUNCHARD, E. G., D.D.—**Christ of Contention.** Three Essays. Fcap. 8vo, 2s.

PUSEY, Dr.—**Sermons for the Church's Seasons from Advent to Trinity.** Selected from the Published Sermons of the late EDWARD BOUVERIE PUSEY, D.D. Crown 8vo, 5s.

RANKE, Leopold von.—**Universal History.** The oldest Historical Group of Nations and the Greeks. Edited by G. W. PROTHERO. Demy 8vo, 16s.

Realities of the Future Life. Small crown 8vo, 1s. 6d.

RENDELL, J. M.—**Concise Handbook of the Island of Madeira.** With Plan of Funchal and Map of the Island. Fcap. 8vo, 1s. 6d.

REYNOLDS, Rev. J. W.—**The Supernatural in Nature.** A Verification by Free Use of Science. Third Edition, Revised and Enlarged. Demy 8vo, 14s.

REYNOLDS, Rev. J. W.—continued.
>The Mystery of Miracles. Third and Enlarged Edition. Crown 8vo, 6s.
>The Mystery of the Universe; Our Common Faith. Demy 8vo, 14s.

RIBOT, Prof. Th.—Heredity: A Psychological Study on its Phenomena, its Laws, its Causes, and its Consequences. Second Edition. Large crown 8vo, 9s.

RIMMER, William, M.D.—Art Anatomy. A Portfolio of 81 Plates. Folio, 70s., nett.

ROBERTSON, The late Rev. F. W., M.A.—Life and Letters of. Edited by the Rev. STOPFORD BROOKE, M.A.
>I. Two vols., uniform with the Sermons. With Steel Portrait. Crown 8vo, 7s. 6d.
>II. Library Edition, in Demy 8vo, with Portrait. 12s.
>III. A Popular Edition, in 1 vol. Crown 8vo, 6s.

>Sermons. Four Series. Small crown 8vo, 3s. 6d. each.
>The Human Race, and other Sermons. Preached at Cheltenham, Oxford, and Brighton. New and Cheaper Edition. Small crown 8vo, 3s. 6d.
>Notes on Genesis. New and Cheaper Edition. Small crown 8vo, 3s. 6d.
>Expository Lectures on St. Paul's Epistles to the Corinthians. A New Edition. Small crown 8vo, 5s.
>Lectures and Addresses, with other Literary Remains. A New Edition. Small crown 8vo, 5s.
>An Analysis of Tennyson's "In Memoriam." (Dedicated by Permission to the Poet-Laureate.) Fcap. 8vo, 2s.
>The Education of the Human Race. Translated from the German of GOTTHOLD EPHRAIM LESSING. Fcap. 8vo, 2s. 6d.
>The above Works can also be had, bound in half morocco.

*** A Portrait of the late Rev. F. W. Robertson, mounted for framing, can be had, 2s. 6d.

ROMANES, G. J.—Mental Evolution in Animals. With a Posthumous Essay on Instinct by CHARLES DARWIN, F.R.S. Demy 8vo, 12s.

Rosmini's Origin of Ideas. Translated from the Fifth Italian Edition of the Nuovo Saggio *Sull' origine delle idee.* 3 vols. Demy 8vo, cloth, 16s. each.

Rosmini's Psychology. 3 vols. Demy 8vo. [Vols. I. and II. now ready, 16s. each.

Rosmini's Philosophical System. Translated, with a Sketch of the Author's Life, Bibliography, Introduction, and Notes by THOMAS DAVIDSON. Demy 8vo, 16s.

RULE, Martin, M.A.—The Life and Times of St. Anselm, Archbishop of Canterbury and Primate of the Britains. 2 vols. Demy 8vo, 32s.

SAMUEL, Sydney M.—Jewish Life in the East. Small crown 8vo, 3s. 6d.

SARTORIUS, Ernestine.—Three Months in the Soudan. With 11 Full-page Illustrations. Demy 8vo, 14s.

SAYCE, Rev. Archibald Henry.—Introduction to the Science of Language. 2 vols. Second Edition. Large post 8vo, 21s.

SCOONES, W. Baptiste.—Four Centuries of English Letters: A Selection of 350 Letters by 150 Writers, from the Period of the Paston Letters to the Present Time. Third Edition. Large crown 8vo, 6s.

SÉE, PROF. GERMAIN.—Bacillary Phthisis of the Lungs. Translated and edited for English Practitioners by WILLIAM HENRY WEDDELL, M.R.C.S. Demy 8vo, 10s. 6d.

SHILLITO, Rev. Joseph.—Womanhood : its Duties, Temptations, and Privileges. A Book for Young Women. Third Edition. Crown 8vo, 3s. 6d.

SIDNEY, Algernon.—A Review. By GERTRUDE M. IRELAND BLACKBURNE. Crown 8vo, 6s.

Sister Augustine, Superior of the Sisters of Charity at the St. Johannis Hospital at Bonn. Authorised Translation by HANS THARAU, from the German "Memorials of AMALIE VON LASAULX." Cheap Edition. Large crown 8vo, 4s. 6d.

SKINNER, James.—A Memoir. By the Author of "Charles Lowder." With a Preface by the Rev. Canon CARTER, and Portrait. Large crown, 7s. 6d.

*** Also a cheap Edition. With Portrait. Crown 8vo, 3s. 6d.

SMITH, Edward, M.D., LL.B., F.R.S.—Tubercular Consumption in its Early and Remediable Stages. Second Edition. Crown 8vo, 6s.

SMITH, Sir W. Cusack, Bart.—Our War Ships. A Naval Essay. Crown 8vo, 5s.

Spanish Mystics. By the Editor of "Many Voices." Crown 8vo, 5s.

Specimens of English Prose Style from Malory to Macaulay. Selected and Annotated, with an Introductory Essay, by GEORGE SAINTSBURY. Large crown 8vo, printed on handmade paper, parchment antique or cloth, 12s. ; vellum, 15s.

SPEDDING, James.—Reviews and Discussions, Literary, Political, and Historical not relating to Bacon. Demy 8vo, 12s. 6d.

Evenings with a Reviewer; or, Macaulay and Bacon. With a Prefatory Notice by G. S. VENABLES, Q.C. 2 vols. Demy 8vo, 18s.

STAPFER, Paul.—Shakespeare and Classical Antiquity : Greek and Latin Antiquity as presented in Shakespeare's Plays. Translated by EMILY J. CAREY. Large post 8vo, 12s.

STATHAM, F. Reginald.—**Free Thought and Truth Thought.** A Contribution to an Existing Argument. Crown 8vo, 6s.

STEVENSON, Rev. W. F.—**Hymns for the Church and Home.** Selected and Edited by the Rev. W. FLEMING STEVENSON. The Hymn Book consists of Three Parts :—I. For Public Worship.—II. For Family and Private Worship.—III. For Children. SMALL EDITION. Cloth limp, 10d.; cloth boards, 1s. LARGE TYPE EDITION. Cloth limp, 1s. 3d.; cloth boards, 1s. 6d.

Stray Papers on Education, and Scenes from School Life. By B. H. Second Edition. Small crown 8vo, 3s. 6d.

STREATFEILD, Rev. G. S., M.A.—**Lincolnshire and the Danes.** Large crown 8vo, 7s. 6d.

STRECKER-WISLICENUS.—**Organic Chemistry.** Translated and Edited, with Extensive Additions, by W. R. HODGKINSON, Ph.D., and A. J. GREENAWAY, F.I.C. Second and cheaper Edition. Demy 8vo, 12s. 6d.

Suakin, 1885; being a Sketch of the Campaign of this year. By an Officer who was there. Crown 8vo, 2s. 6d.

SULLY, James, M.A.—**Pessimism :** a History and a Criticism. Second Edition. Demy 8vo, 14s.

Sunshine and Sea. A Yachting Visit to the Channel Islands and Coast of Brittany. With Frontispiece from a Photograph and 24 Illustrations. Crown 8vo, 6s.

SWEDENBORG, Eman.—**De Cultu et Amore Dei ubi Agitur de Telluris ortu, Paradiso et Vivario, tum de Primogeniti Seu Adami Nativitate Infantia, et Amore.** Crown 8vo, 6s.

On the Worship and Love of God. Treating of the Birth of the Earth, Paradise, and the Abode of Living Creatures. Translated from the original Latin. Crown 8vo, 7s. 6d.

TACITUS.—**The Agricola.** A Translation. Small crown 8vo, 2s. 6d.

TAYLOR, Rev. Isaac.—**The Alphabet.** An Account of the Origin and Development of Letters. With numerous Tables and Facsimiles. 2 vols. Demy 8vo, 36s.

TAYLOR, Jeremy.—**The Marriage Ring.** With Preface, Notes, and Appendices. Edited by FRANCIS BURDETT MONEY COUTTS. Small crown 8vo, 2s. 6d.

TAYLOR, Sedley. — **Profit Sharing between Capital and Labour.** To which is added a Memorandum on the Industrial Partnership at the Whitwood Collieries, by ARCHIBALD and HENRY BRIGGS, with remarks by SEDLEY TAYLOR. Crown 8vo, 2s. 6d.

"They Might Have Been Together Till the Last." An Essay on Marriage, and the position of Women in England. Small crown 8vo, 2s.

Thirty Thousand Thoughts. Edited by the Rev. CANON SPENCE, Rev. J. S. EXELL, and Rev. CHARLES NEIL. 6 vols., Super royal 8vo.
[Vols. I.-IV. now ready, 16s. each.

THOM, J. Hamilton.—Laws of Life after the Mind of Christ. Second Edition. Crown 8vo, 7s. 6d.

TIPPLE, Rev. S. A.—Sunday Mornings at Norwood. Prayers and Sermons. Crown 8vo, 6s.

TODHUNTER, Dr. J.—A Study of Shelley. Crown 8vo, 7s.

TOLSTOI, Count Leo.—Christ's Christianity. Translated from the Russian. Large Crown 8vo, 7s. 6d.

TRANT, William.—Trade Unions: Their Origin, Objects, and Efficacy. Small crown 8vo, 1s. 6d.; paper covers, 1s.

TREMENHEERE, Hugh Seymour, C.B.— A Manual of the Principles of Government, as set forth by the Authorities of Ancient and Modern Times. New and Enlarged Edition. Crown 8vo, 3s. 6d. Cheap Edition, limp cloth, 1s.

TUKE, Daniel Hack, M.D., F.R.C.P.—Chapters in the History of the Insane in the British Isles. With Four Illustrations. Large crown 8vo, 12s.

TWINING, Louisa.—Workhouse Visiting and Management during Twenty-Five Years. Small crown 8vo, 2s.

TYLER, J.—The Mystery of Being: or, What Do We Know? Small crown 8vo, 3s. 6d.

VAUGHAN, H. Halford.—New Readings and Renderings of Shakespeare's Tragedies. Vols. I. and II. Demy 8vo, 12s. 6d. each.

VILLARI, Professor.—Niccolò Machiavelli and his Times. Translated by LINDA VILLARI. 4 vols. Large post 8vo, 48s.

VILLIERS, The Right Hon. C. P.—Free Trade Speeches of. With Political Memoir. Edited by a Member of the Cobden Club. 2 vols. With Portrait. Demy 8vo, 25s.
₄ People's Edition. 1 vol. Crown 8vo, limp cloth, 2s. 6d.

VOGT, Lieut.-Col. Hermann.—The Egyptian War of 1882. A translation. With Map and Plans. Large crown 8vo, 6s.

VOLCKXSOM, E. W. v.—Catechism of Elementary Modern Chemistry. Small crown 8vo, 3s.

VYNER, Lady Mary.—Every Day a Portion. Adapted from the Bible and the Prayer Book, for the Private Devotion of those living in Widowhood. Collected and Edited by Lady Mary Vyner. Square crown 8vo, 5s.

WALDSTEIN, Charles, Ph.D.—The Balance of Emotion and Intellect; an Introductory Essay to the Study of Philosophy. Crown 8vo, 6s.

WALLER, Rev. C. B.—**The Apocalypse,** reviewed under the Light of the Doctrine of the Unfolding Ages, and the Restitution of All Things. Demy 8vo, 12s.

The Bible Record of Creation viewed in its Letter and Spirit. Two Sermons preached at St. Paul's Church, Woodford Bridge. Crown 8vo, 1s. 6d.

WALPOLE, Chas. George.—**A Short History of Ireland from the Earliest Times to the Union with Great Britain.** With 5 Maps and Appendices. Second Edition. Crown 8vo, 6s.

WARD, William George, Ph.D.—**Essays on the Philosophy of Theism.** Edited, with an Introduction, by WILFRID WARD. 2 vols. Demy 8vo, 21s.

WARD, Wilfrid.—**The Wish to Believe.** A Discussion Concerning the Temper of Mind in which a reasonable Man should undertake Religious Inquiry. Small crown 8vo, 5s.

WARTER, J. W.—**An Old Shropshire Oak.** 2 vols. Demy 8vo, 28s.

WEDDERBURN, Sir David, Bart., M.P.—**Life of.** Compiled from his Journals and Writings by his sister, Mrs. E. H. PERCIVAL. With etched Portrait, and facsimiles of Pencil Sketches. Demy 8vo, 14s.

WEDMORE, Frederick.—**The Masters of Genre Painting.** With Sixteen Illustrations. Post 8vo, 7s. 6d.

What to Do and How to Do It. A Manual of the Law affecting the Housing and Sanitary Condition of Londoners, with special Reference to the Dwellings of the Poor. Issued by the Sanitary Laws Enforcement Society. Demy 8vo, 1s.

WHITE, R. E.—Recollections of Woolwich during the Crimean War and Indian Mutiny, and of the Ordnance and War Departments; together with complete Lists of Past and Present Officials of the Royal Arsenal, etc. Crown 8vo, 2s. 6d.

WHITNEY, Prof. William Dwight.—**Essentials of English Grammar,** for the Use of Schools. Second Edition. Crown 8vo, 3s. 6d.

WHITWORTH, George Clifford.—**An Anglo-Indian Dictionary:** a Glossary of Indian Terms used in English, and of such English or other Non-Indian Terms as have obtained special meanings in India. Demy 8vo, cloth, 12s.

WILLIAMS, Rowland, D.D.—**Psalms, Litanies, Counsels, and Collects for Devout Persons.** Edited by his Widow. New and Popular Edition. Crown 8vo, 3s. 6d.

Stray Thoughts from the Note Books of the late Rowland Williams, D.D. Edited by his Widow. Crown 8vo, 3s. 6d.

WILSON, Lieut.-Col. C. T.—**The Duke of Berwick, Marshal of France, 1702-1734.** Demy 8vo, 15s.

WILSON, Mrs. R. F.—**The Christian Brothers.** Their Origin and Work. With a Sketch of the Life of their Founder, the Ven. JEAN BAPTISTE, de la Salle. Crown 8vo, 6s.

WOLTMANN, Dr. Alfred, and WOERMANN, Dr. Karl.—**History of Painting.** With numerous Illustrations. Vol. I. Painting in Antiquity and the Middle Ages. Medium 8vo, 28s., bevelled boards, gilt leaves, 30s. Vol. II. The Painting of the Renascence.

YOUMANS, Eliza A.—**First Book of Botany.** Designed to Cultivate the Observing Powers of Children. With 300 Engravings. New and Cheaper Edition. Crown 8vo, 2s. 6d.

YOUMANS, Edward L., M.D.—**A Class Book of Chemistry,** on the Basis of the New System. With 200 Illustrations. Crown 8vo, 5s.

THE INTERNATIONAL SCIENTIFIC SERIES.

I. **Forms of Water:** a Familiar Exposition of the Origin and Phenomena of Glaciers. By J. Tyndall, LL.D., F.R.S. With 25 Illustrations. Eighth Edition. Crown 8vo, 5s.

II. **Physics and Politics;** or, Thoughts on the Application of the Principles of "Natural Selection" and "Inheritance" to Political Society. By Walter Bagehot. Seventh Edition. Crown 8vo, 4s.

III. **Foods.** By Edward Smith, M.D., LL.B., F.R.S. With numerous Illustrations. Eighth Edition. Crown 8vo, 5s.

IV. **Mind and Body:** the Theories of their Relation. By Alexander Bain, LL.D. With Four Illustrations. Seventh Edition. Crown 8vo, 4s.

V. **The Study of Sociology.** By Herbert Spencer. Eleventh Edition. Crown 8vo, 5s.

VI. **On the Conservation of Energy.** By Balfour Stewart, M.A., LL.D., F.R.S. With 14 Illustrations. Sixth Edition. Crown 8vo, 5s.

VII. **Animal Locomotion;** or Walking, Swimming, and Flying. By J. B. Pettigrew, M.D., F.R.S., etc. With 130 Illustrations. Third Edition. Crown 8vo, 5s.

VIII. **Responsibility in Mental Disease.** By Henry Maudsley, M.D. Fourth Edition. Crown 8vo, 5s.

IX. **The New Chemistry.** By Professor J. P. Cooke. With 31 Illustrations. Eighth Edition, remodelled and enlarged. Crown 8vo, 5s.

X. **The Science of Law.** By Professor Sheldon Amos. Sixth Edition Crown 8vo, 5s.

XI. **Animal Mechanism**: a Treatise on Terrestrial and Aerial Locomotion. By Professor E. J. Marey. With 117 Illustrations. Third Edition. Crown 8vo, 5s.

XII. **The Doctrine of Descent and Darwinism.** By Professor Oscar Schmidt. With 26 Illustrations. Sixth Edition. Crown 8vo, 5s.

XIII. **The History of the Conflict between Religion and Science.** By J. W. Draper, M.D., LL.D. Nineteenth Edition. Crown 8vo, 5s.

XIV. **Fungi**: their Nature, Influences, Uses, etc. By M. C. Cooke, M.D., LL.D. Edited by the Rev. M. J. Berkeley, M.A., F.L.S. With numerous Illustrations. Third Edition. Crown 8vo, 5s.

XV. **The Chemical Effects of Light and Photography.** By Dr. Hermann Vogel. With 100 Illustrations. Fourth Edition. Crown 8vo, 5s.

XVI. **The Life and Growth of Language.** By Professor William Dwight Whitney. Fourth Edition. Crown 8vo, 5s.

XVII. **Money and the Mechanism of Exchange.** By W. Stanley Jevons, M.A., F.R.S. Sixth Edition. Crown 8vo, 5s.

XVIII. **The Nature of Light.** With a General Account of Physical Optics. By Dr. Eugene Lommel. With 188 Illustrations and a Table of Spectra in Chromo-lithography. Third Edition. Crown 8vo, 5s.

XIX. **Animal Parasites and Messmates.** By P. J. Van Beneden. With 83 Illustrations. Third Edition. Crown 8vo, 5s.

XX. **Fermentation.** By Professor Schützenberger. With 28 Illustrations. Fourth Edition. Crown 8vo, 5s.

XXI. **The Five Senses of Man.** By Professor Bernstein. With 91 Illustrations. Fourth Edition. Crown 8vo, 5s.

XXII. **The Theory of Sound in its Relation to Music.** By Professor Pietro Blaserna. With numerous Illustrations. Third Edition. Crown 8vo, 5s.

XXIII. **Studies in Spectrum Analysis.** By J. Norman Lockyer, F.R.S. With six photographic Illustrations of Spectra, and numerous engravings on Wood. Third Edition. Crown 8vo, 6s. 6d.

XXIV. **A History of the Growth of the Steam Engine.** By Professor R. H. Thurston. With numerous Illustrations. Third Edition. Crown 8vo, 6s. 6d.

XXV. **Education as a Science.** By Alexander Bain, LL.D. Fifth Edition. Crown 8vo, 5s.

XXVI. **The Human Species.** By Professor A. de Quatrefages. Third Edition. Crown 8vo, 5s.

XXVII. **Modern Chromatics.** With Applications to Art and Industry. By Ogden N. Rood. With 130 original Illustrations. Second Edition. Crown 8vo, 5s.

XXVIII. **The Crayfish**: an Introduction to the Study of Zoology. By Professor T. H. Huxley. With 82 Illustrations. Fourth Edition. Crown 8vo, 5s.

XXIX. **The Brain as an Organ of Mind.** By H. Charlton Bastian, M.D. With numerous Illustrations. Third Edition. Crown 8vo, 5s.

XXX. **The Atomic Theory.** By Prof. Wurtz. Translated by G. Cleminshaw, F.C.S. Fourth Edition. Crown 8vo, 5s.

XXXI. **The Natural Conditions of Existence as they affect Animal Life.** By Karl Semper. With 2 Maps and 106 Woodcuts. Third Edition. Crown 8vo, 5s.

XXXII. **General Physiology of Muscles and Nerves.** By Prof. J. Rosenthal. Third Edition. With Illustrations. Crown 8vo, 5s.

XXXIII. **Sight**: an Exposition of the Principles of Monocular and Binocular Vision. By Joseph le Conte, LL.D. Second Edition. With 132 Illustrations. Crown 8vo, 5s.

XXXIV. **Illusions**: a Psychological Study. By James Sully. Second Edition. Crown 8vo, 5s.

XXXV. **Volcanoes: what they are and what they teach.** By Professor J. W. Judd, F.R.S. With 92 Illustrations on Wood. Third Edition. Crown 8vo, 5s.

XXXVI. **Suicide**: an Essay on Comparative Moral Statistics. By Prof. H. Morselli. Second Edition. With Diagrams. Crown 8vo, 5s.

XXXVII. **The Brain and its Functions.** By J. Luys. With Illustrations. Second Edition. Crown 8vo, 5s.

XXXVIII. **Myth and Science**: an Essay. By Tito Vignoli. Second Edition. Crown 8vo, 5s.

XXXIX. **The Sun.** By Professor Young. With Illustrations. Second Edition. Crown 8vo, 5s.

XL. **Ants, Bees, and Wasps**: a Record of Observations on the Habits of the Social Hymenoptera. By Sir John Lubbock, Bart., M.P. With 5 Chromo-lithographic Illustrations. Seventh Edition. Crown 8vo, 5s.

XLI. **Animal Intelligence.** By G. J. Romanes, LL.D., F.R.S. Third Edition. Crown 8vo, 5s.

XLII. **The Concepts and Theories of Modern Physics.** By J. B. Stallo. Third Edition. Crown 8vo, 5s.

XLIII. **Diseases of the Memory**; An Essay in the Positive Psychology. By Prof. Th. Ribot. Second Edition. Crown 8vo, 5s.

XLIV. **Man before Metals.** By N. Joly, with 148 Illustrations. Third Edition. Crown 8vo, 5s.

XLV. **The Science of Politics.** By Prof. Sheldon Amos. Third Edition. Crown 8vo, 5s.

XLVI. **Elementary Meteorology.** By Robert H. Scott. Third Edition. With Numerous Illustrations. Crown 8vo, 5s.

XLVII. **The Organs of Speech and their Application in the Formation of Articulate Sounds.** By Georg Hermann Von Meyer. With 47 Woodcuts. Crown 8vo, 5s.

XLVIII. **Fallacies.** A View of Logic from the Practical Side. By Alfred Sidgwick. Crown 8vo, 5s.

XLIX. **Origin of Cultivated Plants.** By Alphonse de Candolle. Crown 8vo, 5s.

L. **Jelly-Fish, Star-Fish, and Sea-Urchins.** Being a Research on Primitive Nervous Systems. By G. J. Romanes. With Illustrations. Crown 8vo, 5s.

LI. **The Common Sense of the Exact Sciences.** By the late William Kingdon Clifford. Second Edition. With 100 Figures. Crown 8vo, 5s.

LII. **Physical Expression: Its Modes and Principles.** By Francis Warner, M.D., F.R.C.P. With 50 Illustrations. Crown 8vo, 5s.

LIII. **Anthropoid Apes.** By Robert Hartmann. With 63 Illustrations. Crown 8vo, 5s.

LIV. **The Mammalia in their Relation to Primeval Times.** By Oscar Schmidt. With 51 Woodcuts. Crown 8vo, 5s.

LV. **Comparative Literature.** By H. Macaulay Posnett, LL.D. Crown 8vo, 5s.

MILITARY WORKS.

BARRINGTON, Capt. J. T.—**England on the Defensive**; or, the Problem of Invasion Critically Examined. Large crown 8vo, with Map, 7s. 6d.

BRACKENBURY, Col. C. B., R.A. — **Military Handbooks for Regimental Officers.**

I. **Military Sketching and Reconnaissance.** By Col. F. J. Hutchison and Major H. G. MacGregor. Fourth Edition. With 15 Plates. Small crown 8vo, 4s.

II. **The Elements of Modern Tactics Practically applied to English Formations.** By Lieut.-Col. Wilkinson Shaw. Fifth Edition. With 25 Plates and Maps. Small crown 8vo, 9s.

Kegan Paul, Trench & Co.'s Publications. 35

Military Handbooks—*continued.*

III. **Field Artillery.** Its Equipment, Organization and Tactics. By Major Sisson C. Pratt, R.A. With 12 Plates. Second Edition. Small crown 8vo, 6s.

IV. **The Elements of Military Administration.** First Part: Permanent System of Administration. By Major J. W. Buxton. Small crown 8vo. 7s. 6d.

V. **Military Law:** Its Procedure and Practice. By Major Sisson C. Pratt, R.A. Second Edition. Small crown 8vo, 4s. 6d.

VI. **Cavalry in Modern War.** By Col. F. Chenevix Trench. Small crown 8vo, 6s.

VII. **Field Works.** Their Technical Construction and Tactical Application. By the Editor, Col. C. B. Brackenbury, R.A. Small crown 8vo.

BROOKE, Major, C. K.—**A System of Field Training.** Small crown 8vo, cloth limp, 2s.

CLERY, C., Lieut.-Col.—**Minor Tactics.** With 26 Maps and Plans. Seventh Edition, Revised. Crown 8vo, 9s.

COLVILE, Lieut.-Col. C. F.—**Military Tribunals.** Sewed, 2s. 6d.

CRAUFURD, Capt. H. J.—**Suggestions for the Military Training of a Company of Infantry.** Crown 8vo, 1s. 6d.

HAMILTON, Capt. Ian, A.D.C.—**The Fighting of the Future.** 1s.

HARRISON, Col. R.—**The Officer's Memorandum Book for Peace and War.** Fourth Edition, Revised throughout. Oblong 32mo, red basil, with pencil, 3s. 6d.

Notes on Cavalry Tactics, Organisation, etc. By a Cavalry Officer. With Diagrams. Demy 8vo, 12s.

PARR, Capt. H. Hallam, C.M.G.—**The Dress, Horses, and Equipment of Infantry and Staff Officers.** Crown 8vo, 1s.

SCHAW, Col. H.—**The Defence and Attack of Positions and Localities.** Third Edition, Revised and Corrected. Crown 8vo, 3s. 6d.

WILKINSON, H. Spenser, Capt. 20th Lancashire R.V.—**Citizen Soldiers.** Essays towards the Improvement of the Volunteer Force. Crown 8vo, 2s. 6d.

POETRY.

ADAM OF ST. VICTOR.—**The Liturgical Poetry of Adam of St. Victor.** From the text of GAUTIER. With Translations into English in the Original Metres, and Short Explanatory Notes, by DIGBY S. WRANGHAM, M.A. 3 vols. Crown 8vo, printed on hand-made paper, boards, 21s.

AUCHMUTY, A. C.—**Poems of English Heroism :** From Brunanburh to Lucknow; from Athelstan to Albert. Small crown 8vo, 1s. 6d.

BARNES, William.—**Poems of Rural Life, in the Dorset Dialect.** New Edition, complete in one vol. Crown 8vo, 8s. 6d.

BAYNES, Rev. Canon H. R.—**Home Songs for Quiet Hours.** Fourth and Cheaper Edition. Fcap. 8vo, cloth, 2s. 6d.

BERANGER.—**A Selection from his Songs.** Translated by W. TOYNBEE. Small crown, 8vo.

Bertha : a Story of Love. Crown 8vo, 3s. 6d.

BEVINGTON, L. S.—**Key Notes.** Small crown 8vo, 5s.

BLUNT, Wilfrid Scawen.—**The Wind and the Whirlwind.** Demy 8vo, 1s. 6d.

    The Love Sonnets of Proteus. Fourth Edition, 18mo. Cloth extra, gilt top, 5s.

BOWEN, H. C., M.A.—**Simple English Poems.** English Literature for Junior Classes. In Four Parts. Parts I., II., and III., 6d. each, and Part IV., 1s. Complete, 3s.

BRYANT, W. C.—**Poems.** Cheap Edition, with Frontispiece. Small crown 8vo, 3s. 6d.

CAILLARD, Emma Marie.—**Charlotte Corday, and other Poems.** Small crown 8vo, 3s. 6d.

Calderon's Dramas : the Wonder-Working Magician—Life is a Dream—the Purgatory of St. Patrick. Translated by DENIS FLORENCE MACCARTHY. Post 8vo, 10s.

Camoens Lusiads.—Portuguese Text, with Translation by J. J. AUBERTIN. Second Edition. 2 vols. Crown 8vo, 12s.

CAMPBELL, Lewis.—**Sophocles.** The Seven Plays in English Verse. Crown 8vo, 7s. 6d.

CERVANTES.—**Journey to Parnassus.** Spanish Text, with Translation into English Tercets, Preface, and Illustrative Notes, by JAMES Y. GIBSON. Crown 8vo, 12s.

    Numantia : a Tragedy. Translated from the Spanish, with Introduction and Notes, by JAMES Y. GIBSON. Crown 8vo, printed on hand-made paper, 5s.

Chronicles of Christopher Columbus. A Poem in 12 Cantos. By M. D. C. Crown 8vo, 7s. 6d.

CLARKE, Mary Cowden.—**Honey from the Weed.** Verses. Crown 8vo, 7s.

COXHEAD, Ethel.—**Birds and Babies.** Imp. 16mo. With 33 Illustrations. Gilt, 2s. 6d.

DENNIS, J.—**English Sonnets.** Collected and Arranged by. Small crown 8vo, 2s. 6d.

DE VERE, Aubrey.—**Poetical Works.**
I. THE SEARCH AFTER PROSERPINE, etc. 6s.
II. THE LEGENDS OF ST. PATRICK, etc. 6s.
III. ALEXANDER THE GREAT, etc. 6s.

The Foray of Queen Meave, and other Legends of Ireland's Heroic Age. Small crown 8vo, 5s.

Legends of the Saxon Saints. Small crown 8vo, 6s.

DOBSON, Austin.—**Old World Idylls** and other Verses. Fifth Edition. 18mo, gilt top, 6s.

At the Sign of the Lyre. Elzevir 8vo, gilt top, 6s.

DOMET, Alfred.—**Ranolf and Amohia.** A Dream of Two Lives. New Edition, Revised. 2 vols. Crown 8vo, 12s.

Dorothy: a Country Story in Elegiac Verse. With Preface. Demy 8vo, 5s.

DOWDEN, Edward, LL.D.—**Shakspere's Sonnets.** With Introduction and Notes. Large post 8vo, 7s. 6d.

Dulce Cor: being the Poems of Ford Berêton. With Two Illustrations. Crown 8vo.

DUTT, Toru.—**A Sheaf Gleaned in French Fields.** New Edition. Demy 8vo, 10s. 6d.

Ancient Ballads and Legends of Hindustan. With an Introductory Memoir by EDMUND GOSSE. Second Edition, 18mo. Cloth extra, gilt top, 5s.

EDWARDS, Miss Betham.—**Poems.** Small crown 8vo, 3s. 6d.

EGAN, Maurice Francis.—**Songs and Sonnets;** and **Carmina,** by CONDÉ BENOIST PALLEN. Small crown 8vo, 1s. 6d.

ELDRYTH, Maud.—**Margaret,** and other Poems. Small crown 8vo, 3s. 6d.

All Soul's Eve, "No God," and other Poems. Fcap. 8vo, 3s. 6d.

ELLIOTT, Ebenezer, The Corn Law Rhymer.—**Poems.** Edited by his son, the Rev. EDWIN ELLIOTT, of St. John's, Antigua. 2 vols. Crown 8vo, 18s.

English Verse. Edited by W. J. LINTON and R. H. STODDARD. 5 vols. Crown 8vo, cloth, 5s. each.
I. CHAUCER TO BURNS.
II. TRANSLATIONS.
III. LYRICS OF THE NINETEENTH CENTURY.
IV. DRAMATIC SCENES AND CHARACTERS.
V. BALLADS AND ROMANCES.

ENIS.—**Gathered Leaves.** Small crown 8vo, 3s. 6d.

EVANS, Anne.—**Poems and Music.** With Memorial Preface by ANN THACKERAY RITCHIE. Large crown 8vo, 7s.

FERGUSON, Tom.—**Ballads and Dreams.** Crown 8vo, 5s.

FORSTER, the late William.—**Midas.** Crown 8vo, 5s.

GOODCHILD, John A.—**Somnia Medici.** Two series. Small crown 8vo, 5s. each.

GOSSE, Edmund W.—**New Poems.** Crown 8vo, 7s. 6d.

Firdausi in Exile, and other Poems. Elzevir 8vo, gilt top, 6s.

GRINDROD, Charles.—**Plays from English History.** Crown 8vo, 7s. 6d.

The Stranger's Story, and his Poem, The Lament of Love: An Episode of the Malvern Hills. Small crown 8vo, 2s. 6d.

GURNEY, Rev. Alfred.—**The Vision of the Eucharist,** and other Poems. Crown 8vo, 5s.

A Christmas Faggot. Small crown 8vo, 5s.

HENRY, Daniel, Junr.—**Under a Fool's Cap.** Songs. Crown 8vo, cloth, bevelled boards, 5s.

HEYWOOD, J. C.—**Herodias,** a Dramatic Poem. New Edition, Revised. Small crown 8vo, 5s.

Antonius. A Dramatic Poem. New Edition, Revised. Small crown 8vo, 5s.

HICKEY, E. H.—**A Sculptor,** and other Poems. Small crown 8vo, 5s.

HOLE, W. G.—**Procris,** and other Poems. Fcap. 8vo, 3s. 6d.

HONEYWOOD, Patty.—**Poems.** Dedicated (by permission) to Lord Wolseley, G.C.B., etc. Small crown 8vo, 2s. 6d.

KEATS, John.—**Poetical Works.** Edited by W. T. ARNOLD. Large crown 8vo, choicely printed on hand-made paper, with Portrait in *eau-forte*. Parchment or cloth, 12s.; vellum, 15s.

KENNEDY, Captain A. W. M. Clark.—**Robert the Bruce.** A Poem: Historical and Romantic. With Three Illustrations by James Faed, Jun. Printed on hand-made paper, parchment, bevelled boards, crown 8vo, 10s. 6d.

KING, Mrs. Hamilton.—**The Disciples.** Seventh Edition, with Portrait and Notes. Small crown 8vo, 5s.

A Book of Dreams. Crown 8vo, 3s. 6d.

KNOX, The Hon. Mrs. O. N.—**Four Pictures from a Life,** and other Poems. Small crown 8vo, 3s. 6d.

LANG, A.—**XXXII Ballades in Blue China.** Elzevir 8vo, 5s.

Rhymes à la Mode. With Frontispiece by E. A. Abbey. 18mo, cloth extra, gilt top, 5s.

LAWSON, Right Hon. Mr. Justice.—Hymni Usitati Latine Redditi : with other Verses. Small 8vo, parchment, 5*s.*

Lessing's Nathan the Wise. Translated by EUSTACE K. CORBETT. Crown 8vo, 6*s.*

Life Thoughts. Small crown 8vo, 2*s.* 6*d.*

Living English Poets MDCCCLXXXII. With Frontispiece by Walter Crane. Second Edition. Large crown 8vo. Printed on hand-made paper. Parchment or cloth, 12*s.* ; vellum, 15*s.*

LOCKER, F.—London Lyrics. Tenth Edition. With Portrait, 18mo. Cloth extra, gilt top, 5*s.*

Love in Idleness. A Volume of Poems. With an Etching by W. B. Scott. Small crown 8vo, 5*s.*

LUMSDEN, Lieut.-Col. H. W.—Beowulf : an Old English Poem. Translated into Modern Rhymes. Second and Revised Edition. Small crown 8vo, 5*s.*

LYSAGHT, Sidney Royse.—A Modern Ideal. A Dramatic Poem. Small crown 8vo, 5*s.*

MACGREGOR, Duncan.—Clouds and Sunlight. Poems. Small crown 8vo, 5*s.*

MAGNUSSON, Eirikr, M.A., and PALMER, E. H., M.A.—Johan Ludvig Runeberg's Lyrical Songs, Idylls, and Epigrams. Fcap. 8vo, 5*s.*

MAKCLOUD, Even.—Ballads of the Western Highlands and Islands of Scotland. Small crown 8vo, 3*s.* 6*d.*

MC'NAUGHTON, J. H.—Onnalinda. A Romance. Small crown 8vo, 7*s.* 6*d.*

MEREDITH, Owen [The Earl of Lytton].—Lucile. New Edition. With 32 Illustrations. 16mo, 3*s.* 6*d.* Cloth extra, gilt edges, 4*s.* 6*d.*

MORRIS, Lewis.—Poetical Works of. New and Cheaper Editions, with Portrait. Complete in 3 vols., 5*s.* each.
Vol. I. contains "Songs of Two Worlds." Eleventh Edition.
Vol. II. contains "The Epic of Hades." Nineteenth Edition.
Vol. III. contains "Gwen" and "The Ode of Life." Sixth Edition.

The Epic of Hades. With 16 Autotype Illustrations, after the Drawings of the late George R. Chapman. 4to, cloth extra, gilt leaves, 21*s.*

The Epic of Hades. Presentation Edition. 4to, cloth extra, gilt leaves, 10*s.* 6*d.*

Songs Unsung. Fourth Edition. Fcap. 8vo, 6*s.*

The Lewis Morris Birthday Book. Edited by S. S. COPEMAN, with Frontispiece after a Design by the late George R. Chapman. 32mo, cloth extra, gilt edges, 2*s.* ; cloth limp, 1*s.* 6*d.*

MORSHEAD, E. D. A.—**The House of Atreus.** Being the Agamemnon, Libation-Bearers, and Furies of Æschylus. Translated into English Verse. Crown 8vo, 7*s.*

The Suppliant Maidens of Æschylus. Crown 8vo, 3*s.* 6*d.*

MOZLEY, J. Rickards.—**The Romance of Dennell.** A Poem in Five Cantos. Crown 8vo, 7*s.* 6*d.*

MULHOLLAND, Rosa.—**Vagrant Verses.** Small crown 8vo, 5*s.*

NOEL, The Hon. Roden.—**A Little Child's Monument.** Third Edition. Small crown 8vo, 3*s.* 6*d.*

The House of Ravensburg. New Edition. Small crown 8vo, 6*s.*

The Red Flag, and other Poems. New Edition. Small crown 8vo, 6*s.*

OBBARD, Constance Mary.—**Burley Bells.** Small crown 8vo, 3*s.* 6*d.*

O'HAGAN, John.—**The Song of Roland.** Translated into English Verse. New and Cheaper Edition. Crown 8vo, 5*s.*

PFEIFFER, Emily.—**The Rhyme of the Lady of the Rock, and How it Grew.** Second Edition. Small crown 8vo, 3*s.* 6*d.*

Gerard's Monument, and other Poems. Second Edition. Crown 8vo, 6*s.*

Under the Aspens: Lyrical and Dramatic. With Portrait. Crown 8vo, 6*s.*

PIATT, J. J.—**Idyls and Lyrics of the Ohio Valley.** Crown 8vo, 5*s.*

PIATT, Sarah M. B.—**A Voyage to the Fortunate Isles,** and other Poems. 1 vol. Small crown 8vo, gilt top, 5*s.*

Rare Poems of the 16th and 17th Centuries. Edited W. J. LINTON. Crown 8vo, 5*s.*

RHOADES, James.—**The Georgics of Virgil.** Translated into English Verse. Small crown 8vo, 5*s.*

Poems. Small crown 8vo, 4*s.* 6*d.*

ROBINSON, A. Mary F.—**A Handful of Honeysuckle.** Fcap. 8vo, 3*s.* 6*d.*

The Crowned Hippolytus. Translated from Euripides. With New Poems. Small crown 8vo, 5*s.*

ROUS, Lieut.-Col.—**Conradin.** Small crown 8vo, 2*s.*

SCHILLER, Friedrich.—**Wallenstein.** A Drama. Done in English Verse, by J. A. W. HUNTER, M.A. Crown 8vo, 7*s.* 6*d.*

Schiller's Mary Stuart. German Text, with English Translation on opposite page by LEEDHAM WHITE. Crown 8vo, 6s.

SCOTT, E. J. L.—**The Eclogues of Virgil.**—Translated into English Verse. Small crown 8vo, 3s. 6d.

SCOTT, George F. E.—**Theodora and other Poems.** Small crown 8vo, 3s. 6d.

SELKIRK, J. B.—**Poems.** Crown 8vo, 7s. 6d.

Shakspere's Works. The Avon Edition, 12 vols., cloth, 18s. ; and in box, 21s.

SHARP, William.—**Euphrenia**: or, The Test of Love. A Poem. Crown 8vo, 5s.

SHERBROOKE, Viscount.—**Poems of a Life.** Second Edition. Small crown 8vo, 2s. 6d.

SMITH, J. W. Gilbart.—**The Loves of Vandyck.** A Tale of Genoa. Small crown 8vo, 2s. 6d.

The Log o' the "Norseman." Small crown 8vo, 5s.

Songs of Coming Day. Small crown 8vo, 3s. 6d.

Sophocles: The Seven Plays in English Verse. Translated by LEWIS CAMPBELL. Crown 8vo, 7s. 6d.

SPICER, Henry.—**Haska**: a Drama in Three Acts (as represented at the Theatre Royal, Drury Lane, March 10th, 1877). Third Edition. Crown 8vo, 3s. 6d.

Uriel Acosta, in Three Acts. From the German of Gatzkow. Small crown 8vo, 2s. 6d.

SYMONDS, John Addington.—**Vagabunduli Libellus.** Crown 8vo, 6s.

Tares. Crown 8vo, 1s. 6d.

Tasso's Jerusalem Delivered. Translated by Sir JOHN KINGSTON JAMES, Bart. Two Volumes. Printed on hand-made paper, parchment, bevelled boards. Large crown 8vo, 21s.

TAYLOR, Sir H.—**Works.** Complete in Five Volumes. Crown 8vo, 30s.

Philip Van Artevelde. Fcap. 8vo, 3s. 6d.

The Virgin Widow, etc. Fcap. 8vo, 3s. 6d.

The Statesman. Fcap. 8vo, 3s. 6d.

TAYLOR, Augustus.—**Poems.** Fcap. 8vo, 5s.

TAYLOR, Margaret Scott.—**"Boys Together,"** and other Poems. Small crown 8vo, 6s.

TODHUNTER, Dr. J.—Laurella, and other Poems. Crown 8vo, 6s. 6d.

Forest Songs. Small crown 8vo, 3s. 6d.

The True Tragedy of Rienzi: a Drama. 3s. 6d.

Alcestis: a Dramatic Poem. Extra fcap. 8vo, 5s.

TYLER, M. C.—Anne Boleyn. A Tragedy in Six Acts. Small crown 8vo, 2s. 6d.

TYNAN, Katherine.—Louise de la Valliere, and other Poems. Small crown 8vo, 3s. 6d.

WEBSTER, Augusta.—In a Day: a Drama. Small crown 8vo, 2s. 6d.

Disguises: a Drama. Small crown 8vo, 5s.

Wet Days. By a Farmer. Small crown 8vo, 6s.

WOOD, Rev. F. H.—Echoes of the Night, and other Poems. Small crown 8vo, 3s. 6d.

Wordsworth Birthday Book, The. Edited by ADELAIDE and VIOLET WORDSWORTH. 32mo, limp cloth, 1s. 6d.; cloth extra, 2s.

YOUNGMAN, Thomas George.—Poems. Small crown 8vo, 5s.

YOUNGS, Ella Sharpe.—Paphus, and other Poems. Small crown 8vo, 3s. 6d.

A Heart's Life, Sarpedon, and other Poems. Small crown 8vo, 3s. 6d.

WORKS OF FICTION IN ONE VOLUME.

BANKS, Mrs. G. L.—God's Providence House. New Edition. Crown 8vo, 3s. 6d.

Danish Parsonage. By an Angler. Crown 8vo, 6s.

HUNTER, Hay.—The Crime of Christmas Day. A Tale of the Latin Quarter. By the Author of "My Ducats and my Daughter." 1s.

HUNTER, Hay, and WHYTE, Walter.—My Ducats and My Daughter. New and Cheaper Edition. With Frontispiece. Crown 8vo, 6s.

INGELOW, Jean.—Off the Skelligs: a Novel. With Frontispiece. Second Edition. Crown 8vo, 6s.

KIELLAND, Alexander L.—Garman and Worse. A Norwegian Novel. Authorized Translation, by W. W. Kettlewell. Crown 8vo, 6s.

OLIVER, Pen.—"All But." A Chronicle of Laxenford Life. With 20 Illustrations by the Author. Crown 8vo, 6s.

MACDONALD, G.—**Donal Grant.** A Novel. Second Edition. With Frontispiece. Crown 8vo, 6s.

Castle Warlock. A Novel. Second Edition. Crown 8vo, 6s.

Malcolm. With Portrait of the Author engraved on Steel. Seventh Edition. Crown 8vo, 6s.

The Marquis of Lossie. Sixth Edition. With Frontispiece. Crown 8vo, 6s.

St. George and St. Michael. Fourth Edition. With Frontispiece. Crown 8vo, 6s.

MALET, Lucas.—**Colonel Enderby's Wife.** A Novel. New and Cheaper Edition. With Frontispiece. Crown 8vo, 6s.

PALGRAVE, W. Gifford.—**Hermann Agha**; an Eastern Narrative. Third Edition. Crown 8vo, 6s.

SHAW, Flora L.—**Castle Blair**; a Story of Youthful Days. New and Cheaper Edition. Crown 8vo, 3s. 6d.

STRETTON, Hesba.—**Through a Needle's Eye**: a Story. New and Cheaper Edition, with Frontispiece. Crown 8vo, 6s.

TAYLOR, Col. Meadows, C.S.I., M.R.I.A.—**Seeta**; a Novel. With Frontispiece. Crown 8vo, 6s.

Tippoo Sultaun: a Tale of the Mysore War. With Frontispiece. Crown 8vo, 6s.

Ralph Darnell. With Frontispiece. Crown 8vo, 6s.

A Noble Queen. With Frontispiece. Crown 8vo, 6s.

The Confessions of a Thug. With Frontispiece. Crown 8vo, 6s.

Tara: a Mahratta Tale. With Frontispiece. Crown 8vo, 6s.

Within Sound of the Sea. With Frontispiece. Crown 8vo, 6s.

BOOKS FOR THE YOUNG.

Brave Men's Footsteps. A Book of Example and Anecdote for Young People. By the Editor of "Men who have Risen." With 4 Illustrations by C. Doyle. Eighth Edition. Crown 8vo, 3s. 6d.

COXHEAD, Ethel.—**Birds and Babies.** Imp. 16mo. With 33 Illustrations. Cloth gilt, 2s. 6d.

DAVIES, G. Christopher.—**Rambles and Adventures of our School Field Club.** With 4 Illustrations. New and Cheaper Edition. Crown 8vo, 3s. 6d.

EDMONDS, Herbert.—**Well Spent Lives**: a Series of Modern Biographies. New and Cheaper Edition. Crown 8vo, 3*s.* 6*d.*

EVANS, Mark.—**The Story of our Father's Love,** told to Children. Sixth and Cheaper Edition of Theology for Children. With 4 Illustrations. Fcap. 8vo, 1*s.* 6*d.*

JOHNSON, Virginia W.—**The Catskill Fairies.** Illustrated by Alfred Fredericks. 5*s.*

MAC KENNA, S. J.—**Plucky Fellows.** A Book for Boys. With 6 Illustrations. Fifth Edition. Crown 8vo, 3*s.* 6*d.*

REANEY, Mrs. G. S.—**Waking and Working**; or, From Girlhood to Womanhood. New and Cheaper Edition. With a Frontispiece. Crown 8vo, 3*s.* 6*d.*

Blessing and Blessed: a Sketch of Girl Life. New and Cheaper Edition. Crown 8vo, 3*s.* 6*d.*

Rose Gurney's Discovery. A Story for Girls. Dedicated to their Mothers. Crown 8vo, 3*s.* 6*d.*

English Girls: Their Place and Power. With Preface by the Rev. R. W. Dale. Fourth Edition. Fcap. 8vo, 2*s.* 6*d.*

Just Anyone, and other Stories. Three Illustrations. Royal 16mo, 1*s.* 6*d.*

Sunbeam Willie, and other Stories. Three Illustrations. Royal 16mo, 1*s.* 6*d.*

Sunshine Jenny, and other Stories. Three Illustrations. Royal 16mo, 1*s.* 6*d.*

STOCKTON, Frank R.—**A Jolly Fellowship.** With 20 Illustrations. Crown 8vo, 5*s.*

STORR, Francis, and TURNER, Hawes.—**Canterbury Chimes**; or, Chaucer Tales re-told to Children. With 6 Illustrations from the Ellesmere Manuscript. Third Edition. Fcap. 8vo, 3*s.* 6*d.*

STRETTON, Hesba.—**David Lloyd's Last Will.** With 4 Illustrations. New Edition. Royal 16mo, 2*s.* 6*d.*

Tales from Ariosto re-told for Children. By a Lady. With 3 Illustrations. Crown 8vo, 4*s.* 6*d.*

WHITAKER, Florence.—**Christy's Inheritance.** A London Story Illustrated. Royal 16mo, 1*s.* 6*d.*

www.ingramcontent.com/pod-product-compliance
Lightning Source LLC
Chambersburg PA
CBHW020828230426
43666CB00007B/1153